DATE DUE

The Terrorist Prince

The Terrorist Prince
The Life and Death of Murtaza Bhutto

◆

Raja Anwar

Translated by Khalid Hasan

V

VERSO

London · New York

First published by Verso 1997

© Raja Anwar 1997

Verso
UK: 6 Meard Street, London W1V 3HR
USA: 180 Varick Street, New York NY 10014–4606

Verso is the imprint of New Left Books

ISBN 1–85984–886–9

British Library Cataloguing in Publication Data
A catalogue record for this book is available from the British Library

Library of Congress Cataloging-in-Publication Data
A catalog record for this book is available from the Library of Congress

Typeset in 10pt Janson by
SetSystems Ltd, Saffron Walden, Essex
Printed by Biddles Ltd, Guildford and King's Lynn

Contents

Foreword

This book furnishes a riveting account of the activities of Al-Zulfikar, the armed group formed by Murtazar Bhutto to avenge the judicial killing of his father, Zulfikar Bhutto, the Prime Minister of Pakistan first deposed and then killed by General Zia al-Huq in 1977. Al-Zulfikar was set up in 1981 and not finally wound up until the gunning down of Murtaza Bhutto in December 1996, though its period of greatest activity was the early and middle 1980s. When reading Raja Anwar's often chilling account of the exploits of this terrorist group the Western reader should bear in mind that the West itself during these years not only backed atrociously repressive governments like that of General Zia, but also supplied terroristic groups, such as those unleashed on Afghanistan, whose activities were to be vastly more destructive than those of Al-Zulfikar.

The eleven-year dictatorship of Zia (1977–89) was one of the most squalid episodes in Pakistan's unhappy history. It brutalized the country and its ruling elite beyond redemption and permitted the birth of a ubiquitous heroin mafia which still dominates the political and business life of the country. The toppling of an elected government and the hanging of Zulfiqar Ali Bhutto inaugurated this degradation. At the same time martyrdom provided the Bhutto family with a halo which has only recently lost its shine.

The Bhuttos were landlords from Sind, a province where the peasants were treated as serfs and where the *droit de seigneur* was not simply a phrase from the history books. The Sindhi landlords were, and remain, amongst the most rapacious and cruel in Asia, inhabiting a world of their own and exercising total dominion over the lives of all those who lived on their lands. The landlord's word is the law.

Zulfiqar Ali Bhutto was born and brought up in this landlord milieu, though he spent a great deal of time in the pre-Partition years in Bombay. He subsequently studied at Oxford and Harvard and became a barrister. While still in his early thirties, he was recognized as a clever young man by General Ayub Khan, the first of Pakistan's many uniformed despots who, in 1958, made Bhutto a Minister in his Cabinet. He never looked back. In 1965, Bhutto, then Foreign Minister of Pakistan, was sacked by Ayub (who had by now promoted himself to Field Marshal). Bhutto formed his own party, the Pakistan People's Party, and when students rose in opposition to the dictatorship, it was Bhutto who became their leader in West Pakistan. He was imprisoned for a short time. The adulation of the crowd had changed him. He enjoyed his rapport with the crowds, he openly baited the rich in town and country. He promised food, clothes and shelter for all. He threatened to occupy the mansions of the rich and change them into hospitals and clinics for the poor. Rhetoric of this sort had never been heard in Pakistan before and when the student-worker insurrection finally toppled Ayrub, it was Bhutto's party that swept the board in West Pakistan, defeating all the big landlords in the crucial Punjabi province. He had promised everyone a slice of the cake and the people had begun their patient wait.

It was at this time that Raja Anwar, one of the more dynamic student leaders from Rawapindi, met Bhutto and was entranced by his skills in the art of mass manipulation. Anwar, like millions of others, believed that this patrician character, though he had not changed his outlook completely, could nonetheless bring about a radical social transformation. There was an excitement that had gripped the whole country in 1968–69 which was never to return again. Those days of hope were drowned in the blood of the Bengalis of East Pakistan. Following the break-up of Pakistan in 1971 Bhutto came to power in the Western half, partly because he enjoyed support from the Army but also because of the strength of the popular support he commanded. After six years in office he was overthrown by his favourite General, Zia al-Haq. This clash between the patrician Bhutto and the Uriah Heepish Zia is vividly drawn by Anwar. Bhutto had promoted Zia over the heads of six senior generals and against the advice of his closest colleagues. He thought Zia was a simpleton who could be easily manipulated. Bhutto's arrogance was bad enough but it was his failure to understand that in the new Pakistan it was the army that had become the central political institution.

This army, after its defeat in Bangladesh, could have been reduced in size, its character and function totally altered and its budget cut by half and used to fund 'food, clothes and shelter' for all, but Bhutto was simply not prepared for this, even though he was the only political leader with the popular support necessary to the task. Instead he believed that he could play one general off against another and in this way keep himself in power indefinitely.

Raja Anwar decided to throw in his lot with Bhutto and agreed to become an official adviser to his government. When General Uriah Heep finally ejected Bhutto and executed him, Anwar was desolated. In his despair he decided to join Murtaza Bhutto, the son-in-exile. This book is a gripping and fascinating account for anyone who wishes to understand the dynamics of a terrorist organisation. The great majority of the young men who lost their lives in the service of al-Zulfikar were dedicated, courageous and idealistic. Unfortunately their leader was a prey to grandiose delusions and utterly careless of the lives of his followers. Since the West backed Zia, Murtaza turned to the authorities in Kabul and Moscow, Damascus and New Delhi, for covert sponsorship. There are times when one feels that the spirit of Nicolo Macchiavelli is haunting the proceedings. Farce and tragedy are willing or unwilling bedfellows in *The Terrorist Prince*. As Raja Anwar's story shifts from the jagged front line of the Cold War in the Hindu Kush to the guerrilla training camps of Syria and Libyai he introduces us to an extraordinary cast of characters – conniving statesmen, sinister intelligence chiefs, idealistic thugs, aristocratic bagmen and duped peasant boys.

Taken as a whole, the story of the Bhutto family and its followers is a Greek tragedy. Zulfiqar Ali Bhutto declares for the people, is hoisted to power by a popular rebellion, misuses that power and is overthrown by a man he had thought of as his creature. He is hanged. His youngest son Shahnawaz Bhutto is poisoned in mysterious circumstances on the French Riviera. The older son, Murtaza, sets up a terrorist group which often scales the pinnacles of absurdity, but also hijacks planes, obtains the release of political prisoners and, as Anwar vividly relates, comes close on at least two occasions to assassinating the Pakistani military dictator. The oldest child, Benazir, stays at home, is arrested many times, allowed out into exile, returns home, takes on the generals and is locked up again. Then Zia's plane is blown up by unknown assailants. Following his death the generals permit the calling of elections. Benazir wins the elections and becomes Prime Minister. She is dismissed, out of power for a few years and then wins again. Murtaza returns home and quarrels publicly with his sister and her husband, Asif Zardari, who is accused of riotous corruption. A sulphurous family feud ensues, ending with Murtaza being shot dead outside his home in Clifton, Karachi, by armed policemen. His sister is the Prime Minister. She is distraught. Soon she is dismissed from power by one of her creatures, President Farooq Leghari, and her husband Asif Zardari is imprisoned. As I complete this preface her husband has been charged with involvement in the killing of Murtaza Bhutto. The story is not yet over.

Tariq Ali
18 July 1997
London

Preface

In March 1981, after the successful hijack of a Pakistan International Airlines aircraft from Karachi to Kabul, and then to Damascus, Murtaza Bhutto announced proudly that I had been shot dead. To him, this was no empty boast but a certainty ready to happen: after getting me thrown into Kabul's infamous Pul-i-Charkhi prison, he had even had a grave dug for me in the city's Karta Chahar quarter. I consider it nothing short of a miracle that in 1983 I rejoined the living by finally obtaining release from prison. Some time later, I went to look at the grave I had cheated.

It is said that idiots and children do not lie. All I would like to add to this is that neither do the dead, as long as life provides them with an opportunity to speak. The book that follows is a result of the opportunity that fell to me. I have written about the events as I saw them, without keeping anything back and without adding to the truth or taking anything away from it. This book has forced me to exhume a part of my life which I had managed to bury deep in my memory. Thus, once again, I have had to undergo the unbearably painful experience of my days in prison. I had begun to believe that I had forgotten them. I had not realized that they were burnt so indelibly into my soul.

Had this book been published five or seven years ago, it would have created a political upheaval, but that was not my aim. I have no political or personal axe to grind. My only purpose has been to record the truth. Much time has passed, so I would urge that the account that follows should be read in its historical context. In a way, what better time could there be for this book to appear than when the Bhutto family has come full circle? Murtaza Bhutto was killed in a shootout in Karachi in September 1996 and Benazir Bhutto, his sister and political rival, was removed from office by Farooq Leghari, her hand-picked President. As I write these lines, I find my country caught in a crisis as deep as the one that broke it up in 1971, following Benazir Bhutto's defeat in elections that focused on the wholesale corruption of Pakistan's political system.

In a way this is not the story of Murtaza or the Bhutto family or Al-Zulfikar, but of the revolutionary movements of those times which became the graveyard of their workers. This book holds up a mirror to the populist revolutionary thinking of the decades of the seventies and the eighties. It explains the central tragedy of our national life in those years. This tragedy consisted in the paradox that the people's longing for democracy and social justice only seemed likely to succeed if it found a feudal champion, since the feudal layer of big landlords monopolized access to political power and social influence. And while our undemocratic rulers could draw on an extended network of influence within the country they also enjoyed support abroad. Notwithstanding the absence of democracy Pakistan was regarded by the West as a pillar of the Free World. The political landscape of the globe was obscured for fifty years by the propaganda smokescreen laid down on both sides of a Cold War fought by proxy in countries that were pawns in the Western–Soviet game. Now that the fog is lifting, we can begin to count the casualties.

Khalid Hasan, the book's translator, and I go back many years. Both of us worked for Zulfikar Ali Bhutto, Khalid as his first press secretary and I as his adviser on student and labour affairs. We earlier collaborated on another book, *The Tragedy of Afghanistan: A First-hand Account*, published by Verso in 1987. I would like to thank my friend for all his hard work spread over the years.

All I have tried to do is to pay my small debt to history. That has been the only motivation for this book.

Raja Anwar
February 1997
Pakistan

Raja Anwar

Raja Anwar attracted notice in the late sixties as a student leader from Rawalpindi who was one of the first among the younger, progressive and politically motivated idealists to join Zulfikar Ali Bhutto who at the time looked like the 'promised socialist messiah'. Raja threw himself into the movement against President Ayub Khan which was gathering momentum, with Bhutto the principal symbol of resistance against the praetorian rule of the man who had become Pakistan's first military ruler in 1958.

Raja served as Bhutto's adviser on student and labour affairs for some years, but like all his left-wing followers remained essentially on the outside, used by the leader but never quite identified with. When Bhutto fell from power in 1977, Raja became one of the principal organizers with Begum Nusrat Bhutto and the young Benazir of a failed bid to save the former Prime Minister's life. He escaped from Pakistan to Germany a year later and flew to Kabul to join Murtaza Bhutto at his invitation. The association did not last as Raja felt that the path being taken by the young Bhutto would only lead to disaster. Raja was jailed by the Afghan authorities at Murtaza's behest, who had earlier sentenced his 'political commissar' to death.

Finally released in 1984, Raja sought asylum in Germany where he has lived until 1992. In 1987, he published *The Tragedy of Afghanistan*, a first-hand account of the Afghan revolution, Soviet and Western intervention and the ensuing civil war. He is the author of five other books, one of which, *Jhootay Roop Ke Darshan (Beauty)*, a love story, is very popular among young Pakistanis.

Khalid Hasan

Kashmir-born Pakistani journalist and writer, Khalid Hasan has published just over twenty-five books, including several translations from Urdu and Punjabi. He has produced eight collections of his own writings on various aspects of Pakistani political and social life, translated two collections of Saadat Hasan Manto's stories, edited two anthologies of modern Pakistani stories, and put together a collection of the poetry of Faiz Ahmed Faiz. He is also the translator of Raja Anwar's *The Tragedy of Afghanistan*. Hasan's latest book is his translation from Urdu of Ghulam Abbas's *Hotel Moenjodaro and Other Stories*. He is currently working on a collection of Manto's partition of India stories and sketches to mark the fiftieth anniversary in 1997 of the end of the Raj and the emergence of India and Pakistan as independent states.

Now living in Washington, he is the US correspondent of the independent Pakistani English daily, *The Nation*.

1

The Fall of Zulfikar Ali Bhutto

The memory of the hot and oppressive evening of 4 July 1977 has always stayed with me. I can still see General Zia-ul-Haq as he walks out of Prime Minister Bhutto's office and climbs into his black army staff car. This was to be General Zia's last meeting as a subordinate of the Prime Minister. Few possibilities could have been more remote, for me at least, than that in just seven hours, the General would become Pakistan's new ruler and Bhutto his prisoner, let alone that in less than two years' time Bhutto would go to the gallows at the hands of his chosen Chief of Army Staff.

After Zia's departure, Bhutto emerged from his room with his retired Chief of Army Staff, General Tikka Khan. He looked at Tikka. 'Well, General, do you recall how you opposed Zia being promoted Chief of Staff? You will now have to concede that I made the correct choice. Had it been another army chief, he would have long since grabbed power by taking advantage of the current law and order situation.'

Tikka Khan was not trained to engage in debate or to argue, so he kept shaking his head affirmatively and saying: 'Yes, sir, yes sir.' Not that Bhutto actually expected a response: rather, he seemed to be reassuring himself. This was Bhutto's way of dealing with difficult questions. He would often think out loud as he was doing now, going over the pros and cons of a given problem. I had heard him speaking to himself about the complex aspects of internal and external situations while his valet Noor Muhammad Mughal, 'Noora', would be giving his shoes a final buff and saying: 'Balley Sain, Balley Sain', Sindhi for 'Well said, sir'.

Events were to contradict Bhutto's over-confidence, and to show that the pattern of military dominance was still built into the fabric of a nation not yet thirty years old (and in one sense only six years old) when he was deposed. To set the stage of this story, it is worthwhile to sketch some features of the birth and early history of a nation that had never existed before the partition of India in 1947. Both Pakistan and the new India were pieced together in haste out of the patchwork of provinces and principalities that the British had ruled as a loose confederacy rather than the monolith that had suited the Raj. Their division on a dualist, Hindu-Muslim basis

1

imposed an unprecedentedly religious national logic on both of the new nations.

A Young and Malformed Country

Right from the start, our country was plagued by centrifugal forces within and geopolitical pressures from outside. As a designedly Muslim nation, with some key exceptions, it contained most of the areas in the outgoing Raj where Muslims were in the majority. It happened that these areas were not joined: a thousand miles separated the two halves called East and West Pakistan. Even the name Pakistan is both an ironic pun and a prophetic acronym. It comes from the initial letters of the western areas – *P*unjab, the *A*fghan frontier, *K*ashmir and *S*ind, plus Baluchi*stan*, but can also be read as a combination of the Urdu *pak* (pure) and *stan* (land). So it contained no trace either of the eastern wing later to secede as Bangladesh, or of its principal language, Bengali.

Inside Western Pakistan there were tensions between Punjab – much the most populous and influential province – and the other areas. Sind absorbed many of the seven and a half million Muslims who fled from India to both parts of Pakistan at the time of partition. The province had its own traditions, and a historic antagonism to Punjab, and its problems were deepened by having to make room for the needs and ambitions of the new immigrants, known as Mohajirs, Urdu-speaking and of Indian birth. The tribal Frontier region between Pakistan and Afghanistan had never been governable from outside, and some of its inhabitants wanted to establish a separate state of 'Pushtunistan' (land of the Pushtuns or Pathans), encouraged by the Afghan government. Baluchistan too, the largest but least populous province of West Pakistan, had separatist ambitions.

When the Hindu ruler of the disputed state of Kashmir and Jammu refused to commit his country to Pakistan at partition despite its three-quarters Muslim population, a Muslim rebellion led to the first brief war between India and Pakistan. It ended on 1 January 1949 with a ceasefire agreement that split Kashmir into unequal halves. Much of the state, including the fabled Kashmir Valley, fell under Indian control while the rest, Azad (Free) Kashmir, lay in the hands of local rebels who had been backed by Pakistan and Pushtun tribesmen. The United Nations passed a series of resolutions in 1948 and 1949 which required the two countries to allow a plebiscite to choose between India and Pakistan. The plebiscite has never been held.

Inner divisions and territorial disputes were bound to give far more power to the army of this new and artificial nation than in a country with long-established boundaries and a unified tradition and culture. In India the Congress party was able to stabilise civilian rule and promote agrarian reform. By contrast, in Pakistan the great feudal landowning families still had virtually undisturbed power and influence. History and geography further aggravated the problems of the new state. Pakistan is bordered to the west by Iran, to the north by Afghanistan, to the north-east by China and to the south and east by the Arabian Sea and India. It was born at much the same time as the Cold War, and quickly became a focus of superpower rivalry. Like Tsarist Russia before it, the Soviet Union had influence and ambitions in Afghanistan, and control of neighbouring Pakistan would have brought access to the oil-rich Middle East where the United Kingdom and United States were determined to reinforce their own economic and strategic interests. In the 1950s Pakistan became a member of the Western-dominated South East Asia Treaty Organization (SEATO 1954–75) and Central Treaty Organization (CENTO 1955–79), both collective defence pacts now defunct.

The West's main aim in Pakistan was a government and armed force that would pursue a reliably anti-Soviet policy. Here as elsewhere, if that meant backing the authoritarian and conservative loyalties of the armies they supplied and the soldiers they hosted and trained, neither the UK nor the US were likely to feel more inhibited by the repercussions on domestic issues such as civil liberties and social justice than the Soviets. Real or imagined, the threat from the much larger nation of India to Pakistan's territorial and Islamic integrity further reinforced the influence and prestige of the armed forces.

My generation, born with Partition, saw our country struggling to find a national and international identity. The British Raj had left us with no democratic tradition, no solid industrial base, and a system of feudal landlordism so stubborn that even in the 1970s and 1980s, four fifths of the members of Pakistan's parliament owned holdings of more than a hundred acres. The peasants needed freedom from a system of virtual serfdom. Both they and the urban poor had to improve their standards of living. Some tentative beginnings were made with trade union organization and political agitation, often stimulated by a middle class that had ambitions of its own.

The country's entrenched conservative order and hidebound military failed either to consolidate a sense of national identity or to respond to popular aspirations for a better and freer life. The early years were marred by the death of the founder, Mohammad Ali Jinnah, in 1948, and by the assassination of the first prime minister, Liaquat Ali Khan, in 1951. No constitution had been agreed when in 1954 the Governor General dissolved the constituent assembly and declared a state of emergency. Iskander Mirza, an officer of the Indian Political Service, succeeded Ghulam Muhammad as the Governor General and emerged as the strong man of the country.

The Rise of Zulfikar Ali Bhutto

Zulfikar Ali Bhutto had a close-up view of the birth and early struggles of his country. He was born to a Sindhi landlord, Sir Shahnawaz Bhutto, diwan or prime minister of the small principality of Junagarh, in 1928. The young Zulfikar was sent to the University of California at Berkeley, from where he graduated. He returned to Pakistan after spending time at Oxford and Lincoln's Inn, where he obtained degrees in political science and law. Although he set up a legal practice in Karachi, he was not much interested in it. Politics were his passion. Karachi was still the capital of Pakistan – the shift to the new city of Islamabad came in the 1960s – and the hub of political and economic activity, and Bhutto's youth and brilliance soon brought him to General Mirza's notice. Both the Governor General's wife, Naheed, and his own, Nusrat, were of Iranian origin, and it seems that Naheed was his passport to Mirza's court.

In 1954, Bhutto was sent as a delegate representing Pakistan to the Law of the Sea Conference, which the young and ambitious lawyer saw as a great honour as well as a recognition of his talent. It was around this time that he wrote a letter to Mirza calling him a greater leader than even Jinnah himself, the founder of Pakistan. This would be cited later on in his career to damage his democratic credentials.

In 1955, tensions between East and West Pakistan caused the government to merge the provinces and princely states of West Pakistan into a so-called 'One Unit', so as to counterfeit parity with the more populous but less powerful East Pakistan. Both the western and eastern wings of the country received equal representation in the new legislature, though the census of 1961 put their respective populations at forty-three and fifty-one million. This spurious 'balance' flouted the principle of democratic proportionality. It offered the people of East Pakistan no chance to reform a system that siphoned off the foreign earnings of the area to subsidize the then less prosperous West, and in which Bengali officers held less than four per cent of the commissioned ranks in the armed forces. Another effect was to exacerbate inter-ethnic antagonisms among the provinces crammed into the new structure.

By the terms of the first constitution, adopted in February 1956, Pakistan became an Islamic republic under its first president, General Mirza. On 7 October 1958, Mirza abrogated the constitution, dismissed the government and declared martial law with General Ayub Khan, the commander-in-chief of the army, as his chief martial law administrator (CMLA).

Mirza gave the young Bhutto his first political break by appointing him minister for commerce. The choice was approved by Ayub, and this was fortunate for Bhutto because his mentor's ride on the tiger was a brief one.

4

Mirza had overthrown the government with the help of the army. Now the army, or more precisely its chief, had decided to get rid of him. The constitution that might have sustained Mirza in power, he had already abrogated. He lasted just twenty days. On 27 October 1958, he was deposed by Ayub and put on a London-bound flight. He never returned and died in exile in London, where he had worked as hotel manager.

Bhutto did not waste time in regrets, but began to cultivate Ayub and win his confidence. Reportedly, he used to call him 'Daddy'. Ayub took a shine to the bright young man, who was ultimately to oust him from power. In 1963, Bhutto was made foreign minister, an appointment that put him in the spotlight, since during those years Pakistan was an important US ally as a member of the anti-communist CENTO and SEATO. However, he was farsighted enough to see that Pakistan would have to broaden its choices and not remain attached to the US camp only. He tried to create a niche for his country in the Non-Aligned Movement, and also took up the cause of Kashmir against India in a vigorous and emotional style that won him much public support and admiration.

From independence right through the decade of the 1950s, India and China had maintained the most cordial relationship. However, when India granted asylum to the Dalai Lama in 1959, their relationship soured. Late in 1962, the two countries fought a brief war along their border in India's northeast. India suffered humiliating reverses at the hands of the better-prepared and more motivated Chinese force. Bhutto felt that the time was right to wrest Kashmir from India. However, since both the Soviet Union and the United States were on India's side, no adventurist intervention into Kashmir by Pakistan would have been tolerated. In order to assuage Pakistan, the Americans assured Ayub Khan that if he created no difficulties for the beleaguered Indians and avoided the temptation of taking advantage of the traditional enemy, New Delhi would be persuaded to hold meaningful negotiations over Kashmir once the crisis was over. After the end of Sino-Indian hostilities, Jawaharlal Nehru, the Indian prime minister, paid a visit to Pakistan. In 1964, the two principal Kashmiri leaders, Sheikh Mohammad Abdullah and Mirza Afzal Beg, were sent by Nehru to Pakistan, reportedly with a peace formula. Unfortunately, only days after their arrival, Nehru died suddenly and the peace mission had to be aborted. Never again were India and Pakistan to come so close to a settlement over Kashmir.

It was Bhutto's assessment that India was vulnerable after its conflict with China, and if Pakistan played its cards right it could still snatch Kashmir. A half-baked plan called 'Operation Gibraltar' was drawn up mainly under Bhutto's guidance and set in motion. It involved the dispatch of Pakistani and Azad Kashmiri irregulars into Indian-held Kashmir with orders to ignite an uprising that would force India either to pull out or to make a settlement with Pakistan on the latter's terms. It was assumed that there would be no war as such between India and Pakistan, since the entire action would take place in disputed territory and India would not be so reckless as to attack Pakistan across the agreed international frontier of the two countries. Ayub Khan, always a pragmatic man, was reluctant to accept the plan, which he found full of pitfalls and questionable assumptions, but went along with it in the end because both his brilliant foreign minister and one of his top military commanders, Major-General Akhtar Hussain Malik, were strongly in favour of going ahead. Pakistan ignored the Indian Prime Minister Lal Bahadur Shastri's repeated warnings that if Pakistan did not bring its adventurist incursion into Kashmir to an immediate end, India would take appropriate action to defend itself.

On 6 September 1965, India attacked Pakistan at three points across the international border both in Kashmir and further south. The seventeen-day war that both sides claimed to have won was actually indecisive. However, Bhutto emerged as a star from the 1965 conflict, and his emotional performance in the UN Security Council while pleading Pakistan's case was lapped up by a nation swayed by tales of glory and overcome with patriotism. Bhutto declared that Pakistan would fight a thousand-year war with India, then he paused, and pulled from his pocket a telegram containing instructions from Ayub Khan about the acceptance of the ceasefire. By reading it out dramatically he created the impression back home in Pakistan that it was the President who had 'surrendered' to India – had it been left to him, he would have fought on until victory. This single act was to endear Bhutto to the people of Punjab forever. That province had not only been arbitrarily divided in 1947, thanks to Lord Mountbatten, but had suffered the worst communal rioting in India. The wounds of partition had not healed, nor the bitterness against India subsided.

This time the peace between India and Pakistan was brokered by the Soviet Union, and an accord was signed between Ayub and Shastri at Tashkent on 10 January 1966 under which both countries had agreed to settle their disputes through peaceful means rather than war. Bhutto, sensing that the accord would be viewed as a national disgrace, distanced himself from it even while it was being signed. Pictures flashed back to Pakistan showed a crestfallen foreign minister whose face told the story of national humiliation. In June 1966, Ayub sacked Bhutto, although the official announcement said that he had resigned on grounds of 'ill health'. Once he was out of government, he warned against Indian inducements to peaceful cooperation, openly denounced the Tashkent accord as a symbol of Pakistan's humiliation, and promised to tell the 'real story' behind that 'shameful betrayal'. He also managed to disassociate himself from the military regime he had served just at a time when its incompetence, rigidity and conservatism were becoming increasingly obvious and unpopular.

People who had had enough of Ayub Khan's paternalistic rule for eight long years greeted the new Bhutto as a choking man greets oxygen. He appeared to offer hope and the opportunity for a new start to students and to other sections of the population who were awakening into political life as their military rulers stumbled from disaster to humiliation.

Bhutto Boards the *Khyber Mail*

I first met Bhutto in Rawalpindi on the night of 20 June 1966, when I and some other students boarded the train – the *Khyber Mail* – that was taking the fallen foreign minister to Lahore. Why was I on that train? Because it had been my ambition since the end of the 1965 war to see Bhutto from close quarters, and if possible, meet him. He was already my hero. I had been waiting on the platform since 10 pm. Bhutto arrived an hour later, although his train was not due to leave until 2.30 am. There were no more than twenty people to see him off, most of them from the Foreign Office. Bhutto shook hands with them one by one and walked into his first-class carriage. I rushed forward and greeted him. He looked at me with questioning eyes. 'I am a student at Gordon College and I am going with you, sir, up to Lahore to see you off', I stammered. He looked pleased and gave me his hand.

This journey proved to be a turning-point in Bhutto's life. When the train reached Jhelum it was five in the morning, but the platform was thronged with students who began to shout slogans in his praise. Some of them began to knock at the door of his carriage. After a few minutes Bhutto appeared wearing a long shirt and baggy trousers, the traditional *shalwar kamiz*. The moment they saw him, the students began to curse Ayub. One young man shouted: 'You said you were going to fight for a thousand years. Why have you abandoned us?' Bhutto was so overcome that tears welled up in his eyes. He raised his finger to the sky and replied: 'I leave you in the hands of God.' This was Bhutto's first real contact with the people.

All along the route, there were more and more people because word had spread that Bhutto was on the train. As we moved forward, the crowds grew larger. When we arrived at Gujarat, scores of people poured into Bhutto's carriage, two of them carrying that morning's Urdu daily *Nawai Waqt*, in which the popular and progressive poet Habib Jalib had written a poem entitled *Chhor ke na ja* – don't leave us. They read out that poem to Bhutto who in those days did not speak or understand a great deal of Urdu. These two men were later to join the Pakistan People's Party (the PPP). Their names were Professor Mohammad Usman and Masood Sarwar Rathore.

The *Khyber Mail* slunk into Lahore at 9 am and was received by thousands of people, most of them students who were shouting slogans against Ayub and beating their breasts, a traditional gesture of denunciation. Since the proclamation of martial law, Ayub had banned all political parties. Hence it was left to the young students to struggle for the restoration of democracy, and since 1962 they had been spearheading the movement against military dictatorship. In Bhutto they found a leader, a real answer to Ayub Khan's government. Bhutto pulled out his handkerchief and dried his eyes, so overwhelmed was he. We learnt later that someone removed the handkerchief, and that it had been auctioned for thousands of rupees. Bhutto's plan was to break his journey at Lahore before proceeding to Karachi. He was led away from the rear of the train as the crowds were so dense and emotionally wrought.

Years later, I asked Bhutto why he had chosen to travel by train that night. He told me that he wanted to measure the people's 'temperature' and read their mood. I can recall his words.

Since my journey was to begin at 2.30 am and end at nine in the morning, I wanted to know if there would be people to greet me at those ungodly hours. I had argued to myself that if people were prepared to turn up at such inconvenient hours, they would also be willing to take to the streets against Ayub Khan.

That one journey made up Bhutto's mind for him. He now knew that the masses were hankering after a new leader and that he met the specifications.

The stage was set and on 30 November 1967 he founded the Pakistan People's Party in Lahore. It was the first party in Pakistan's history that fired the imagination of the urban lower middle class and poor. Its cadres were and remain to this day emotionally charged, courageous but foolhardy, ready to follow but disorganized, rowdy and anger-prone. The new party received massive support in Punjab, especially in areas which had been directly affected by the 1965 war. Bhutto, however, began his campaign from Peshawar, in the North-West Frontier Province, where he held a public meeting on 5 November 1968. From there he was expected to arrive by road in Rawalpindi on 7 November and go straight to the Hotel Intercontinental. A day earlier, he had sent on two of his party men and close friends, Mumtaz Ali Bhutto and Ghulam Mustafa Khar, as an 'advance party'. Later, they were to be made chief ministers of Sind and Punjab respectively. Part of their mission was to go to Gordon College and contact me, as vice-president of the student union and already an informal member of the PPP. They told me to see to it that Bhutto received a big welcome from the students when he arrived next day.

As it was, I had already been organizing a welcome march for Bhutto. We had a good excuse to stage it. Two months earlier a group of students from Gordon College had taken a day trip to Landi Kotal on Pakistan's Afghan frontier. The town was part of the tribal areas where the normal laws of Pakistan did not apply and smuggled goods from all over the world could be purchased. The students had bought some odds and ends from the bazaar and customs men had confiscated them on the farcical ground that the entry of smuggled goods into the country was banned. We planned to protest against the high-handedness of the customs officials and demand the return of our goods. At a student assembly held on the morning of 7 November, a student called Khalid Latif Thulla[1] made a strong speech against Ayub Khan. From the college we marched to the Hotel Intercontinental to welcome Bhutto when he arrived. There was a lot of police activity. At 3 pm we were still waiting and Bhutto had not turned up. Suddenly, without provocation, the police fell on us with steel-tipped sticks and a rain of teargas shells. As Bhutto arrived at the hotel through clouds of tear gas, word reached us that the police had fired on the students of the Polytechnic Institute, a couple of miles from the hotel, and killed a student by the name of Abdul Hamid. That was enough to set off widespread student rioting in the city.

On 9 November, I along with some other Gordon College students was arrested by the police. They took us to the Bagh Sardaran interrogation centre, where they kept us for ten days in squalid conditions. We were also roughed up. As it turned out, the Rawalpindi incident touched off a countrywide protest movement against Ayub. The time was ripe; we had provided the spark.

On 19 November we were released. The first thing we did after coming out was to form an action committee representing student unions from all Rawalpindi colleges. Our lead was followed by students all over the country, and action committees sprang up overnight. In the next few weeks, lawyers, civil servants, doctors, engineers, journalists and labour unions joined what was now a mass movement against Ayub Khan and his misrule.

On 23 March 1969, Ayub Khan stepped down. He also destroyed his own 1962 constitution, which had created a selective presidency, against the principle of one man one vote, by handing over power to his army chief, General Yahya Khan. The new man placed a ban on all strikes, marches and public protest demonstrations. He also disbanded the 'One Unit' and so restored their autonomy to the four provinces of Frontier, Punjab, Sind and Baluchistan, and declared 1970 'election year'. A new National Assembly was to devise a new constitution for the country. East Pakistan would hold more seats than the West in the Assembly – 162 against 138. By now, though, it was too late to heal the rift between the separate halves of Pakistan, and a decisive split was only a matter of time. Nonetheless the junta, feudal lords and mullahs from West Pakistan refused to acknowledge the mounting tragedy.

In 1970, although political activity was restored, it was forbidden to criticize the martial law under which the country was being ruled. I spent that year in jail in Bahawalpur for ignoring the ban. Other PPP men held there for the same crime included Mairaj Mohammad Khan, Mukhtar Rana, Pervez Rashid and Maulana Kausar Niazi, all of whom were to play important roles when the party came to power a year later after Pakistan's dismemberment. Yahya and his generals had gambled that no single party would be able to win decisively in the elections of 7 December which would leave the army in the driving seat. However, the results of the first direct universal elections since independence were completely otherwise. Sheikh Mujibur Rahman's Awami League made a clean sweep in East Pakistan with 160 seats, a clear majority in the Assembly. Bhutto's PPP won 81 seats – a decisive victory in the Punjab and Sind. In Baluchistan and Frontier, Abdul Wali Khan's National Awami Party won enough seats to be able to form governments.

It was Yahya Khan's duty to invite the majority party led by Mujib to form the new government of the country and give the people a new constitution. He did no such thing, because he did not really wish to part with power. Mujib had fought the election on the basis of his Six Points, which laid down a confederal formula for the governance of Pakistan with the federal government responsible only for defence and foreign affairs. Yahya, who should have formed a bridge between the major contenders for power, instead did everything to divide them further. In the struggle that followed, Bhutto sided with Yahya and the army. The new, elected National Assembly never met. On 25 March 1971, Yahya ordered a massive army crackdown in East Pakistan. The Awami League was banned and wide-scale arrests of its leaders and workers made. Bhutto was in Dhaka at the time. He flew to Karachi next day and his first words on arrival were: 'Thank God, Pakistan has been saved.'

However, God did not agree to save Pakistan, thanks to the generals, landlords and bureaucrats whose greed for power and callous short-sightedness had brought the situation to this tragic pass. India took full advantage of the mess, and began to arm Bengali dissidents. In the short civil war that followed, millions of refugees from East Pakistan fled to West Bengal in India and thousands of civilians were killed by the Pakistan army. The situation was geared for disaster and it finally overtook Pakistan. On 4 December 1971, in a mystifying move Yahya attacked India – ostensibly from West Pakistan to relieve pressure on his beleaguered troops in the East but perhaps to jettison that troublesome part – and within two weeks, Pakistan had lost the war. The army surrendered to the Indians in East Pakistan and over ninety thousand of its officers and men were taken prisoner. East Pakistan had become Bangladesh. During the short-lived war, General Yahya Khan set up a so-called civilian government with the old and ailing Bengali politician Nurul Amin as prime minister and Zulfikar Ali Bhutto as his deputy as well as foreign minister. If General Yahya Khan had thought that Bengali masses would accept Nural Amin as a substitute for their independence, then he was the biggest fool ever born on Pakistan soil.

Bhutto was blamed by some in the Army for the loss of East Pakistan. His opponents believe to this day that he allowed Pakistan to be destroyed rather than stay out of power. The breakup also weakened if not utterly demolished the rationale on the basis of which Pakistan itself had come into being. The founder of Pakistan had conducted the struggle to establish a new Muslim state in the subcontinent on the precept that India contained two nations – Hindu and Muslim. Twenty-four years later, the majority province of Muslim Pakistan had seceded on the strength of Bengali nationalism.

Bhutto's Fateful Misjudgements

Bhutto became the new president, and the first civilian chief martial law administrator of what he called the New Pakistan. It was a quirk of history that the man who had vowed to fight India for a thousand years in 1965 was appealing to India six years later to release ninety thousand Pakistani POWs. The man who had denounced the Tashkent accord as humiliating had to travel to India in 1972 to sign the Simla Agreement. The Pakistan Army had ruled the country from 1958 until 1971, and it only ceded power because of its military fiasco in East Pakistan. In its heart, it never accepted responsibility for losing half of Pakistan and consigning so many of its men and officers to Indian POW camps. (It was not till August 1973 that the two countries came to an agreement for the release of these prisoners and the exchange of refugee populations displaced by the war of independence.) Nevertheless, when Bhutto became president the army was diminished and demoralized, and this may have blunted his alertness about its future role.

An allied misjudgement was to lead to his eventual destruction, in the form of Zia-ul-Haq. When Bhutto became president he promoted Zia from brigadier to major-general, after King Hussein of Jordan had put in a word for him. Had that not happened, Zia would probably have retired as a brigadier. Zia, who was in Jordan in 1970 at the time of the Black September operation against the Palestinians, was believed to have taken part in the massacre on the orders of Hussein, in blatant violation of his charter of duties as an officer seconded to Jordan from the Pakistan army. Hussein had now returned the favour. It was a signal to Bhutto that Zia was the kind of man who would go to any length for him too. Soon the time came to test that loyalty.

11

In 1973, as many as 122 army officers were arrested and charged under Article 6 of the new constitution with conspiring to overthrow Bhutto's government. This episode came to be known as the Attock conspiracy case. It was at Bhutto's suggestion that Zia was made president of the military court where these officers were tried. To impress Bhutto with his devotion to constitutional government and democracy, and as a gesture of appreciation for his promotion, Zia passed overly harsh sentences against the accused. His way to the next rank was now assured, and before long he was promoted to Lieutenant-General. In February 1976, Bhutto made him head of the Pakistan army. Zia was the most junior in rank of the Lieutenant-Generals and could never have dreamt of winning the top job. Fifteen months after his elevation, he had become the sole ruler of Pakistan, and for the next eleven years, his every word was the law. It is ironic that after doling out heavy punishment to those accused in the Attock conspiracy case, Zia's conspiracy toppled the government only two years later. Better yet, after he took over, Zia reprieved the men he had sentenced in the Attock trial. One of them, Raja Nadir Pervez, became a minister in his cabinet.

There were other reasons for Zia's promotion. Bhutto was well aware of one unpleasant fact of Pakistani political life, namely that no politician could hope either to get into power or to rule effectively without the good will, support, and indeed permission of the army. Therefore he was looking for an army chief who would remain obedient to him, like Tikka Khan. Another factor was Zia's public persona, which was more akin to an NCO's than to those of the generals mythologized in Pakistan at the popular level. For Bhutto, Zia's superficially weak personality was an asset. On top of that, he came from a non-military background in East Punjab, whereas the army establishment traditionally belonged to North Punjab. Bearing these points in mind, especially as Zia was a refugee from what was now Indian Punjab, Bhutto persuaded himself that his hand-picked man would not take over as Ayub Khan had done in 1958.

Punjab, admittedly, was Bhutto's power base, but after a revolt by his most trusted deputy, Ghulam Mustafa Khar, in 1974 he no longer felt too easy with the country's largest and most formidable province. Punjab, in Bhutto's own words, was one of the two 'bastions of power' containing sixty-two per cent of the country's population. Khar, his most trusted lieutenant and friend, fell out of favour because he raised the banner of Punjabi nationalism, which Bhutto as a populist leader could not tolerate. The defection of such a strong and popular leader from the Punjab could only mean that a potential rival and co-claimant had been born. Bhutto's appointment of the lackadaisical Nawab Sadiq Hussain Qureshi as Punjab Chief Minister, and of former Brigadier Muzzaffar, a pliant officer, as Chief Secretary can only be understood against this background. He thought he had learnt from his bitter experience with Khar. In Bhutto's view, Zia belonged to the same semi-paralytic category.

General Zia was always a practising Muslim. He did not drink and he had no interest in women or other diversions much loved by young army officers, at least of his time. After promoting Zia, Bhutto was often heard saying, as if to reassure himself, that the army needed an abstemious leader like him. Army messes began to turn dry after Zia took over, and what had been an officer crop with liberal traditions increasingly began to cast off what were considered the un-Islamic ways of the West. When General Zia moved into Army House in Rawalpindi, the Chief of Staff's official residence, he had all pictures taken off the walls. In their place he ordered photographs of religious shrines and mosques. I was present during a visit when Bhutto noticed the walls and remarked, 'General, you have turned your living-room into a mosque'.

In the same room, Bhutto could also have seen the complete set of Abu Ala Maududi's writings. Zia was the first head of the Pakistan army whose idea of a prize on special occasions was Maududi's books, which advocated a return to religion and the establishment of an Islamic state. Bhutto should have sensed the danger. What clearer signal could he have received about Zia's extremely right-wing views! However, his court of sycophants continued to assure him that his personality transcended all ideologies. Only that can explain why Bhutto continued to consider Zia personally loyal to him despite once severely insulting him in front of others.[2]

Bhutto admitted after his removal that Zia's appointment had been his greatest mistake. He misread him on several counts. First, on the question of personality, he compared Zia's grey subservience with his own assertive brilliance and found no competition. Not only did he underestimate Zia's long-term vision, cunning and cold ruthlessness, but he failed to recognize that the armed forces would obey orders from the top regardless of personality. Second, he did not recognize the threat of Mullahism as a political force in Pakistan. Here he was not alone, and it must be remembered that the Shah of Iran was on the throne, Sadat was President of Egypt and Beirut was still standing. Yet in Pakistan as elsewhere what is now known as 'Islamic fundamentalism' could tap the social frustrations bred by half-baked reform and botched modernization. Zia was not socially radical but neither was he feudal; upwardly-mobile junior officers often shared his outlook, with its characteristic mixture of resentment and subservience towards the old ruling families. Third, martial law regimes were integral to the Cold War world: US governments instinctively preferred the devil they knew, especially in military dress, to maverick politicians, no matter how autocratic. For this particular ailing ally, the unholy troika of generals, mullahs and landlords was the remedy of choice: safety first.

But there was one great achievement that Bhutto could justly claim – the 1973 constitution, Pakistan's third, which was adopted unanimously. When it was brought in, he proudly announced that he had laid the curse of martial law to rest forever in the Arabian Sea. In those days, Bhutto was seen as the only man who could build a new Pakistan and restore national honour. Surely the army had learnt from its recent débâcle and past experience, and would not try to take over again. If it did, there was Article 6, which laid down capital punishment for overthrowing the government by violent means and annulling the constitution.

I was appointed adviser on student and labour affairs by Bhutto in October 1973. Although I had been publicly critical of many of his policies, my services to the party and various stints in prison had in his book counter-balanced my dissidence. He reminded me the day he appointed me: 'We were both on that train in June 1966. I am sure you will never get off the revolutionary train of the Pakistan People's Party.' I recall replying: 'Sir, as long as you are in the driving seat, I am sure neither will our train go in the wrong direction nor will it occur to me to step off it.' Bhutto smiled and patted me on the back affectionately.

Looking back, the biggest mistake made by the PPP was that instead of ending feudalism, it went ahead with the nationalization of industry and other sectors, handing over the control of these fledgling sectors to the bureaucracy. The bureaucracy failed to come up to the expectations of the working class, and its lack of experience brought Pakistan's industry to the point of near-collapse. The PPP taught the workers how to ask for their rights but did not teach them the work ethic. While they demanded wage increases, it never occurred to them to step up production, nor were they asked to do so. In the 1970 elections, for the first time in Pakistan's history, the feudal classes in Sind and Punjab had been trounced, while ordinary people representing the interests of the underprivileged were returned to the assemblies. Once the PPP took power, the very elements which it had defeated began to fill its ranks. Soon they were controlling the levers of power in the party and the government. Right up to Bhutto's fall in 1977, most of the ministers and governors came from the same feudal class against which the PPP had originally risen.[3] The land reform announced by Bhutto in 1972 was hamstrung by these same powerful vested interests.[4]

Early in 1977, Bhutto announced his intention to hold general elections on 7 March. Nine mostly right-wing political parties now formed a movement, the Pakistan National Alliance (PNA), to mobilize the general public disaffection with Bhutto's harsh rule. The electoral strategy perfected for Bhutto by his feudal-minded advisers and intellectually barren bureaucrats proved to be his political undoing. All four provincial chief ministers and the Prime Minister himself were elected 'unopposed' when the opposition candidates from their constituencies were physically prevented from handing in their nomination papers. A number of seats from Sind were similarly acquired. Even before the elections there was nationwide condemnation of these arrogant tactics.

Bhutto's advisers had assured him that these electoral walkovers would be seen abroad as evidence of his popularity, while at home people would conclude that it was futile to oppose a party whose leadership had been returned without a contest. One of the co-authors of this advice asserted that the average citizen invariably sided with the powerful and the victorious.[5] His views said more about his class background than his powers of objective observation, for while the feudal landlords and assorted khans, nawabs, sardars, jagirdars and tribal chieftains of Pakistan have always kowtowed to the ruler of the day, the masses tend to side with the oppressed. In a fair election a man like Maulana Jan Muhammed Abbasi, who was physically prevented from running against Bhutto in his home town of Larkana, would in any case have gained a negligible vote. The shame of the 1977 elections was that the PPP set out to rig them. The irony is that Bhutto allowed himself to be deprived of what would have been a genuine victory. The tragedy is that the elections defiled the institution of a fair vote.

While Bhutto had come to realize by February 1977 that his, and his chief ministers', 'unopposed' victory had been a mistake, he was not in a position to undo what had happened. However, it was now his intention that the general polls to federal and provincial assemblies, due to take place on 7 and 10 March, should be free and above-board. Accordingly, he issued strict instructions to the administration, right down to the lowest level, that there should be absolutely no irregularity in the vote. However, some members of the ruling party, notwithstanding their leader's orders, committed the most blatant irregular acts on election day, even replacing sealed ballot boxes. Bhutto's position was much like that of the legendary Iranian king Nowsherwan, who once accepted the gift of an egg from a villager, only to find that by doing so he had prompted his troops to rob the whole village of its entire stock of cattle.

The PNA had stood no chance of victory, but when it was announced on 8 March that in a National Assembly of two hundred seats the PNA had won only 36, and the PPP 155, there was outrage at the scale of the illegalities committed and the contempt they showed for the electorate. The opposition exploited public anger by declaring a boycott of the 10 March elections to the provincial legislatures. Strike calls received tremendous support. In order to break this cycle, Bhutto decided to stretch out the negotiations he had begun with the opposition to settle differences, but while these stalling tactics did succeed in lowering the tempo of the protest, the political uncertainty they created brought the country several steps closer to an army takeover. When Bhutto spoke to Tikka Khan on the evening of 4 July about the wisdom of his choice of Chief of Staff, he was reassuring himself that the spectre of martial law did not really exist. He was confident that Zia would never be part of an attempted coup against him, though he was not so sanguine about some of the other generals.

The Pakistan army, as mentioned earlier, had ruled the country from 1958 until 1971 and had only ceded power because of the military collapse in East Pakistan. In its heart, however, it had never accepted civilian rule or responsibility for defeat, which it attributed to Bhutto's greed for power and the insidious influence of General Yahya Khan. To the army Bhutto was a scapegoat for the 1971 defeat. Bhutto, having failed to quell the PNA movement through civilian law and order agencies, had increasingly begun to depend on the army for his political survival. On 21 April he had martial law proclaimed in Karachi, Lahore and Hyderabad, but the army was not ready to shoot the people in order to keep a civilian in power. Like all armies, it was terrified of a revolt within its ranks following the action of four brigadiers in Lahore who resigned in protest because they felt that their oath did not include the obligation to kill the people of Pakistan. A man of Bhutto's intelligence and experience failed to grasp that while it was easy to order the army out, it would be harder to order it back to barracks.

The Coup and its Aftermath

But let us return to the evening of 4 July, as the clock ticked away the remaining hours in office of the Bhutto government. After talking to Tikka Khan, he turned to me and asked: 'Have you already seen Benazir?' I told him that I was due to meet her at 11 am the next day. When in 1976 Benazir Bhutto had become president of the Oxford Union, her father's eyes had glowed with pride, and he had news of this 'electoral victory' well publicized. Several of his ministers offered him their congratulations, which Bhutto accepted with pleasure. He wanted his daughter, educated abroad, to become a symbol of progress, modernity and equal rights for the downtrodden women of Pakistan, and he had just appointed her his adviser on youth, an office I had held for several years.[6] I had been asked to ease Benazir into her new job and help her get acquainted with things. I was to continue my job as adviser on labour to the Prime Minister. As it was, before she could start working in her post, the army had overthrown her father. Her appointment lasted two and a half days.

It may be mentioned that Bhutto had had a secret alarm system installed in the Prime Minister's house which had a three-way connection. He could alert the Pakistan Army Chief and the Director of the Federal Security

Force (FSF), Masood Mahmood, by pressing a red button in case there was an emergency. They could both do the same. This system was only to be used in case of grave danger or a direct threat to the life of the Prime Minister. That one line connected to the head of the FSF could not have been much to the generals' liking. It was meant to be a warning to them by Bhutto that if they tried to overthrow him, they would have to contend with the FSF which was well-equipped and supposedly an 'elite' force, though actually quite untried. On the eve of the coup d'état there were said to be at least ten thousand FSF men in the capital. The generals wished to avoid a clash with what was popularly known as 'Bhutto force'.

Lieutenant-General F.A. Chisti was in charge of the operation that night and keen to know how long it would take Masood Mahmood to come 'on line' when Bhutto pressed the panic button. That was why four hours before the Prime Minister's house was surrounded, the emergency red button was pressed from General Zia's room at the GHQ. Within seconds, both Bhutto and Masood Mahmood had picked up their special phones. There was an immediate apology, 'Sir, it was a mistake,' but what the generals wanted to know they now did. Before 'Operation Fair Play' got underway, Masood Mahmood was arrested. He began to tremble when he saw the soldiers move into his house. He offered no resistance, nor did his much vaunted 'elite' force. The way was now clear for Brigadier Warraich – later General – to surround the Prime Minister's house and inform Bhutto that 'the tea party was over'. It is strange that a man of Bhutto's wisdom and experience could consider Masood Mahmood, who became the main witness against him in the murder trial, as his friend and defender.

Overnight General Zia-ul-Haq initiated his 'Operation Fair Play', which removed the stricken government of Zulfikar Ali Bhutto, weakened immeasurably by countless strikes, protest marches and demonstrations. The moment the army moved into the Prime Minister's house, his loyal valet Noora rushed into his bedroom and told him in a trembling voice: 'Sain, the police post at the outer gate has phoned to report that the Prime Minister's house has been completely surrounded by army soldiers. The key to the locked gate has also been taken away from the police.'

Since he was not even prepared to consider the possibility of a coup while General Zia was in charge, Bhutto's first reaction was that some Bonapartist general must have removed his Chief of Army Staff. So he picked up the red emergency telephone and rang Zia, who answered himself, 'Hello sir.' Bhutto was relieved. 'Are you still awake?' he asked. 'Do you know what is going on outside?' Adopting his usual obedient tone, Zia answered: 'Sorry sir, I had to do that.'

'So it was you,' Bhutto said as he put the phone down.[7] The castles he had built on Zia's loyalty had suddenly crumbled. The shock of martial law was less painful than the realization that his hand-picked general had betrayed him. This was what made him psychologically unable to have a dialogue with Zia in the months ahead.

The entire Bhutto family was up and had assembled in one room. After a few minutes, when Bhutto had recovered some composure, he called Zia again and told him that he would like to go to Larkana with his family. Zia's reply, delivered with the utmost obsequiousness, was: 'Sir, take a rest in Murree for just fifteen days; afterwards you may go wherever you wish.' Murtaza Bhutto later told me that he was about to take on the soldiers with the one revolver that was available in the Prime Minister's house, but was prevented by his father and mother. The story need not be disbelieved, because in the near and later future his behaviour was consistently reckless.

When martial law was first declared, it was widely believed in Pakistan that Zia was merely carrying out Bhutto's orders. The reason for this rumour lay in the public's perception of Zia as weak and indecisive, a sycophant who by grovelling to Bhutto's huge ego had more than made up for his lack of seniority and modest talent. There were others who believed that Zia was in league with the PNA. Ten days after taking power, Zia said in a speech: 'To some I am Mr Bhutto's protégé. Can a man of his stature share power with me? Am I a PNA man as I go to the mosque regularly?'[8]

Both the PPP and the PNA misread the apparently humble and harmless General who promised on the first day that he would hold elections in ninety days' time, and stated unequivocally that the only purpose of the army was to hold free elections. Ten days after taking over, he repeated this: 'They [the politicians] have got to look after the country and its future and not I. I am here only for ninety days.'[9] It was the first of a series of broken promises made with the synthetic sincerity that was Zia's stock-in-trade. In reality, the first words he excised out of his political lexicon were elections, constitution and transfer of power.

Bhutto was in 'protective custody' at the hill resort of Murree, and he was bristling. On 12 July, Zia flew by helicopter from Rawalpindi to visit him. I was present at Murree. A more awkward, difficult and strange encounter is hard to imagine. Only seven days earlier, Bhutto had been the Prime Minister of Pakistan and Zia his faithful Chief of Army Staff; today Zia was the all-powerful ruler and Bhutto his prisoner. No other general would have come to face a man he had so recently deposed. Few people could exert such close control over their emotions and inner thoughts as Zia-ul-Haq. His face never gave anything away: no tell-tale impassivity, but a mask of bumbling mediocrity. Bhutto found it hard that day to disguise his anger, frustration and impatience. His face told the story.

When General Zia entered the room, he came smartly to attention and saluted Bhutto. He did not take the chair until Bhutto had taken his, and called him sir throughout their meeting. In order to placate him, he kept on professing that the army had taken the step with the utmost reluctance. Bhutto's cold reply was: 'If elections are held in time, I will not raise the question of this constitutional violation.' He stressed the possible consequences of overthrowing the elected government, and made it a point to look stern when he was having his picture taken with Zia. The next day's newspapers ran the shot of the Chief Martial Law Administrator and the deposed Prime Minister on their front pages. Bhutto's deliberately grim expression sent the message that it was not his martial law. What he felt was unmistakable. This was the last picture taken of the two men. They met twice more, but Zia did not risk having another picture taken with his patron-turned-prisoner.

There was no chance that Zia could have failed to grasp the implication of Bhutto's words. The reference to the constitution was a reminder to Zia that if he did not hold elections and hand over power, then under Article 6 of the constitution of Pakistan he could be hanged for treason. It was for violating Article 6 that Zia himself had jailed over a hundred officers in the Attock conspiracy trial only two years earlier. Zia's arrival in Murree so soon after evicting Bhutto's government suggests that he was still questing for a lead. He had taken over power but he still felt uncertain about the future course of events. Supposing that he had flown to Murree to renew what had been a close relationship, it must have been obvious to him that he had failed. Although Bhutto was no longer the country's Prime Minister, he still considered Zia his subordinate.

This meeting became the turning-point for Zia. He had felt a sense of fear in Murree, and as time passed this feeling grew. His reaction came shortly afterwards when he had an old murder case against Bhutto revived. He wanted to remind the deposed Prime Minister that he too could face the ultimate punishment. Had General Zia had any intention of holding elections, that stern response from Bhutto must have exploded the idea. On 14 July, two days after meeting with Bhutto in Murree, he told a news conference: 'Our acts and deeds will demonstrate whether we were usurpers or traitors or whether we violated the constitution or not.'[10]

On 29 July, Bhutto was released from 'protective custody' and had a brief meeting with General Zia. On travels through Larkana, Karachi, Multan, Peshawar and Lahore, he was greeted by enthusiastic crowds. The people had opted for Bhutto against martial law. In the weeks following, the tension soared between Bhutto and the generals. On 24 August, Zia announced that a report on the irregularities of the Bhutto government was under preparation and would be released before the promised October 1977 elections. At 2.30 pm on 28 August, Bhutto held a meeting with Zia and General F.A. Chisti, Zia's right-hand man, at army headquarters in

Rawalpindi. This was to be Bhutto's last meeting with Zia. Bhutto was staying at Pir Safiuddin Makhad's house in Islamabad. On return, he told party leaders waiting at the residence:

> The generals asked me to provide them with constitutional and legal guidance because they had no experience of running a government. I told them that it was their decision to take over the government and it was now up to them to solve the problems associated with it. I told them that I could help them to the extent that if they held the elections they had promised, I would not raise any constitutional issues.

If the generals were looking for a deal, then this last meeting was a total failure too. Bhutto could not stomach his removal from power, and continued to address them in his customary stand-offish manner. There is no question that in his presence the generals felt the chill of the hangman's noose around their necks. They were forced to the conclusion that to restore Bhutto to power would amount to digging their own graves. Bhutto always believed in speaking from a position of strength. He now believed strongly that Article 6 was his strong point: its presence would deter the Generals from scrapping the constitution or ruling the country under martial law. Given his conviction that they had no choice but to hold elections and cede power, then he himself, Zulfikar Ali Bhutto, was their only hope of survival. He simply failed to perceive that it was his own life which was on the line. The constitution was his own creation. How could it work against him?

Bhutto had forgotten that a Supreme Court which during his days of power had felt no compunction about declaring Pushtun opposition politician Wali Khan and his National Awami party traitors[11] would hardly hesitate to brand him as a murderer and to declare the rape of the constitution under Zia permissible under the 'doctrine of necessity'. There were only two ways in which the impasse could have been resolved. One, that Bhutto should reprieve the generals for removing him in return for power; two, that he should leave the political field, keep his head down and wait for the chance to strike back. He would not opt for either course. The lines between Bhutto and Zia were now drawn, and there could be no going back.

The first poisoned fruit of the Bhutto-Zia meeting appeared on the night of 3 September 1977, when Bhutto was arrested at his residence in Karachi for the murder of Nawab Muhammad Ahmed Khan Kasuri. The generals had decided that the only way to save themselves from a resurgent, vengeful Bhutto was to wring his neck. A bail application was moved at the Lahore High Court before Justice Samdani, who happened to be a Sindhi like Bhutto and was also believed to be one of his admirers. He released Bhutto on bail ten days after his arrest, but the reprieve proved temporary. On the night of 16 September, Bhutto was picked up again under a number of martial law regulations which could not be challenged in any court of law, nor were the offences bailable. Bhutto had been gagged and tied and thrown at the mercy of the Lahore High Court. His release came only with his death.

The election campaign had begun officially on 15 September 1977 – an additional reason to sideline Bhutto. Zia did not want him on the streets. He knew that if Bhutto was allowed to mobilize public opinion, it would not be possible to arrest him. Since his removal and imprisonment, the graph of his popular standing, which had fallen so low during the agitation, had shot up again. It was clear within two weeks from the start that a free vote would favour the PPP. That was too dangerous for Zia, so on 1 October he postponed the elections on the pretext that the law and order situation was not yet normal. His task was made easier because the opposition leaders were demanding that 'accountability' should precede elections – Bhutto and his colleagues must 'justify' their actions while in office. This could only mean one thing: that Bhutto should be removed from the scene before staging a vote.

As soon as the October elections had been put off, a witch hunt began. This was a shameful period in Pakistan's history. The mere mention of the word constitution, or election, or Bhutto, was enough for a person to be picked up and punished. The brazen manner in which General Zia used the Jamaat-i-Islami (Party of Islam) for his purposes has few examples in recent political history. This Muslim revivalist party was founded in 1941 by Maulana Abu Ala Maududi because he believed that the Muslim nationalism advocated by Mohammad Ali Jinnah's All-India Muslim League ran counter to the true spirit of Islam. The Jamaat now declared Zia the great Islamic defender, and lent its blind support to every sinister martial law enactment and measure of his. Wherever people turned out on the streets to protest against martial law, the baton-swinging 'Danda Force' of the Jamaat would appear on the scene and beat up the demonstrators. If the day ever comes when the Jamaat can bring itself to examine its past conduct honestly, it will struggle to acquit itself of the charge of having acted as martial law's concubine. Scores of appeals to hang Bhutto were made by its members to General Zia.

As for Zia, he disgraced Islam and distorted its revolutionary social and economic edicts. What he called Islam was in reality authoritarianism, mullahism and retrogression. He claimed to 'implement' Islam, but his Islam was no more than sectarianism, the worship of dead symbols, savage physical punishments and ignorance-ridden superstition. His 'Islamization' sowed the seeds of religious intolerance and hatred whose fruit continues to blight national life in Pakistan. The medieval punishments that Zia ordered – meted out in public – including lashings and even hangings, were invariably the lot of the poor and members of the working class. During his eleven years' rule, not a single jagirdar, general or big civilian figure was even arrested, much less punished, for corruption and dishonesty. If Zia was an Islamic ruler, then he was one who made people turn away from Islam rather than move towards it.

Postponed October elections, the murder case against Bhutto and the witch hunt against the PPP in the name of accountability all showed that General Zia would not risk parting with power or letting Bhutto walk out of prison alive. Yet Bhutto was oblivious to the danger he was in, and his wife and daughter equally unwary. That same month, Benazir was made a member of the PPP central committee. However, she was no more than a spare wheel to her mother. Like everyone else at the time, Begum Bhutto lacked the insight to foresee her husband's fate, and therefore to plan to circumvent it. As for the PPP, it was more a rabble than a party. Bhutto had never encouraged party democracy, or a strong local structure with solid grass-roots links. He once claimed that, 'I am the People's Party and they are all my creatures', a lesson that his heirs learned only too well. For most of the PPP's young members, a political act consisted of leaping in the air and dancing as their leader made his characteristic fire-breathing speeches. Because of its infantile chemistry and psychological limitations, the party was not equipped to deal with martial law in an organized and effective manner. With no tradition of local initiative, it was only natural that the rank and file would become the victims of Zia's brutal repression.

After the postponement of the October 1977 elections, the PPP's central committee broke into two rival factions. The right wing was formed by former federal minister Maulana Kausar Niazi, former Sind Chief Minister Ghulam Mustafa Jatoi, Ghulam Mustafa Khar and Kamal Azfar, a PPP senator from Karachi. They opposed Begum Nusrat Bhutto's confrontationist stance and advocated a working arrangement with the army. This faction believed that the party's leadership belonged in the hands of someone like Jatoi, who did not upset the army. It argued for compromise. Bhutto might go into exile for a while – he could always return when the situation changed for the better.

Looking back, that seems to have been the only way of saving Bhutto's life. Assuming, as was claimed at the time, that these men from the PPP did have a secret link with the army, it indicates that the army was also seeking an honourable way out and did not want Bhutto's blood on its hands. However, the Bhutto ladies denounced all these suggestions as an army plan to deprive the Bhutto family of the leadership of the PPP and oust it from the politics of Pakistan. Would it be fair to say that in the keenness of his family's ambition, Pakistan's unique son was sacrificed? Fair or not, it is a fact that the Bhutto ladies had created such a grief-laden atmosphere around the issue that it appeared to the people of Pakistan that their only objective should be to prevent the leadership of the party from going into the hands of a non-Bhutto.

It was Bhutto's misfortune that while, on the one hand, the United States had turned against him because of his nuclear ambitions for an 'Islamic bomb', on the other, Zia and his cabal of generals lived in fear of Bhutto's political return and public influence. Both wanted to see the last of him. Bhutto had been allowed to remain alive on the night of the coup because he was considered politically defused. Had there been the slightest doubt on this point, he would been done away with, like Allende in Chile in 1973 and Sheikh Mujibur Rahman in Bangladesh in 1975. The army generals and their American patrons were neither so naive as to reprieve an opponent who would malign and attack them before the world for the next two years, nor so unwise as to deliberately invite universal condemnation by hanging Bhutto after a long and controversial trial which could not establish his guilt. They must have assumed that he would bow to the inevitable.

It seems reasonable to conclude that the forces that feared Bhutto's return should have been assured that he was prepared to play the game and go into voluntary exile. For some Pakistanis, it is hard to understand why ten years after his execution, the Bhutto ladies were prepared to cooperate both with the generals and with US interests to put Benazir on the throne. If this was how it was going to be, why was this spirit of 'realism' not evident when the deposed Prime Minister's life could have been saved? Did the generals, the party and the family only need a dead Bhutto?

In an address to party workers at Sheikhupura near Lahore on 5 January 1978, Begum Bhutto's answer to the right-wing leaders of her party who were advocating compromise was: 'Instead of bowing our head, we will prefer to have it chopped off.' She also described such thinking as virtual treachery and denounced the compromise faction as agents of the army, wheeler-dealers and guns for hire. Some were even thrown out of the party. So vicious were these attacks that the ordinary PPP worker and many in the media believe to this day that these men were actually responsible for the execution of Bhutto, through their failure to launch a protest move-ment. Was a movement to be launched at the push of a magic button? If so, then where was Begum Bhutto's index finger? As I will show later, Bhutto's wife made several unsuccessful attempts to start a movement against the military regime. The truth is that the disorganized PPP's weak structure simply did not have the capability of staging a movement against the powerful and well-oiled army machine.

I would like to admit at this point that I was a great supporter of Begum Bhutto's confrontationist policy. Nevertheless, a pragmatic analysis of these events would be bound to conclude that while some leaders of the PPP central committee were willing to sacrifice Bhutto's political career in order to save his life, the policy of confrontation adopted by others destroyed not only Bhutto's political career but Bhutto himself. The only beneficiary besides General Zia was Begum Bhutto, whose family claim on the party came to be accepted. The tragic price was Bhutto's physical elimination.[12]

Soon after Bhutto's overthrow, Ghulam Mustafa Khar came to the conclusion after meeting Zia's closest companion, Lieutenant-General F.A. Chisti, that if Bhutto dug in his heels, he would not be spared. Accordingly, he advised him at the end of July 1977 to leave Pakistan so that he could 'live to fight another day'. Was Bhutto afraid that if he fled the country, his opponents would denounce him as a coward? Was it his ego that prevented him from reaching an understanding with his COAs? Bhutto never accepted until the end that he had been permanently deprived of power by the army. He believed that he would be able to outwit and outmanoeuvre Zia, calling his bluff. Convinced that Zia would never have the nerve to do him grave or fatal injury, he considered that the murder charge against him was nothing but a ploy to damage his reputation or to put a psychological lock on him. Perhaps that was why he fought his case not so much on legal as on political grounds. Or is it possible that inside the jail he was given a false impression of the state of affairs outside? Whatever the reasons, his decision to stand firm was to prove fatal.

2

Al-Nusrat:
The Campaign to Save Bhutto

Zia's postponement of the October 1977 elections delivered the clear message that he had no intention of parting with power. The murder case instituted against Bhutto in the Lahore High Court warned of a tragic end to the drama whose first scene had been the coup of 4 July, and it was under this grim threat that in November 1977 Begum Bhutto started a movement whose goal was to challenge and undermine the martial law regime. Her tactic was to deflate the popular fear of martial law's excesses by planning a series of voluntary arrests every day in Lahore and extending them to other cities as time passed. She drew up a list of five or six hundred party leaders said to be willing to court arrest and thus set in motion a campaign that would eventually lead to full-scale opposition to martial law. As was to be expected, most of these leaders were former ministers, prospective legislative candidates, and members of the PPP Central Committee favoured by the Bhutto family. The first man to volunteer arrest was the retired General Tikka Khan in Lahore's Anarkali area. The next day, not one volunteer set foot in the public domain. It turned out that most PPP leaders had phoned the police and requested to be collected from their homes. Others had been picked up anyway. There may have been other factors too, but it was obvious that the movement Begum Bhutto wanted to launch had backfired on the launching pad.

Begum Bhutto swallowed her disappointment and decided to launch a secret cell within the PPP to take up the fight against Zia. The idea came from a former deputy chairman of the Senate, Tahir Muhammad Khan, so she asked him to organize the cell, to be known as Al-Nusrat. Others involved with the effort included Qazi Anwar, a former student leader,[1] and the rather mysterious Dr Zafar Niazi.[2] Al-Nusrat was divided into two wings: political and armed. The first was assigned the task of organizing the labour force and other supporters in urban centres and bringing them out on the streets, while the armed wing was to 'deal with' the generals and judges connected with the Bhutto murder case. Al-Nusrat was never short of funds. There was plenty of money in party coffers as well as from direct donations by some of the Gulf sheikhs, notably Sheikh Zayed bin Sultan al-Nahyan of Abu Dhabi.

Although the aims and objectives of Al-Nusrat were ambitious, its performance was feeble. Before it could get organized even in a rudimentary way, Begum Bhutto announced that 5 January 1978 – Bhutto's birthday – would be celebrated as Democracy Day. In order to make it a success, she channelled a lot of money to the professional labour leadership of Lahore. I was with her that day in Sheikhupura, where she addressed party workers. She expected the labour movement to stage widespread protest marches to mark the occasion, especially in Lahore, and did not wish to be directly associated with the demonstrations.

However, on 5 January not a single factory closed, nor did any labour union organize street marches. The naive Begum Bhutto had little experience of practical politics. She did not know how difficult it was to put professional labour leaders to use, and did not understand that these cautious worthies never jumped into the fray when the odds were stacked against them. They kept the rank and file happy by issuing rousing slogans while holding hands in private with the administration and its various agencies. While this class of men was perfectly willing to take Begum Bhutto's money, it was not prepared to come out on the streets and get shot. As for the ordinary worker, he was committed to Bhutto to the extent that he would vote for him in an election.

The PPP had never taken any direct part in the inner politics of labour unions. When I was his adviser on Youth and Labour Affairs, Bhutto used to tell me: 'Instead of ourselves becoming a part of trade unions, we should keep good relations with the workers in a general, collective way to get their votes.' This made good sense as an electoral strategy, but the PPP's reluctance to play a direct role in the labour movement had caused the leadership of the movement to be divided into three groups. The first represented professional labour leaders who were agents of the local administration; the second consisted of ideologically committed men who were under the influence of various communist factions; while the third group, though small, was aligned with the right-wing Jamaat-i-Islami.[3]

Obviously, not one of these groups was willing to go marching under the Al-Nusrat banner. Tahir Muhammad Khan came from Quetta and did not really know the labour leaders of Lahore, nor had he ever had anything to do with the labour movement. However, to his credit he did manage to bring various labour leaders to call on Begum Bhutto at Khagga House in Lahore. Unfortunately, instead of trying to analyse the reasons for the failure on 5 January, Begum Bhutto held Tahir personally responsible for the fiasco. She accused him of diverting the money meant as payment to labour leaders. It is interesting that everyone whom Begum Bhutto threw out of the party she accused either of embezzling funds or of being an enemy agent. By the latter she meant that the person involved was in the pay of the other side. In her world, differences on the basis of political belief cut no ice. Tahir Muhammad Khan was an honest man who had kept his hands clean all through Bhutto's days in power. He was so shocked by Begum Bhutto's charge that he parted ways both with the party and with politics itself, so her reckless behaviour deprived the PPP of a sincere and honest leader.

It was about this time that Qazi Anwar arrived in Lahore from Peshawar with a consignment of arms acquired from the tribal areas of the Frontier province and paid for by Begum Bhutto. These arms were supposed to be distributed among the armed wing of Al-Nusrat, except that the wing did not exist, nor had any arrangement been made to train eventual recruits in the use of weapons. Qazi Anwar stayed at Lahore's Hotel International on the Upper Mall, but as soon as he tried to make contact with his consignee the police staged a raid and he was arrested. Either the Peshawar police had kept an eye on him and alerted its colleagues in Lahore, or his contact in Lahore was already under surveillance. One can only guess at the truth, although Begum Bhutto hit on the explanation that both Qazi Anwar and Dr Zafar Niazi were in league with the secret police or CID, and between them had arranged to have the arms discovered and confiscated. She said they were 'enemy-paid agents', an old charge.

The arrest of these two men was the end of the 'armed wing' of Al-Nusrat, and the organization folded before it had taken off. Dr Niazi was released in March 1981 as part of the Al-Zulfikar hijacking deal and was flown to Damascus, and from there to Kabul. I heard from Al-Zulfikar people that he went through a hazardous time there. Early on, he had found that if you wanted to be close to the Bhuttos you must learn to disregard snubs and ignore major insults. This lesson came in useful in Kabul.

In short, the party was incapable either of organizing mass voluntary arrests or of running Al-Nusrat, its phantom secret arm, and this thwarted Begum Bhutto in between 1977 and 1978. The army regime traded on the PPP's paralysis to peddle the impression both at home and abroad that there was absolute peace in the country, that Bhutto was being tried as an ordinary criminal, and that the public was in favour of such accountability. Zia further reinforced this veneer of normalcy by arranging a series of cricket Test matches in December 1977 which had the whole country under its spell, cricket being the popular craze in Pakistan.

It was painful to see that while Bhutto stood trial for murder in Lahore, the people of the city were showing greater interest in the Test match being played there. To break down this apathy, the Bhutto ladies decided to stage a demonstration during the match. Lahore's Gaddhafi stadium stands in the Gulberg area of the city, ten minutes away from Khagga

House, where both Begum Bhutto and Benazir were staying. On 16 December they got into two cars and headed for the stadium together with a group that included myself, the journalist Zia Iqbal Shahid, and Bashir Bhutta, who was acting as their bodyguard.[4] A sprinkling of workers was already at the stadium waiting for the two women to appear.

The cars drove up to the entrance to the stadium's general enclosure and disgorged their passengers, who walked towards the entrance shouting slogans against General Zia and martial law. This was the cue for the PPP workers already inside to move towards the exit and echo the slogans. There was much noise and even more confusion. In the mêlée, one of the gates to the stadium was smashed and Begum Bhutto entered shouting 'Jiye Bhutto', followed by about three hundred people chanting the same slogan. Now the police on duty took their turn. They moved into action and began to beat the crowd with steel-tipped sticks. Benazir Bhutto was next to me and was hit on the shoulder and back. She ran towards the steps that led into the ground, where play was in progress. A big crowd was propelling us forward, and the police were beginning to get its rhythm right. Someone stuck a helmet on Benazir's head, which saved her from serious injury. Another supporter pushed her out of reach of the charging policemen.

Begum Bhutto was now beside herself with fury. As she pressed forward she uttered a steady stream of abuse against the police. The uneducated and underpaid policemen did not realize perhaps that it was Begum Bhutto who was moving towards them, so they kept hitting everything and everyone who they thought was in their way and part of the disorder. Soon Begum Bhutto took a blow to the head, and blood gushed out. She did not stop but tried to attack the policeman who had hit her. There was no quelling the torrent of her rage. Even Benazir did not dare pull her mother back. We wanted to take Begum Bhutto to the hospital, but she wanted instead to go to the Governor's House, always popularly seen as the seat and symbol of state power, which was where all marches and demonstrations traditionally ended.

We rushed out of the stadium pell-mell, piled into cars and drove towards the Governor's House. Begum Bhutto was bleeding profusely but she seemed oblivious to it, and when we stepped out of our cars at the main gate of the House she began to curse Governor General Iqbal Khan. 'Thank you for this gift,' she screamed, pointing to her head. Then she reminded the General – who was not there, of course – that it was 'we' who had got his fellow soldiers released from Indian POW camps in 1973 and it would be 'we' again who would spring them from Afghan jails tomorrow. What Begum Bhutto had in mind was the ever-present spectre of a Soviet-backed Afghan invasion from the north which would overrun Pakistan. I was standing right next to Begum Bhutto, but could not persuade her to let us take her to hospital. When General Iqbal was informed of what was happening outside, he ordered that no matter what Begum Bhutto said or did, she must be taken to hospital.

Begum Bhutto had succeeded in getting the match interrupted and play called off for the day. By publicly clashing with the police, she had demonstrated that Zia's pretence of a country at peace was false. Later, the Bhutto ladies said that they had gone to the Gaddhafi stadium only to watch the cricket, and by beating them with sticks and batons, the government had insulted and abused them. This proved effective propaganda. The foreign press was covering the match and reported the incident. The personal courage and aristocratic manners of the Begum and her daughter made their point but failed in any way to sway the regime.

In March 1978, by a unanimous verdict, the High Court sentenced Bhutto to death. There was hardly any public reaction, and this was a dangerous sign because it implied that the regime could send him to the gallows with confidence. Bhutto had to be saved, and practicality demanded that an urgent effort should be made to come to some arrangement or understanding with the military government. It was Bhutto's ill luck that while there appeared to be no move afoot to reach a compromise with the army, the chances of launching a public movement looked non-existent.

This desperate situation led the PPP to opt for religious intervention to save the leader, and every shrine and holy place in Pakistan was used to seek the intercession of dead saints on Bhutto's behalf. By this appeal, the People's Party was effectively admitting that it had thrown in the towel. One day someone told Benazir that there was a holy man in Karachi whose prayers on the supplicant's behalf never went unanswered. This spiritual master would need to be paid a tribute of Rs 3.4 million (about £170,000), half in advance, the rest when the prayer was answered. Had it been up to Benazir, she would have gone along, but Begum Bhutto (who told me this story) did not wish to part with so much money. Benazir has always felt drawn to such other-worldly methods involving amulets, star readings and other airy-fairy devices – an aspect of her personality with which the West is not so familiar.

After the sentencing of Bhutto by the Lahore High Court, foreign governments began to send appeals to Zia-ul-Haq to reprieve the deposed Prime Minister. Not only was Bhutto a well-known international figure, but his murder trial had received a lot of coverage in the world media. Then there was the work done outside Pakistan by Murtaza Bhutto, Ghulam Mustafa Khar (who was in London) and Husna Sheikh, reportedly Bhutto's secret third wife. The party newspaper *Musawaat* now began to sell its readers in Pakistan the line that because of intense international pressure, the army junta would not dare harm Bhutto. This acted as a kind of tranquilliser for both party leaders and workers, who began to believe in Zia's powerlessness when faced with such persistent international pressure.

They thought a mouse-like Zia could not eat up Bhutto, who is taller than the Himalayas.

And what about Bhutto's foreign friends? During his five and a half years in power, the Pakistani Prime Minister had established close ties with the nouveaux riches Arab sheikhs, the Shah of Iran, the Saudi ruling family and Colonel Moammar Gaddhafi. They all had two things in common: oil and autocracy. They could only lose their power through death, natural or imposed. Because of the general longevity of regimes in that area, friendship with these rulers could be expected to be long-lasting. No outside capitalist was prepared to put money into Bhutto's party, but Sheikh Zayed bin Sultan al-Nahyan of the United Arab Emirates and Colonel Gaddhafi made generous contributions to PPP funds. These two also funded Murtaza Bhutto in his efforts to save his father's life. They personally made every sincere attempt to ensure Bhutto's physical survival. However, it somehow did not occur to anybody to ask these influential Arab rulers to act as peacemakers between Bhutto and the Pakistan army.

Begum Bhutto's refusal to give up the confrontationist position she had taken against the army can be attributed either to sheer courage or to her habit of digging in her heels regardless of the consequences. As for Bhutto's hot-headed party workers, popularly known as *jiyalas*, if faulty wiring caused a blaze somewhere, they would rush to the Bhutto ladies and claim credit for yet another act of revolutionary heroism. At the end of 1977, a part of the Prime Minister's house in Rawalpindi caught fire by accident. Quite a few *jiyalas* assured the Bhutto ladies that it was their work. If a train got derailed, several PPP leaders would inform Begum Bhutto that it was their revolutionary act. There is an Urdu proverb about men who want to join the ranks of martyrs while doing no more than daubing themselves with a bit of blood. The PPP was full of such people.

3

The Human Torches

'Eight of my party workers committed self-immolation. This
was no joke; one does not even singe one's finger for another's
sake.'

Zulfikar Ali Bhutto in the Supreme Court[1]

The years 1977 and 1978 were perhaps the most turbulent in Pakistan's
history. I spent them in close proximity to the Bhutto ladies and enjoyed
their complete trust. Nevertheless, while I fully supported Begum Bhutto's
confrontationist strategy and bold stance towards the martial law regime,
in my view her tactical mistake lay in trying to run a protest movement
through a nominated central committee or relying mainly on former
ministers and members of the defunct assemblies. The total number of
such people at local, provincial and federal levels was at no time more than
six hundred, hardly any of them willing to undergo the least personal
inconvenience for the sake of Bhutto. Since it was a small and well-
identified group, the government's intelligence agencies could easily keep
watch on the activities of its members. This was one reason why every
protest activity staged by Begum Bhutto was known to the authorities
before it was undertaken.

These failures underscored the lesson that an effective movement against
an unabashed military government could only be run with the help of rank-
and-file workers from the backstreets, and not through bigwigs whom
everyone knew. The police have no record of ordinary party workers, nor
are the intelligence agencies prepared to admit that the common man is
capable of doing anything effective against the state machinery, or leading
a movement. The state agency radar does not register the faceless, shirtless,
powerless worker, so it cannot apprehend him when he gets into the act.

In April 1978, I advised Begum Bhutto to set up secret action committees
numbering ten to twelve workers in every town and city in the country. If
instead of persuading party leaders to volunteer arrest we were to ask these
workers to do so, they would respond to the last man. When that happened,
the state agencies would be overwhelmed. I told Begum Bhutto that once
we had workers offering arrest in every city and town of Pakistan for a

period of four weeks on end, it would ignite a popular movement which alone could safeguard Bhutto's life. If the people rose, the army would not be able to gun them down, nor would Zia have the power to hang Bhutto. However, if four weeks of countrywide arrests should fail to trigger a popular uprising, then we must find some other means of saving Bhutto from the gallows.

Begum Bhutto not only liked my plan but asked me to pursue it. I soon realized that while it was easy to draft a plan on paper, its execution was another matter. To find even a handful of workers in a town or city willing to run the risk of being awarded twenty-five lashes and serving two years' hard labour was difficult, especially if it was to be done without recourse to the established local leadership. There was another snag. The People's Party teemed with disorganized rabble-rousers who represented elements fatal to creating and preserving an in-house secret cell. I decided to perform this task myself, and after making some changes in my physical appearance intended to ward off arrest, I set out on an organizing and recruiting tour of scores of towns and cities in the fiery summer of 1978, travelling always by bus or train. By August 1978, we had secret cells in place in most of Pakistan's cities. Not only were the intelligence agencies of the government unaware of our network, but the local PPP leaders were also in the dark.

In the Punjab, the People's Action Committee was organized by Pervez Rashid and Rana Shaukat Ali from Lahore, Sheikh Gul, Sheikh Iqbal and Lala Fazil from Gujranwala, Nek Muhammad Maghmoom alias Saeed Khan from Sialkot, Mehr Abdul Rashid from Faisalabad, Chacha Hamdani and Mushtaq Butt from Rawalpindi, Arshad Awan and Rana Farooq from Punjab University, and Qazi Ghiasuddin Janbaz from Toba Tek Singh. In the Frontier province, all the work was done by Muzaffar Shah from Nowshera, Shaista Khan from Dera Ismail Khan, and Qamar Abbas and Hamidullah Zahid from Peshawar. In charge in Sind were Syed Pervez Ali Shah, Masroor Ahsen and Sardar Hanif. The Baluchistan committee was the responsibility of Sadiq Umerani and Khalid Khan.[2]

The agreed plan called for the Action Committee to begin offering arrests from the middle of August 1978, but Benazir Bhutto's tour of the Frontier caused us to postpone D-Day until the middle of September.[3] Since Bhutto was incarcerated in Rawalpindi, it was decided for the sake of symbolism that the first arrest should be volunteered in that city. Each day, two workers would choose a popular spot there and start to raise slogans in Bhutto's favour till the police moved in and removed them. For the first two weeks, only Rawalpindi was to be activated. Other cities would be brought on line afterwards.

A large number of volunteer workers were assembled in Lahore before the Rawalpindi launch – enough reserves to keep the process of arrests unbroken. A party friend had taken responsibility for putting up and feeding all these men. The factory he had recently established was turned into a secret workers' hostel. This was a great risk, because in the event of exposure he stood to lose not only his personal liberty but his means of livelihood as well, which was exactly what happened. He had to undergo great hardship on the party's account. Sheikh Gul and Nek Muhammad Maghmoom had taken the responsibility of transporting the workers from Lahore to Rawalpindi, and arrangements for their stay had been made by Khwaja Samad in Gujjar Khan and Mushtaq Butt. Ghiasuddin Janbaz was in charge of press and publicity, which really meant only the party paper *Musawaat*, since no other newspaper in the country was allowed to print any story that favoured or promoted the PPP.

On 15 September 1978, a day before Zia's promotion to President, the first arrests were staged at Fawara Chowk, Rawalpindi's central square. This was the city's busiest area and also home to two or three cinema houses. As the six o'clock show ended and crowds came out of the auditoriums, two Action Committee volunteers suddenly appeared calling for Bhutto's release and the end of martial law in screaming voices. The police appeared at once and picked them up. As they were thrown into a van and taken away, the large crowd that had by now assembled began to cheer. This was not a bad beginning: the first stir in the deathly stillness of martial law. For the next five days, Fawara Chowk remained the venue of arrests, two every day. On the seventh day, the Committee shifted the action to the city's famous Committee Chowk, and this remained the venue for many days. By evening, a large crowd would gather at the site and as the two men stepped forward to raise anti-martial law slogans, the crowd would cheer and join them in calling for an end to martial law and the release of Bhutto.

The intelligence agencies were at a loss because they did not know where the volunteers were coming from with such regularity. They tried very hard to unearth the organizers of this increasingly effective form of protest, but had no luck, much to their confusion and embarrassment. They did not know either how workers from other cities were reaching Rawalpindi to offer arrest, or who was behind the effort.

The Action Committee's work was secret, but the intelligence agencies had learned that the chief organizer was none other than Raja Anwar, because it was in my name that press statements were issued on behalf of the People's Action Committee. We knew that the police would use every method to extract information from the arrested workers, and to deal with that eventuality we had asked every worker to say something along the lines of: 'Some time ago, I ran into Raja Anwar, who persuaded me to join the protest. He it was who told me the day, time and place of the event. He even gave me my train and bus fare, so that is how I am here.'

As a further sop to the police, some of the workers would name a local party leader known to have sold out to the authorities. The government agencies always fell for this, and instead of seeking out the real organizers, would pick up party leaders, none of whom had any connection with what was happening. A few years later, the Al-Zulfikar operatives adopted the same practice when arrested by giving the police the names of PPP leaders they disliked. Although so far it was only in Rawalpindi that arrests were being volunteered, it was no small achievement given the terror in which the military regime was held.

Fifteen days after the start of daily arrests at Rawalpindi, the party paper *Musawaat* wrote proudly:

> It is significant that these heroes of democracy today came forward to offer arrest before the cinema shows had begun, rather than after they were over, but those who were there to receive and welcome them were far more in number than on any previous occasion. Yesterday, the three workers who offered arrest were Muhammad Siddiq, Muhammad Riaz and Muhammad Rashid, all from Faisalabad. When they were taken in they were raising slogans against martial law.[4]

During the first fifteen days, forty people volunteered to be arrested, including four women led by Sardar Begum from Faisalabad. Each one of them was sentenced to ten lashes and one year's hard labour in prison, except the women who were imprisoned but not lashed. While people were now gathering every day in anticipation of what they knew would take place, we were not satisfied with the results. After the workers were taken by the police, the crowd would disperse and go home. They would not march into the city or create a civil disturbance.

Meanwhile, two of the Action Committee workers, Rashid Nagi and Waheed Qureshi, decided on a more dramatic form of protest. If the military government did not announce the holding of general elections in the country, they declared that they would set themselves on fire publicly. The idea of self-immolation came from these two workers, not from the Committee. It was their belief that if they could save Bhutto's life by offering their own, it was a price worth paying. They were confident that their sacrifice would jolt the common people into action. The Zia government did not take the announcement seriously.

On 1 October 1978, Nagi and Qureshi got ready in Lahore to set out for Rawalpindi. Qureshi's wife had died some time earlier, leaving four daughters behind and he alone was now responsible for their care. The youngest was no more than four: she was the one most attached to him. Qureshi worried about her, and instructed Lala Fazil in Gujranwala, where I was present: 'Lala, please tell Apa [Qureshi's sister] that she must have the youngest sleep with her at night because she is not used to sleeping by herself. I don't want her to be crying all night.' He must have repeated this message several times before leaving for Rawalpindi, but he just could not get away from the thought of his youngest girl. That scene is carved into my memory forever.

Before he left, Qureshi embraced me, and just as he got into the car that was to drive him to Rawalpindi, he said to Sheikh Gul once more: 'You'll be back by tomorrow after dropping us. Please don't forget to remind Baji, if the youngest gets restless at night, to let her sleep in her bed.' Before he was driven off, everyone said to him that the self-immolation bid was to be symbolic rather than real, and he should take care. 'Don't any of you worry,' he replied, laughing. We believed him. We were all naive. We thought we were helping create another newspaper story that would hasten Bhutto's release. No one seemed to realize that playing with fire was a dangerous, lethal game.

That same evening in the middle of Committee Chowk, Rawalpindi, the two men set themselves on fire. When those gathered there saw Nagi and Qureshi burning, they began to dance around them raising excited slogans. Sheikh Gul and Nek Muhammad Maghmoom managed with some difficulty to put out the fire in which Nagi was engulfed, but Qureshi was lost in ecstasy, caught in a kind of transcendental state. He was so carried away by the slogans all around him that he went on dousing himself with petrol. He was terribly burnt, and died after fifteen days, never again to have his little, motherless daughter fall asleep with her head on his chest. Nagi lost one leg.

On 7 October, Mehr Abdul Rashid Ajiz from Faisalabad and Pervez Yaqub Khokhar Masih, a Christian from Gujranwala, set fire to themselves in Lahore. They were like men possessed as they danced around dousing their bodies with petrol. They had reached that strange mystical state where the most unbearable pain provides joy beyond comprehension. The Action Committee men were unable to put out the fire. Unconscious and badly burnt, they were taken to the hospital where they died. Ajiz was the father of seven children and used to make a living selling odds and ends from a hand barrow. Khokhar left a young wife and a daughter just eighteen months old, plus his old parents. Before the fire brought him to the ground, he was heard intoning Christ's moving words on the cross: 'Eloi, Eloi, lama sabach thani' (My God, my God, why hast Thou forsaken me?).

By the beginning of October, Action Committee volunteers were courting arrest not only in Lahore and Karachi but in Peshawar, Quetta and Karachi. By 7 October, our cells were fully operational in every town and city. Arrests were being invited according to the by now established pattern from one end of the country to the other. Slowly but gradually, this was also having an effect on the actual cadres of the PPP. I should mention in passing that wherever our people offered themselves for arrest, the workers of the Jamaat-i-Islami would join the police in beating them up. I state this to underline the fact that it took a lot of courage in those dark days to court arrest.

Without the patronage of Begum Bhutto and Benazir Bhutto, this movement would not have gathered such widespread appeal. They toured Punjab extensively, going from town to town and city to city. I was still writing their speeches. Without naming the Action Committee, they would appeal to the workers to come forward and do their bit for democracy. Pakistan's martial law rulers began to get worried and decided to act. Begum Bhutto was arrested and Benazir was picked up as she arrived in Multan. With the arrest of the two ladies, we were in a now-or-never situation. We did not want the daily arrests to come to be treated as a matter of routine and thus lose their impact. We had managed to build up a tempo. Now we should use it to do something major.

The Action Committee called for a countrywide day of protest against Pakistan's 'jungle law' on 14 October. An appeal to this effect was published in the press under my name. We asked for a total strike, and even urged those serving prison terms to abstain from eating that day. I consider that day historic because even Zulfikar Ali Bhutto staged a hunger strike in Rawalpindi jail.[5] Begum Bhutto and Benazir, who were under detention, also joined the rest and went on a hunger strike.[6] Marches were organized and party workers went on the streets in defiance of martial law. Hundreds were arrested. There were two self-immolations: in Rawalpindi, Abdul Aziz, a press photographer; in Okara, Munawwar Hussain. Both men burned themselves to death. In Lahore, Mai Pathani tried to set herself on fire but was arrested before she could harm herself. The march in Lahore was led by Abida Malik.[7] In Sahiwal district the Action Committee was led by Mohammad Sardar and Ijaz Athar. Both of them were picked up by the police, and Ijaz Athar is still missing today, a victim of the regime's extra-judicial killings.

It was typical of the lack of concern and commitment shown by established PPP leaders and members of various assemblies that with the exception of Rao Hashim, a member of the National Assembly, not one man came forward to court arrest. During Bhutto's five and a half years in power, hundreds of these MNAs and MPAs had received personal and official benefits, including cabinet posts, thanks to him, but none of them was today prepared to stand up for him. The workers who burnt themselves to death or got lashed had never even seen Bhutto at close quarters. To them he was an infallible, almost mythological figure. Perhaps this mesmeric effect can only exist where those under its spell have never been close to their hero.

After the success of the 14 October protest day, the process of arrests intensified and spread. To kill the Action Committee, the party newspaper

Musawaat was closed down by the government on the charge that it had given extensive coverage to the Committee and thus endangered peace and order. It took about eight weeks for this movement to die out, despite the self-immolations and the public whipping of hundreds of workers. Movements work on the premise of hate rather than love, and hatred against Zia was not yet extreme. The common man was still confident that Bhutto's life was in no danger. Yet the Action Committee had broken the deathlike stillness of martial law in which the country lay, and the sacrifices of the party workers had exposed the military government's claims that all was quiet and peaceful. It was no longer easy after this to persuade the outside world that Bhutto was a common murderer and the people of Pakistan were not behind him. Pictures of those who had burnt themselves in Bhutto's name were published around the world, which made it easier for many heads of government who were still sitting on the fence to send earnest appeals to Zia-ul-Haq to spare Bhutto's life.

The Action Committee was the only movement spawned by the PPP which evaded the secret intelligence agencies of the state. None of them was able to locate the headquarters of the Committee, work out its operational methods, or detect those behind it, barring myself. Not one of the Committee's workers was arrested from his house, and despite frantic efforts the Zia regime was unable to establish the identities of those who had run this successful movement. The Inspector-General of Police of the Punjab, it may be mentioned, had set up a special squad headed by a superintendent of police to arrest my colleagues and me. Months after it was all over, one of our people was arrested, taken to the Lahore Fort and tortured. He told them everything, but it was not much use to them by then.

In Pakistan, contrary to Israel or Iraq for example, intelligence agencies are run by the state bureaucracy, which means that they are more often in the position of responding to events than being able to forestall them. Mostly, they spend their time trying to buy or browbeat political leaders. They have almost no knowledge of what the ordinary citizen does or is like. This was the failing we exploited to run our movement, which cost only the Rs 55,000 (£2,750) that Begum Bhutto sent me in two instalments. This money was used to pay for the workers' travel, food and lodgings. Without it, we could not have run the Action Committee even for a day. It was perhaps the most economically-run political movement of the time anywhere. I should thank my stars that the former First Lady did not charge me, as is the tradition, with having embezzled funds. On the contrary, she sent me a message from jail that the Bhutto family would forever remain grateful for my services.

In October 1978, the American newsweekly *Time* published a letter attacking those who had burnt themselves. Such letter-writing campaigns were run on behalf of the regime by the Jamaat-i-Islami. In the next few weeks, arrests of PPP workers and those suspected of running the People's Action Committee were made at random by the police and security agencies. In January 1979, Begum Bhutto was released and came to Lahore. She told me in a meeting, arranged secretly at one Mian Aslam's house, that she had written several letters to *Time* under different pseudonyms in support of the movement, but only one had been published. However, the fact was that our movement had failed to ignite a countrywide popular protest. I asked Begum Bhutto to find some other avenue to save her husband's life. A tired and anxiety-ridden Begum Bhutto said helplessly: 'I have given an interview to the BBC in which I have said that if the Supreme Court decision goes against us, then those thousands of workers who call me their mother will come out to offer the ultimate sacrifice.' In this meeting she told me to leave the country immediately because if I was arrested the regime would happily hang me.

In those days I had no permanent address and would never spend two consecutive nights in one place. I would arrive unexpected wherever I slept, and by night, never informing anyone in advance nor whether I would return. Most nights I would sleep in the open air in front of a hospital, to take advantage of the camouflage of the crowds – the patients' relatives – waiting there. Like them I would cover my head with a blanket and thus go undetected. This was the safest place for me to sleep, as the police never looked for me in this faceless mass. If I had to meet anyone, I would arrive at a busy urban meeting place two hours ahead and quietly become part of the crowd, watching for any police presence that had been sent to spot me.

Ten years after the Action Committee movement, Benazir Bhutto paid its workers a tribute:

> Pervez's life could have been saved by the crowd which had rushed to put out the flames, but the martial law authorities prevented anyone from reaching him. They wanted the people to watch his agony, in order to scare any other Bhutto loyalist who might want to do the same thing. But the depth of passion intensified. Over the next weeks five more men would burn themselves to death to try to save their leader's life.
>
> The regime claims that those who burned themselves to death were paid to do it by the party. Can there be such a price on human life? Those brave men were idealists whose dedication and decency tran-scends their own pain. We salute them.[8]

Benazir's warm tribute is fine as far as that goes, but it is not hard to imagine the pain and deprivation that must have pursued the orphaned children of Ajiz, the abandoned daughters of Qureshi, and Khokhar's baby girl as they grew up in our indifferent society. Who would have taken care of them or sent them to school, in a country whose rulers think nothing of embezzling money raised in charity for the maintenance of orphans and the destitute? We live in a society where people get killed because they have a fistful of coins that someone else wants. When these girls grew up into young women, who came forward to pay for their marriages? Who knows how many of them were forced into domestic service for a few rupees a month in order to survive? Even after the Bhutto family came to power, its 'salute' to these people remained confined to pathetic little pieces of state land. And what is the certainty that these orphans ever received title to that land, or that it did not stick to the fingers of state and party intermediaries? Those children should have been brought up at the expense of Bhutto's vast lands and large property. They had more right to it than Bhutto's own children, since their fathers had burnt themselves to death to save Bhutto's life. His own children did not offer such a supreme sacrifice.

To discredit the protests, the martial law government accused the PPP of getting people drunk and offering tempting sums of money to set fire to themselves. In order to cover their own apathy and lack of involvement, some leaders of the PPP itself who were secretly hobnobbing with the martial law rulers launched an insidious propaganda campaign which charged that all this drama was happening at the command of General Zia-ul-Haq. In other words, this movement of the small-time worker was being attacked from opposite sides at once. We who were inside it were unable to announce that we had the complete support and patronage of the Bhutto ladies. Had we done that, the two of them would have had scores of cases registered against them under various martial law regulations. Whether out of malice or ignorance, this campaign of abuse against the Action Committee continues to this day, and those involved remain a target of attack. If it continues, perhaps one day someone will come up with the revelation that it was not Zia but those who immolated themselves who should answer for Bhutto's hanging. If the one serious movement launched to save Bhutto's life is to be laid at Zia's door, what legacy but shame attaches to the Pakistan People's Party?

Bhutto's revised petition against his execution was dismissed by the Supreme Court. On 3 April 1979, the Bhutto ladies, until then confined in the Sihala rest house, were taken to Rawalpindi jail. This was to be their last meeting with Bhutto. For the first time, they realized that he was actually going to be hanged.[9] Begum Bhutto left the jail in tears and desperately tried to see Zia, but was told that he was at prayer and could not be disturbed. Bhutto too had been under the illusion until that evening that under the tremendous weight of international pressure, a pygmy like Zia would not dare harm a hair on his head.

As the hour of execution drew closer, Bhutto's nerve started to fail. His condition in the last few hours was such that a man who had always stepped briskly, with his head held high and his back ramrod straight, was unable to walk. The last journey of his life was to be made on a stretcher.[10]

Bhutto was hanged on the night of 3–4 April 1979. For the first time since grabbing office, Zia must have heaved a sigh of relief, finally secure in the knowledge that he had rid himself forever of the threat called Zulfikar Ali Bhutto.Yet in the next nine years and more, no day could have passed when he did not feel that he himself was under a death sentence. There was to be no going back. Only one option was his: to stick to office as long as he was alive and to greet death while in power. That is what he actually did. And then on 17 August 1988 his C-130 aircraft crashed mysteriously over Bahawalpur minutes after taking off. There were no survivors.

Zia had said goodbye to power and life at the same time.

4

Kabul Hosts People's Liberation Army

In April 1978, soon after the Lahore High Court presided over by Maulvi Mushtaq Hussain had found Bhutto guilty of murder and sentenced him to death, Murtaza Bhutto flew to Beirut and asked Yasser Arafat for armed help to rescue his father.[1] If he had expected that Arafat would immediately place a team of PLO commandos at his disposal, he was mistaken. Arafat at forty-eight years old was much more experienced than Murtaza at twenty-three. The Palestinian leader had spent his entire life in such operations and he knew that to stage such a mission could also result in Bhutto's death. While tactfully refusing to involve the PLO, he made a large quantity of arms and ammunition available to Murtaza, to be used as he saw fit. The wily Arafat must have known that not only would it be diffi-cult to smuggle these lethal and sophisticated weapons into Pakistan, but that it would be harder still to find people who would know how to use them. Where was Murtaza going to get hold of trained commandos who would pull Bhutto out alive from the steel trap in which the army had placed him?

Nevertheless, Murtaza came to see the arms bestowed by Arafat as the first diplomatic victory of his life. Straight away he sent a message to inform his mother that he would soon be sending a useful packet of medicines to her.[2] While these medicines could not reach Pakistan in time, the wide-spread rumour that the PLO would soon spring Bhutto from jail caused the army to tighten its security arrangements. In a book he published some years later, the man in charge, Colonel Rafi, wrote:

> I was summoned to the office of the Deputy Martial Law Adminis-trator (DMLA) and told by the General (Maj. Gen. Khwaja Rahat Latif) that at a party somewhere, a number of PLO men had bragged that they could pull Bhutto out of jail whenever they wanted. He questioned me closely about the means I would adopt were such a move to be made. In the end, he instructed me to take special precautions.[3]

41

Bhutto was hanged in April 1979. A month later, Murtaza arrived in Kabul seeking help from the Afghan authorities. He was accompanied by a Greek woman by the name of Daila, married, well connected and fifteen years older than him. Her husband was among the three army officers who had played a direct role in the overthrow of civilian government in Greece in the sixties. During the Colonels' regime, he was said to have been in charge of intelligence and espionage operations. When democracy returned to Greece, he was arrested along with many others and was still in jail in 1979. His wife was spending some of her time in exile with Murtaza, who could have been no more than a callow spring chicken as far she was concerned. Where he had met her or how was never clear. However, anyone who saw her could not fail to notice the striking resemblance she bore to Begum Nusrat Bhutto in her younger days. Leaving aside the Oedipal aspect of this combination, Murtaza used to introduce her as his fiancée. Between 1977 and 1981, she made at least three trips to Pakistan carrying Murtaza's messages, staying each time at 70 Clifton, Bhutto's private residence in Karachi.

The region was growing more and more unstable. In April 1978, a coup in Kabul had killed President Muhammed Daud Khan and brought the Soviet-backed People's Democratic Party of Afghanistan (PDPA) to power. In February 1979 a revolution in Iran led by Ayatollah Khomeini had overthrown the Shah. A referendum in April had approved the declaration of the Islamic Republic of Iran. Both Soviet and Western eyes were focused on events in neighbouring Pakistan.

In May 1979 Murtaza went to Kabul and met the new President Nur Muhammad Taraki and Prime Minister Hafizullah Amin. He asked for permission to open a camp there. He told them that he had a huge arms cache in Beirut and would not be asking the Afghan government for any help on that count. However, he would need assistance to put shipments into Pakistan. He also promised to bear all expenses and seek no financial aid from his hosts. What Murtaza failed to realize was that the moment he set foot on Afghan soil his main source of funding, Sheikh Zayed of Abu Dhabi, would cast him aside. Later, he had to eat his words and beg for financial assistance. The Afghans, thanks to poor Pakistan–Afghan relations, did not take long to say yes, and he was allotted the annexe to the palace of Taimur Shah, brother of the wife of the deposed King Zahir Shah. The owner was in jail at the time, while the comrades were having the time of their lives in the royal palace. However, for the record, the former royal palace had been renamed 'Khana-i-Khalq', the people's house. In Pakistan General Zia had already begun to set up camps and reception centres for Afghan rebels and the Afghan government felt that the presence of Bhutto's son in Afghanistan would act as a counterbalancing factor.[4]

Murtaza Bhutto had a gift for selling fishy stories most convincingly if the occasion demanded it. To establish himself as a genuine and experienced revolutionary to his Afghan hosts, he told them that he already had a fully operational secret organization in Pakistan. Later, he earned much ridicule because of this empty claim. Half his time in Kabul was spent concocting such tall stories, and the other half in telling more lies to shore up the earlier ones. Afghan intelligence officials used to ask him tongue in cheek: 'Do you really have an organization on the ground in Pakistan?' He would reply, slapping his knee: 'You will see for yourself.'

After the Afghans said yes, Murtaza returned to Kabul to see about transferring the arms promised by the PLO. Around the end of May 1979, a Syrian aircraft delivered the consignment, which consisted of several hundred Kalashnikovs, hand-grenades, machine pistols, anti-tank RPGs and SAM-7s. Afghan intelligence provided the necessary storage. Murtaza had the arms now, but he needed men to use them. Major-General Imtiaz Ali, Bhutto's former military secretary, was the first Pakistani to come to Kabul at Murtaza's invitation in June 1979. He had sought asylum in Dubai soon after the overthrow of the Bhutto government. Imtiaz had served as a commando and knew a lot about the business his former chief's son was getting into. Rejecting Murtaza's offer to make him the commandant of the camp, he advised him that instead of taking on the Pakistan army, he should set up a powerful transmitter near Pakistan's border and broadcast calls to the people to rise against the military regime. He tried to convince Murtaza that it would be folly to imagine that the Pakistan army could be overcome with the help of this handful of borrowed weapons, or that he could drum out Zia-ul-Haq. In those days it was Murtaza's philosophy that anyone unwilling to pick up a gun might just as well be shot with it, so he ruled out Imtiaz, who returned to Dubai after a few days.

With an AK-47 on his shoulder, Murtaza waited impatiently in the living-room of his Kabul palace for two of his friends from Pakistan, one the grandson of the former Governor of West Pakistan, Nawab Amir Muhammad Khan of Kalabagh, the other the favourite son of the Nawab of Bahawalpur. Murtaza's presumption that these old schoolfellows would be burning to avenge his father's execution exemplifies his poor grasp of his country's class structure, its contradictions, and its system of political values. It had not occurred to him that social change and revolution are of no interest to the sons of princes and nawabs.

In June 1979, Sohail Sethi and Pervez Shinwari, two of Murtaza's close companions, arrived in Kabul at his orders. He had found them good jobs when the PPP held office. The time had come for them to pay him back. No gift was free in Murtaza's book. He had decided to use them to smuggle arms to Pakistan. They were either unaware of the gravity of their assignment or lacked the courage to talk Murtaza out of his feckless scheme. According to Murtaza's instructions, the first consignment of arms was to be stored in the palaces of the Nawab of Kalabagh and the Nawab of Bahawalpur.

The man in charge of this transfer from the Afghan side was Asadullah Sarwari himself, the Afghan chief of intelligence. The Pakistan desk was supervised by Shah Wali, an intelligence officer who walked with a crutch because of a bad leg. He had joined the Afghan intelligence service during the time of the deposed King Zahir Shah, but had survived every upheaval and was to stay on until the last communist ruler of Afghanistan had fled. He was a great survivor. I do not know of his present whereabouts, but would not be surprised if he was performing the same service for Afghanistan's current 'Islamic' government. Using one of his agents from the tribal areas between Pakistan and Afghanistan, Shah Wali had the consignment of arms taken to Landi Kotal, the town that marks the border between the two countries. This semi-buffer zone between the neighbouring states has been the traditional recruiting ground for agents used by the two intelligence establishments, but who bear no special loyalty to either.

It was Pervez Shinwari who was to take charge from that point on. As soon as he learnt that the arms had arrived from the Afghan side, he got in touch with a tribesman who had been engaged by Shah Wali. In order to establish his identity, Shinwari gave him the torn half of a banknote which the carrier matched with the other half that he had been given by Shah Wali. The arms were handed over to Shinwari, and both portions of the torn banknote were returned to Shah Wali back in Kabul to prove that his instructions had been followed and the consignment placed in the hands of the right man.

Shinwari himself was a tribal Pushtun who came from this area and knew it well. He loaded everything into his own car and began to drive through the Khyber Pass towards Peshawar, where Sohail Sethi was waiting. On 20 June 1979, as the sun beat down on the bare metalled road winding on to Peshawar, Shinwari arrived at Jamrud, the check post that marks the end of the tribal belt and the start of what are called settled areas. As he braked to a stop a posse of armed policemen closed in. In desperation, he reversed the car, but before he could turn it back towards the tribal areas he was surrounded and caught.[5] When word reached Sethi in Peshawar that Shinwari had been taken, along with the arms he was carrying, he fled to Karachi and told Begum Bhutto what had happened. She in turn phoned her sister Bejat Harreri in London to give Murtaza the message: 'Your friend's wife in Peshawar has had a miscarriage. Please do not send any more medicines.'

It later turned out that the tribal agent who had carried the arms to Landi Kotal was a double agent, working for the Pakistani customs and security agencies as well. It was he who had informed the Pakistanis about Shinwari and his cargo. Many of the tribesmen who inhabit the

Pakistan–Afghanistan border areas make a good living working both sides of the fence. Since their intelligence is almost always accurate, both governments consider them trustworthy. Their sole and fruitful interest is money. Murtaza's first operation thus ended up with the capture of the arms he despatched and the arrest of the man who carried them. It was an inauspicious beginning. Yet even supposing that Shinwari had managed to clear the border and deliver the arms to Kalabagh and Bahawalpur, the chances are that their most subversive function would have been to kill wild boar, which are plentiful in these areas.

After Shinwari's arrest, the NWFP Governor, General Fazle Haq, asked the Soviet ambassador to Pakistan to come to Peshawar. He showed him the captured material and expressed Pakistan's deep anxiety over its Soviet origin. The ambassador must have seen the joke, because the protesting government was engaged in an international cross-border operation involving the daily smuggling of tons of arms and ammunition into Afghanistan for the Mujahideen resistance. However, his reaction was diplomatic.

'Half the world buys Soviet arms,' he told General Haq, 'and it is impossible to tell where what is bought from us is sold, and to whom. We have no control over that. But let me have the serial markings on the equipment and I will try to determine who the first buyer was. As soon as I have information, it will be passed on to you.'[6]

General Haq must have also been amused because he knew quite well where the arms had come from and why and how they had been smuggled into Pakistan. It is to be assumed that Shinwari had told the police everything he knew. On the other hand, the gist of the conversation between the Soviet ambassador and General Haq must have been passed on by the KGB to Kabul the same evening. If the KGB hoped that this incident would make the Afghans more careful, then it did not really know the head of Afghan intelligence, Asadullah Sarwari. He was not only a braggart but indiscreet to a fault. Caution or prudence were simply not a part of his psychological make-up. He told the above story to Murtaza and me one evening after a couple of drinks, when he was feeling expansive.

The Pakistan government must have known that the arms had come from Beirut originally, but it was easier and more expedient to blame Moscow and Kabul than the PLO. The generals who ruled Pakistan were no fools. They knew what would best induce the Americans to pour more arms and money into Pakistan.

Let me at this point explain how I arrived in Kabul from Pakistan, and why I was on the run after the collapse of political resistance in the country. Knowing that I risked my life if I was caught by the martial law authorities who were looking for me everywhere, I fled from Pakistan in January 1979 on Begum Bhutto's instructions, crossed into Afghanistan and took a flight out of Kabul for Germany. I heard of Bhutto's execution while I was in Berlin.

In May 1979, Bashir Riaz, a Pakistani journalist who was quite close to the Bhuttos, phoned me from London to say that Murtaza was waiting for me in Kabul. He said Begum Bhutto wanted me to join him. I took no more than a couple of minutes to reach the most reckless decision of my life. Riaz sent me an air ticket the next day and I went to the office which was processing my application for political asylum to say that it should be considered withdrawn. This was something the officer who interviewed me had never heard before. He looked at me hard and asked: 'Have you had too much to drink? I have never seen anyone applying for asylum and then withdrawing the request.' Standing perfectly upright, I told him proudly: 'The son of my great leader has sent for me. Instead of being a burden on your country, I am on my way to bring about a revolution in my own homeland, a revolution which will free us of our dependence on others.' The German officer looked at me again, somewhat cynically, pulled out my passport and asylum application from a heap of papers on his desk and said: 'Here you are. And could you please hurry with that revolution and reduce this mountain of applications from your unemployed countrymen that you see on my desk?'

As I walked out of that office, I was quite sure I would never set foot in it again. After all, I was going to a socialist country and, what was more, at the invitation of Murtaza Bhutto. The fate that lay a few years down the road would find my expectations naive and comical. It knew that the same Murtaza who was now summoning me to Kabul would one day pass the sentence of death on me – the same Murtaza whose father I had tried to save from the gallows by putting my own life on the line. It knew that the worst years of my life lay ahead of me in prison in a country which had declared that it was going to establish an idealistic socialist system.

But let me get back to the bright and wonderful summer morning of 26 June 1979 when my Ariana Afghan flight landed at Kabul. The crew outnumbered the passengers, thanks to the Afghan 'revolution'. I had hardly stepped down from the gangway when a short, extremely fair, red-cheeked Pushtun practically leapt towards me. 'Raja Anwar?' he asked. I nodded my head in an affirmative gesture. 'We have been waiting for you for days. You were expected earlier,' he said in perfect English. 'Yes, there was a bit of delay,' I answered. A black Chevrolet was waiting for us. 'Delays are not always bad,' he said good-naturedly. 'In fact in our language there is a saying that what takes more time turns out to be better in the end.'

Then he introduced himself. He came from Asadabad and his name was Azamuddin Alami, a close friend and associate of the then Afghan intelligence chief, Asadullah Sarwari. Both had joined the communist party in 1970 and served as pilots in the Afghan air force. (Two months after my arrival in Kabul, differences developed between Nur Muhammad Taraki, the President, and Hafizullah Amin, his Prime Minister. It had taken only one year of sharing power for these two men, who had been close friends and comrades through thick and thin, to become mortal enemies. Sarwari and Alami sided with Taraki and had to pay a price when he lost out to Amin.) Alami and I became close friends, and have maintained our links as the years have passed. In 1990, he managed to escape from Kabul with his family and sought asylum in Sweden. Both of us in our own ways are victims of what we believed in – he of revolution, I of blind loyalty to the Bhuttos.

It took us about twenty minutes to reach our destination. The car drew into a garage, the driver stepped out, pulled down the shutter-like garage door, and only then did he ask us to get down. Alami whispered to me: 'Comrade, the real problem is that right in front of us is the imperialist German embassy and these people are equipped with all kinds of sophisticated devices. It is better not to be seen by them. That's why we only left the car after the garage had been shuttered.' He was a James Bond-like figure and gave me a long talk on security and tradecraft and what advantages the shuttered garage possessed, almost as if the road to revolution passed right through it.

There was a small side door through which we entered a vast living-room. Right in front of us on a large sofa sat Murtaza wearing a white shalwar and a long shirt of the same colour. A Kalashnikov rested against the sofa, its butt on the floor. To his left, an Alsatian dog was stretched out, half asleep. This was Wolf, who was later to play an important part in the PIA hijack. Despite his wild ancestry, Wolf was an even-tempered and peace-loving beast. He did not bark at us, merely sized us up through half-closed eyes and then appeared to go to sleep as if he had not seen anyone or anything.

Although Murtaza had been awaiting my arrival for the past month, because of Alami's presence he shook hands in a very formal way. He might not know much about politics, but his class origins made it natural for him to give Alami the impression that it was not he who had need of individuals but they who had need of him. Alami made a mental note of it; he had an acute sense of observation. One day he said: 'Bhutto is quite an actor, isn't he? Don't you feel that he puts on a different act for every visitor?' Dry communist that Alami was, he did not know that in Pakistani society, those who came from the privileged classes and entered politics as their birthright inherited a tradition of public performance designed to fool the people into helping them to power.

When I arrived in Kabul, Shinwari had already been in jail for a few days. Murtaza was a worried man. After Shinwari, he was afraid that the next man to be picked up might be Sohail Sethi. In those days, his entire political advice came from such sycophants. In my first meeting with him, he expressed the apprehension that if he also lost Sethi, his revolution would suffer a serious setback right at the outset. He also told me that on arrival in Kabul, he had founded what he called the People's Liberation Army (PLA). He said this with great pride, as if he had already won the first round of the war he had not yet waged. This army – already in existence, according to Murtaza – did not have a single soldier at the time. Then assuming an air of great wisdom he added: 'Have you noticed how close-sounding the two names are? There is our PLA and there is the PLO. What is more, PLA has a Chinese echo to it, though we are in a country which is pro-Moscow.' This may sound absurd to people today, but in the seventies and early eighties it was precisely bunkum of this sort that was confused with revolutionary action. Murtaza was a perfect example of this juvenile adventurism. In 1969, he had a makeshift hut, such as you would find in a slum, constructed in the forecourt of his father's elegant house at 70 Clifton, Karachi. And now, ten years later, housed in a luxurious annexe to a former royal palace, he had hung out a sign saying 'People's Liberation Army' and dreamed of revolution.

Murtaza also told me: 'I wanted to rush to Kabul in 1978 with an arms cache and establish a base, but when papa was told about it in jail, he formally ruled it out because he considered that the new revolutionary Afghan regime would not be able to establish order for a long time. He thought setting up a base in Kabul would be inviting disaster.' Bhutto was to be proved right. What a loss that a populist leader of his insight ended up on the gallows.

They made me stay in the same house as Murtaza. He was not very intelligent, but that was no impediment to his political future, as intelligence is not rated very highly in Pakistani politics. People do not rise to political power there because they are bright, but due to their class. In the past, I had had fairly high hopes of him. When he would come home during holidays, his sympathetic nature endeared him to the junior staff and servants of the Prime Minister's house, and they would make a great fuss over him. He used to take an interest in their problems. He was so friendly with the washermen, barbers, drivers and cooks attached to the Prime Minister's vast establishment that now and then he would even take a few quick drags on the hash-laced cigarettes they smoked during their off-duty hours. Unlike most young men of his class, he kept his arrogance well hidden. He was reluctant to speak his mind or use harsh words, and he had never been caught misbehaving publicly or getting into fist-fights in clubs and cinema houses. Perhaps one reason for this was Bhutto's strictness as a father. Despite being Westernized in a most liberal sense, he never allowed his children to do what they wanted. Convinced that President Ayub Khan had fallen from power because of his sons' misbehaviour, he was determined not to let his children or his family ever place him in such a predicament. I was present one day in 1975 when he gave his younger son, Shahnawaz, exemplary punishment after learning that he had got into a scuffle with the son of a Baluch Sardar.

Ever since my arrival in Kabul, Murtaza and I had been examining the various courses open to us. Our discussions were long and heated. He agreed that unless fortune-hunting generals and unprincipled feudal lords were taken out of the body politic, Pakistan could never hope to become a healthy and democratic state and society. It was an evil system, and it alone was responsible for Bhutto's death. Despite his repeated commitments, when he should have been able to change things, Bhutto had changed very little. My argument was that it was a mistake to hold individual generals, including Zia, or certain judges responsible for Bhutto's execution. Instead of taking revenge on a person or persons, we should change the undemocratic and repressive system under which we lived. Murtaza agreed about the system, but he was set on avenging his father's murder by punishing those whom he held responsible for it. I was hopeful that this angry young man would in time master his personal feelings and begin to see things in a larger perspective. It was only appropriate that he should begin his political journey where Bhutto had left off. After his fall from power, Bhutto had analysed his failure in these words:

> I am undergoing this ordeal because I tried to rebuild this shattered country and tried to resolve its contradictions and establish a fair and honourable order, but it appears as if the middle way or a compromise solution or even the attempt to make peace are no more than a utopian dream. The military revolt shows that class struggle knows no conciliation and it has to end in one or the other class emerging as the victor.[7]

The PPP itself was a bundle of contradictions and clashing interests. The leadership of the extended front of peasants and workers was in the hands of the feudal class, and the lower middle-class component of the party was no more than an ineffective attachment. During his years as its unquestioned head, unfortunately Bhutto never opened the PPP to the necessary discipline of party elections. The first instinct of its nominated functionaries was to stay in their leader's good books. When the generals threw him into jail, the party was paralysed.

Even in 1997, thirty years after the founding of the PPP, it continues to run on undemocratic lines. None of its office-bearers is elected. Bhutto's personality cult has been continued by his daughter, and it remains to be

49

seen whether she will begin to impart some of the benefits of her Harvard and Oxford education to her party. It is the collective tragedy of Pakistani politics that most parties that claim to represent the people have no internal democracy nor an accountable organizational structure. The political leaders perpetuate their hold on power in an autocratic atmosphere that encourages them to appoint whom they like to party posts. It is ironic that while the political activists have often been able to win for the masses the right to vote freely because of their struggle against dictatorships, they have failed to gain the right to elect the office holders of the political parties they belong to.

In the first few weeks after his arrival in Kabul, Murtaza had taken to sleeping on the floor. Perhaps it was a kind of vow that he would not sleep in the comfort of a bed unless he had avenged his father's execution. However, this austerity did not last long, because he soon married an Afghan girl by the name of Fauzia, and the young couple moved to the private comfort of a double bed.

His sister Benazir excelled Murtaza even here. She only married after she had tightened her grip on the party. This result-oriented young woman played a more intelligent game than her brother because she realized that their father, who remained as powerful in death as he had been in life, should be made a stepping-stone to political power rather than a symbol of revenge. The same army which had allowed his dead body to hang from the rope for half an hour after his execution, found itself saluting his daughter twice as the country's Prime Minister. This was Benazir's way of avenging her father's death.

The idea of an armed class struggle which Murtaza had brought to Kabul could only be given practical form by building a political organization on a solid, working-class base. The question was whether, given Pakistan's political traditions, it would be possible to do so with every member, including the leader, adhering to agreed and drawn-up rules, or whether Murtaza's view of group discipline would amount to obeying his word alone, regardless of what it was.

In the end Murtaza agreed on the following points. Due to heavy censorship, the public did not believe the official version of the news. The credibility gap was so wide between the masses and their military masters that people would listen either to the BBC or other foreign radio stations to find out what was happening in their own country. Murtaza said he had the money to buy a powerful radio station. The Afghan government had no objection to its installation near the Pakistan Afghan border; they were in fact more than happy at the idea. Murtaza promised that we would immediately get things moving in the right direction. To free the poor from military dictatorship, we would need to use every available means.

Any decision about the PLA would be made only after the fullest consultation with party workers and associates. The decision to launch the PLA had to be rooted in working-class ideology. No party or organization could ever succeed in bringing about a democratic or revolutionary change in Pakistan unless the vast peasantry was organized against the oppressive feudal system. The trade unions had organized the industrial working class, but the peasantry was never properly organized. We decided that a group of PPP workers should be brought into Kabul for training on how to set up revolutionary cells among small groups of landless peasants. Each cell should comprise three people. Once there were seven or eight thousand such cells, then the PLA could start distributing land. The radio station would play its part in promoting this idea over the air.

In the cities, following Bhutto's execution, there was growing opposition to General Zia's rule. If the peasantry aligned its movement with the democratic struggle being waged in the cities, the night of the generals could come to an end. But revolution never meant just picking up a gun and starting to shoot innocent people. Such madness would never have public support. In Pakistan we were not setting up a national liberation movement against a foreign occupation, so we should not try to ape Yasser Arafat. Our strategy should be different. We were suffering under a military dictatorship. We should organize the people to restore democracy on one hand, and organize them for a revolutionary change on the other. I advocated that the question of armed struggle should be left open for the future. Murtaza agreed that he would never opt for terrorism. I was encouraged by his attitude and began to believe that he had dropped the idea of personal revenge.

We had decided that volunteers should be brought to Kabul. With just two men available to bring them, the question was who should do it. Who could best risk a visit to Pakistan? Murtaza had left the country soon after the removal of the Bhutto government in July 1977, so there were no cases registered against him. In fact, many people had expected him to return after his father's hanging, but he had not. One evening, over a drink, we began to talk about a mission to Pakistan, and it came as a shock to me that Murtaza was terrified of Zia and what he might do to him. As for me, I was wanted at home on many counts. If I was taken they would hang me. So only through sheer stupidity can I have volunteered to return to Pakistan to recruit for our Kabul operation. Describing my decision as an act of valour and an unforgettable favour to the Bhutto family, Murtaza toasted this development all evening. Today when I think of that occasion, I cannot believe that it was really I, Raja Anwar, who offered to go back. I suppose we sometimes do things on the surge of emotion that certain situations generate. Such acts can be called either brave or foolhardy. Everyone has undergone such an experience at some point in his or her life. Anyway, there has never been a shortage in Pakistan of short-sighted, unself-seeking

51

votaries who have considered the goodwill of any member of the Bhutto family as the height of personal achievement. In the *jiyala* culture of the PPP, this kind of lower-middle-class thinking is endemic. Party workers have not hesitated even to risk their lives in the name of the family. That has been our tragedy and undoing.

Before setting out for Pakistan, I changed my appearance as best as I could. Like an ordinary village Pushtun, I put a turban – called a 'lungi' – on my head, found myself a rosary, and gave up cigarettes in favour of the snuff that the tribal people love. I wanted to convey the impression to my tribal guides that I was neither educated nor the political type, and bore no mark of social or official position. I was just an ordinary person who had no special identity or status and if, along the way, they decided to hand me over to Pakistani security, it would bring them no profit because I had no value. Shah Wali was going to introduce me to the tribals who were to be my guides. I asked him to have me meet them not in his office but in some ordinary tea shop or *qehvakhana* in town. Accordingly, he picked out a third-class tea place to introduce me to two men. Their names were Wa'aiz Khan Nadaf (*nadaf* in Persian means one who extracts oil from seeds: his real name turned out to be Amir Muhammad) and Qadir Shah Afridi. They had been told that my name was Aslam Khan and I worked for a travel company that sent Pakistanis via Kabul to the Gulf Emirates for employment. On my way back I might bring a group of Pakistanis who would have to be escorted safely and secretly to Kabul.

On 10 July 1979, we set out on foot for Pakistan. Since I come from a village, I found no difficulty in keeping pace with my hardy Pushtun guides as we negotiated tough, hilly terrain. I could feel that they felt at ease with me because they saw me as one of themselves, fated to suffer the rough and tumble of a difficult life in order to survive. The heat was unbearable but we managed to walk twenty kilometres. My guides stopped at a village named Landi Kili, which turned out to be Qadir Shah's home. I had been drawn to Qadir rather than his companion, and he had taken a liking to me. Like most villagers, he was fond of gossip and telling stories. He told me sadly that he had two grown-up sons who lived at home because there was no work for them in the city. He was the poorest man in his village. The only work he had was the kind he was doing now, small-time assignments for the Afghan intelligence. He was paid no salary but was allowed to smuggle small amounts of food and cloth from across the border.

Qadir Shah appeared to me to be a sincere, straightforward person. I was keen to know if he had any links with the Political Agent of the Khyber Agency on the Pakistani side of the border. 'You should sometimes keep an eye on the other side as well. You wouldn't want notice from the Political Agent for Khyber,' I whispered in his ear in a confidential tone. 'There's nothing to worry about,' he told me. 'My uncle's son sees him now and then, and I've paid my respects to him myself.' In other words, Qadir Shah was in the good books of both governments, in keeping with traditional tribal diplomacy. This shook me, and I probed for information. With some regret, he told me how in 1971 he had been hired to help a Bengali officer to escape from Pakistan to Afghanistan, but instead he had taken his money and handed him over to the Political Agent. I sensed that this incident now weighed on his conscience. It didn't take me long to decide that no matter how dangerous the situation, the personal friendship that we had struck up would give me a chance of getting out.

I needed a persuasive cover story, so I told Qadir Shah that I came from a village near Rawalpindi, where years ago I had mistakenly killed a man. Although the court had found me innocent, the murdered man's family wanted blood. I had run away to Lahore and joined a travel agency. Our owner was an influential man and he had a sound financial arrangement with Shah Wali. Many of our people came to Kabul via Paktia, and Shah Wali had them put on board aircraft flying out of Afghanistan. We had a regular guide but he had been taken ill, which was why Shah Wali had asked him to help me cross into Pakistan. I swore him to secrecy and warned him that under no circumstances should Shah Wali get wind of our conversation.

Qadir Shah listened closely to my story, then thumped me on the shoulder. 'Don't you worry, that lame joker will never come to know of our conversation.' And it is a fact that he never betrayed my confidence, otherwise I would have known it through Shah Wali. He introduced me to his relatives in the village by telling them: 'This Punjabi murdered somebody many years ago and has been on the run since to save his life.' The laws of Pakistan do not apply in the tribal belt. Those who seek shelter there are often fugitive. His relations paid little attention to me because mine was an everyday story.

The next morning we left Landi Kili bound for Ali Masjid, which was another twenty kilometres away. I spent most of this journey trying to deepen my friendship with Qadir Shah. In the end, with great sincerity, he placed his turban on my head; in reply, I placed my own on his, thus formally sealing our friendship in accordance with the age-old tribal custom. His face lit up with joy. 'Look at my luck, God has given me a youthful brother.' As his father's only son, he was painfully aware of the difficulties that a brotherless man faced in a tribal society. He looked at peace. We had exchanged turbans, which meant that from that day on we would have the same friends – and the same enemies. I felt confident now that Qadir Shah would not turn me in.

We arrived at Ali Masjid after several hours. Under the traditional agreement between the Pakistan government and the tribes, the metalled road leading to Peshawar belongs to the former, which means that once you are on it, you are subject to Pakistan's jurisdiction. It followed that I could now be arrested by the Pakistani authorities if anyone informed them of my presence in the country. For a moment I panicked, then looked at Qadir Shah for reassurance. Unaware of what was going on in my mind, he thought I wanted some snuff. Pulling his snuffbox from his pocket, he passed it to me saying: 'Aslam Khan, this exhausting journey is over, now all we need is the Peshawar bus and we will be there soon.' After some time, a bus arrived, packed with people and luggage. The driver asked us to climb onto the roof, which we did. To ride on top of a bus in that hilly and dangerous area with serpentine roads was an adventure in itself.

(While this journey cemented my friendship with Qadir Shah, it led me into many difficulties later. What happened was that in January 1980, Qadir Shah got involved in a bitter dispute with some rival tribesmen in his village. Being his brother under tribal law and tradition, it fell to me to assist him in every way I could. I sent him a great deal of ammunition from Kabul. A few times, I even went to visit him in his village. He had turned out to be a true friend. Once he said to me: 'Tell me where your family is and I will go and get your wife and children. I will help you build a house next to mine.' When he found that I was not married, he said he would find me a match among the tribal girls. He almost ordered me: 'You should get married right away. Later you can take my daughter as your second wife.' I felt that he was eager to establish a blood relationship between us because that would bring us really close. 'But your daughter is only six years old,' I laughed. 'So what?' he replied. 'In ten years she will be perfectly capable of running a household.' In tribal areas, girls are married very young and polygamy is common. Qadir Shah himself had two wives.

Qadir Shah came to know of my real name and identity in 1981, when the Political Agent for the Khyber Agency showed him my photograph and asked him if he knew that man. 'Sure, that's my brother Aslam Khan. He works for some Lahore travel agency.' The Political Agent laughed. 'He is neither Aslam Khan nor your brother. His real name is Raja Anwar and he used to be Bhutto's adviser. The government of Pakistan wants this man, dead or alive.' Qadir Shah said nothing. He was jailed but released after six months. He came straight to Kabul and was greeted by more bad news. Not content with having had me arrested and sent to Kabul's notorious Pul-i-Charkhi jail, Murtaza announced that I had been hanged.

It was a double-edged sword. In Kabul, Murtaza wanted me dead; in Pakistan, the Zia regime had me on its most wanted list. Qadir Shah thought long and hard, and since he now knew who I was, decided to take hostage some of the Al-Zulfikar men who passed through his area after crossing over from Pakistan while on their way to Kabul. He was confident that he would be able to exchange me for these hostages. He had also arranged to keep me in his village, where neither Murtaza, nor Afghanistan nor, for that matter, Pakistan could lay hands on me.

Qadir Shah was mistaken. Murtaza would not have helped obtain my release in return for hostages. Had he had the slightest regard for the lives of his companions, he would not have gone after me in the first place. It was fortunate that Tajbar Khan, who was also president of the Pakistan Students Federation in Mardan, came to seek asylum in Qadir Shah's village during those days. When he learnt what Qadir was planning, he talked him out of it after convincing him that it was not possible to take on both Kabul and Islamabad together. I sometimes think that it is only by luck that Murtaza failed to convince Najibullah to kill me and Tajbar Khan succeeded in talking Qadir Shah out of taking and killing innocent hostages. I learnt all this after I was set free in 1983.)

However, coming back to my first journey to Pakistan in 1979, once we arrived in Peshawar, I let Qadir Shah Afridi and Amir Muhammad Nadaf go. I did not tell them where or when our next meeting would take place. Experience had taught me that a man in my situation needed first of all to keep his movements secret. The task I had come to perform was my first priority, and I had to look out for police and security agents because I was on every wanted list. I had to make contact with people, but I could not afford to have anyone make contact with me. Qadir Shah had a relation living in Peshawar whose address he had given me. I had also paid close attention to the route we had taken into Pakistan, and I was confident that I would be able to return on my own if I had to.

Despite all the care I was taking, I made the mistake of shaking hands with Saeed Khan, a Peshawar shopkeeper and local PPP worker, in the presence of Amir Muhammad, my Afghan guide. Some months later, Amir was picked up by the police. He talked, and Saeed Khan was arrested. He had nothing to do with Murtaza or the PLA, but one slip on my part cost him years of imprisonment.

I made contact with the provincial Pakistan Students Federation chief, Hamidullah, and told him that Murtaza was in Kabul and needed volunteers. He readily arranged for some of his friends to get ready to move to Kabul. I then went secretly to Rawalpindi, Lahore and Multan. It was terribly hot and I had to travel in crowded buses, always in public view, fearful of being caught. It was an excruciatingly painful experience. For years to come, I would have dreams every night of being chased by the police. In about a week, I was able to persuade fifty workers to jump into the blind well that Kabul was to prove. According to the plan, the volunteers were to report to Peshawar's Hilal hotel, which we reckoned as a safe assembling point because it was run by Hamidullah's father, Hazrat Usman, and his brother Moeenullah.[8] Once they had gathered, I made contact with Qadir Khan, who was already in the city.

We split the recruits into small groups and put them on buses bound for Ali Masjid, where we arrived undetected. Qadir Khan was waiting, and our revolutionary caravan set out on foot for Kabul. A forty-mile trek through hilly country is no joke, and many of the youngsters had bloody feet before we reached halfway. When we came to the area called Bazar, ten kilometres from the Pakistan–Afghanistan border, the sun had risen and it was hot. Qadir Khan hired a mule, and two of the volunteers, Tariq Cheema and Rana Farooq, took turns riding it. This was a sight to be seen, because the mule was not strong enough to bear the weight of these two strapping Punjabis. They fell several times along the way, and the unburdened mule would sprint forward with the two running after it. It must have been an auspicious mule, because out of that entire caravan only these two young men survived politically. Tariq Cheema became a minister in the Punjab in 1993, and Rana Farooq got elected to the Punjab Assembly and was made a parliamentary secretary. It was lucky for them that on their first return to Pakistan from Kabul they were arrested and jailed, and so lost contact with Murtaza, otherwise they would have met the same fate as their comrades.

When the first batch of volunteers arrived in Kabul in July 1979,[9] no arrangements had been made for their stay. Murtaza rushed to Shah Wali's office for help, and in what turned out to be a grave breach of security he had them quartered in a number of city hotels that were used to accommodate tribal agents – the last people these workers should have been exposed to.

In 1974, thousands of Baluchis of the Marri tribe had sought shelter in Afghanistan's Kandahar province from the Pakistani army, which was involved in operations against them in Baluchistan.[10] They had a full-scale cantonment of their own, with the entire administration and control of the facility in their own hands. Murtaza won no such concession. Compared to the Baluchis, he had no establishment, or any training ground for his guerrillas-to-be. Inevitably, this harmed his operation. Had he chosen Jalalabad instead of Kabul as his base, he would have enjoyed the great advantage of being only thirty miles from the Pakistan frontier, well positioned for his men to cross to and fro. He might still have ended up the same way, but perhaps some of the young lives lost in ill-planned border crossings would have been saved.

5

Murtaza's Ragtag Army

The years 1979 to 1980 were especially eventful for Afghanistan. The power struggle in Kabul had led the Soviet Union to make the same mistake the US had made in Vietnam, only with much more far-reaching results, because it became a key factor in the destabilization and ultimate collapse of the Soviet regime. The coup of 1978 had brought the People's Democratic Party of Afghanistan (PDPA) into power and made its leader, Nur Muhammad Taraki, president. Taraki and his colleague Hafizullah Amin were the principal leaders of the Khalq faction of the PDPA, which enjoyed considerable Soviet support, both economic and military. However its social reforms, too suddenly introduced and brutally enforced, spurred widespread Mujahideen resistance driven by the growing influence of Muslim Fundamentalism. In September 1979 a split between Taraki and Amin ended in the death of Taraki. Amin took over and one of the first men to be placed on the list of traitors was Asadullah Sarwari.

Amin's three months in power saw three men holding Sarwari's old post – Akbar Azizi, Asadullah Amin and Muhammad Yousuf. No policy was clearly enunciated, either at home or abroad, during Amin's brief fling, and as pressure grew from the Mujahideen, he sought ways of making up with Zia-ul-Haq. In December 1979 the Soviet Union invaded Afghanistan, claiming justification under the terms of the treaty of friendship and cooperation signed between the two countries in 1978. It overthrew Amin and installed Babrak Karmal as prime minister. This was the start of an era of warfare that brought the withdrawal of the Soviet Union in 1989, the fall of the PDPA in 1992, and the defeat of its successor government in 1996 by the fundamentalist Taliban movement.

The Soviet invasion of Afghanistan provoked an almost unanimously hostile international response. Funds and arms poured towards the Muja-hideen, mostly through Pakistan, from a bizarre de facto alliance that included the USA, Saudi Arabia, the Gulf States, China and Iran. The chief beneficiary of the invasion was Zia-ul-Haq, now the chief US ally in the region, able to agree a $3.2 thousand million six-year aid package with the Reagan administration in 1981, and legitimized by the West no matter how repressive his domestic regime.

A lesser beneficiary was Murtaza. Although Afghanistan became a dangerous place from which to operate, the besieged regime was bound to support even its lesser friends. Babrak Karmal appointed Dr Najibullah as head of intelligence, and he was so keen to maintain good relations with Murtaza that he even paid for his first marriage. This was the broad background to Murtaza's debut and brief reign as a leader of armed resistance to the government of his father's executioner.

Murtaza had decided to receive the newly arrived workers and volunteers from Pakistan in a safehouse provided by Afghan intelligence. An hour before the meeting was due, Azamuddin Alami rushed into our residence. He sounded harried.

> Director General Asadullah Sarwari is holding a most important and nationally significant meeting in that safehouse which is expected to last another two to three hours. If you can't wait until then, we can arrange for you to use the house next door.

To establish his own importance, Murtaza told him:

> These men have come at my call after an arduous journey through mountains. I can't keep them waiting longer than I already have. These are the men who will bring a revolution in Pakistan. My meeting too has far-reaching national implications. Please arrange for us to meet in the next house.

The arrangement was made. We also found out soon enough what nationally significant meeting Sarwari was having in the house next door. We saw him leave the place with a pretty young college student.

The stage was now set for Murtaza's first meeting with his troops, and he put up a dramatic show. Not only was he wearing an 'awami' suit, a long kurta and shalwar, in the image of his father, but like him, he had the sleeves unbuttoned. There was only one sofa in the room, which could seat only him. To hammer home his revolutionary credentials, he had a Kalashnikov resting against his left forearm. Sethi sat behind him in an upright chair. He was playing the secretary in this staged performance. Shahnawaz, Murtaza's younger brother, sported an Arab keffiyeh. He was wearing army fatigues, with a string of hand-grenades hanging from his belt and a dagger hugging his right thigh. An extra magazine had been secured to his Kalashnikov with the help of scotch tape. This was something he had seen PLO fighters do. He looked like a fully-trained commando.[1] The men were brought in groups of three, which was to remain their work formation in future. Murtaza's imported dog Wolf was also in attendance,

58

but as usual he lay in a corner quite uninterested in the revolutionary drill in progress.

The first batch of three walked in and, wailing loudly, rushed towards Murtaza to show their grief, as Bhutto had been executed only three months earlier. This was the traditional Pakistani way of condoling a death. Their intention was to throw their arms around the grieving son and weep for the proper time. However, this scene had not been written into the revolutionary script that Murtaza had drafted. He did not want them to weep over him as if he was a helpless orphan. Shahnawaz had been assigned the role of his bodyguard for the duration of the meeting. (This may also have been intended as a clear message that he, Murtaza, and no one else, including his brother, was the rightful heir and successor of Zulfikar Ali Bhutto.) It was the cue that Shahnawaz might have rehearsed, for in a sudden, unexpected intervention, as the first worker advanced towards Murtaza lamenting, Shahnawaz jumped forward and stood between him and his brother, his Kalashnikov levelled. The terrified worker stopped weeping and leapt back. The message was clear, and no one else made the first trio's mistake. Shahnawaz kept his Kalashnikov pointed at everyone who came forward to shake the leader's hand.

These theatrics derived not only from the youth of the Bhutto brothers, but also from the psychological impact of recent events. Until Bhutto's hanging, Zia had been seen by Murtaza and Shahnawaz as a comical figure, but since the night of 4 April he had been transformed into a monstrous devil whose very name sent shudders down their spines. Their fears were only sharpened by messages from their mother that Zia's commandos were out to get them. Since they knew none of the PPP workers, it was natural for them to be suspicious of anyone who approached them. This turned into an obsession that stifled trust and led to many future tragedies.

Murtaza's first words to these men went something like this:

We undertake to complete Bhutto the Martyr's mission and to avenge his blood, even if we have to lose our own lives in the fulfilment of this sacred duty. Our negotiations with the Kabul government are complete. Very soon we are going to establish our own radio station, and with its help we will establish links with our people and issue them with the necessary instructions. You, meanwhile, will undergo a short course of military training.

This seemed to be working well until, after listening to Murtaza, the volunteer Akmal Shah, brother of the PPP leader Muzaffar Shah[2] and the president of the Pakistan Students Federation (PSF) in Nowshehra, asked: 'What is the evidence that you will really bring about a revolution and will do what you are saying when the time comes?' Murtaza was not prepared for this and his reaction was sharp: 'And how can you say that we won't do what we are committing ourselves to?' Akmal at once replied: 'Our history is witness that the Party has not kept to any of its pledges. If it had, we would not be ruled by General Zia today.' Murtaza cut him short: 'Instead of talking about the PPP's past, look forward to the revolution.' Akmal Shah was not to be quelled so easily. 'All I wanted to say was that you do not know me or any of us. You would not even come to know were I to be killed tomorrow, but let this imported dog of yours disappear, and you wouldn't eat for days. How can there be a revolution until you change your imperial style of life and your class conduct?' Murtaza had no answer, but he never forgot what he could not help seeing as Akmal Shah's impertinence. Fourteen months after this exchange, he charged that Akmal Shah had insulted him at my suggestion.

It was Murtaza's decision that all those who had come to Kabul should be given crash military training, but the reality was that these men were no more than living toy soldiers for the Bhutto brothers. Much of their 'training' took place in Kabul hotels. A squad would assemble in a room and one of the Bhuttos would empty and load a Kalashnikov magazine and ask the recruits to repeat the demonstration. In half an hour, this induction course was over. As for practical training, for one day only Asadullah Sarwari had arranged for his guests to use the Kargha firing range in one of Kabul's cantonments. The men were picked up from their hotels in a police bus, driven to the firing range and instructed by the Bhutto brothers. What they were keen to establish was that they, the Bhutto brothers, were the instructors, teachers and leaders in all departments. Murtaza had everyone fire a few shots, and thus in about three hours, the military training of his front-line troops was declared completed.

After this farce, Murtaza almost began to believe or pretend that these fifty men, some hardly out of their teens, were battle-worthy enough to take on Zia's army. In this feat of self-deception, it is difficult to allocate the contribution made by wishful thinking, immaturity, romanticism and simple ignorance. He had gone to bag a wild elephant with equipment hardly fit to catch a mouse. One of Bhutto's most famous remarks made from jail was Murtaza's guiding mantra at the time: 'My sons are not my sons if they do not drink the blood of those who dare shed my blood today.' (Zulfikar Ali Bhutto had been quick to take offence and had often erupted like a volcano. If he had to grapple with a major problem, he would often think aloud. When on trial for his life, helpless and desperate, he had been subjected to constant needling and humiliation. It was natural for him to declare that if he was killed, his sons would avenge him. This was not the first time his anger had taken such a form. In the 1970 election campaign, a right-wing Urdu magazine had made slighting references to his mother being a Hindu. A few days later, at a huge public meeting, Bhutto threatened the editor: 'I will avenge this insult. And if I die, it will be my sons who will avenge this insult. If they fail to do so, they will cease to be my sons.' A sense of insecurity, wounded pride, playing to the gallery – Bhutto's was a complex personality. But although he could be florid in his speech, at heart he was a man of compromise, and his emotional response to provocation may have been misread by his son.)

Murtaza told his volunteer soldiers that after returning to Pakistan, they should stay clear of PPP politics and wait for his instructions. The last group he received was actually the most important It consisted of Moeenullah from Peshawar, Misbahuddin from Dir and Jamal Shah from Nowshehra. They were the first to be given arms supplied by the PLO. Before they left, Murtaza regaled them with a long and rambling lecture on discipline and security matters. After they were gone, Murtaza returned to his residence. As the driver parked the car in the garage and Murtaza stepped out, he was astounded to see a smiling Moeenullah. He had been hiding in the boot of the car. This was in violation of Murtaza's instructions, which had stressed that no one was to try to find his residence. In such operations, the 'need-to-know' principle is safest for everybody. Moeenullah's showed that the volunteers' ten-day stretch in Kabul's third-class hotels had failed to curb the *jiyala* enthusiasm for which PPP cadres were known. This lack of seriousness also heralded the needless hardships many of them would suffer. When Moeenullah was asked why he had performed this caper, he replied with the utmost simplicity: 'Sir, I wanted to see with my own eyes the great place where you were putting up.' He was unaware of his indiscretion, and quite determined to get a guided tour of the place.

The smuggling of PLO arms to Pakistan had become a rite of passage for Murtaza. Pervez Shinwari's arrest had caused bitter exchanges between Murtaza and Sarwari, with Murtaza holding Afghan intelligence responsible for the mishap and Sarwari attributing it to the organizational indiscipline of Murtaza's outfit. The fact was that Sarwari had no experience of intelligence matters. This former Afghan Air Force pilot had no knowledge of Pakistan's internal affairs, and did not grasp the psychology of the tribal agents that he used. A measure of his naiveté is the fact that Murtaza had him running most of the time. Sarwari did not seem to realize that Murtaza had no organized force at all.

In July 1979, when the first group had returned to Pakistan, Murtaza met Sarwari and asked to have the arms delivered in Peshawar instead of the border post of Landikotal. Murtaza was sure that if the arms were taken through the tribal belt and into the settled areas, they would be safe from the police. Sarwari saw no problem with that. Shah Wali now took over, and dispatched Shah Rehman and Amir Muhammad (alias Wa'aiz Nadaf) to Peshawar, where they stayed with Shah Rehman's father-in-law. According to the plan, the arms were to be delivered to Shah Rehman in Peshawar by five tribesmen.[3] He was to pass them on to Moeenullah. The fail-safe feature in this scheme was that in the event of a leak at Peshawar, Afghan agents would be arrested rather than Murtaza's men. Given the Cold War setting of the time, it was clear that any Afghans who were caught would be dealt with harshly by the Pakistanis. Sarwari gave the operation the OK. All intelligence agencies in a way are alike: they consider the individuals that they use expendable.

The man at the other end, NWFP Chief Secretary Captain Isani, who was head of the administration, waited patiently for the arms to reach their destination, and on 6 September 1979, which was also Pakistan's defence day, when the last gun had been delivered, Moeenullah's house was surrounded and he was taken into custody. Ten years later, Moeenullah told me:

> The police raiding party was led by an inspector who had a complete list of the arms which had been delivered to me. He began to check all items against this list, but when it came to the pistols he said one of them was missing, as according to his count, when there were only thirty-three there should have been thirty-four. They started searching everywhere, and finally found the pistol lying under a bed.[4]

Captain Isani was a former army officer who had been inducted into the Civil Service of Pakistan in the 1960s. Originally a Sindhi, he benefited from the meagre number of Sindhi officers in Pakistan's public services, and gained rapid promotion during the Bhutto years (1971 to 1977). When the Zia coup came, he was Joint Secretary at the federal Ministry of Education. The new military ruler appointed him Chief Secretary of the NWFP. In 1985 Pakistan once again got a Sindhi Prime Minister, when Zia chose Muhammad Khan Junejo. He picked up Isani as head of the Prime Minister's secretariat. In 1988, when Benazir Bhutto, another Sindhi, took power, she let him keep his job.

Moeenullah had hidden the arms at three different places, but the police had no difficulty in unearthing them. Shah Rehman and Wa'aiz Nadaf had also been picked up, and for several years they rotted in Pakistani jails. One month after this fiasco, Asadullah Sarwari himself lost his job, and the families of Shah and Nadaf used to seek out Shah Wali in Kabul, begging to have their men brought home from Pakistan.[5] The five Afridi tribesmen who actually brought in the arms had also been arrested by the Peshawar police, and prosecuted under martial law regulations. All these men who ventured their freedom were pawns in a game played by absent political masters. The question was who had blown the operation. The only people who knew all the details were Shah Wali's staff, and it cannot be ruled out that one of them was spying for Pakistani intelligence.

Shah Wali had also assigned Nadir Khan, a tribal agent, to deliver some arms to Misbahuddin in Timargarah, Dir. The carrier turned out to be more resourceful than they expected. First of all, he asked for a mule that would carry the arms to Pakistan. Murtaza himself gave him the money to buy one. Nadir Khan loaded four anti-tank RPG-7 missiles on the animal and delivered only one of them to Misbahuddin in Dir. When he returned, he told an elaborate story of how the mule had later died. Shah Wali duly bought a new mule. This time he was given eight missiles for shipment to the same destination. Instead of delivering them to Misbahuddin, Nadir Khan sold them in Timargarah for Rs 200,000 (about $20,000). Then he went to Misbahuddin and asked him to return the one missile he had brought earlier. When Misbahuddin refused, Nadir Khan went to the police and had Misbahuddin arrested and the missile confiscated.[6]

Having intercepted the arms smuggled from Afghanistan, the NWFP administration turned its attention to Murtaza's operatives and bagged almost all of them quite easily. The few who escaped remained on the run for years to come. The arrest of Moeenullah's father Hazrat Usman was a more painful aspect of this tragedy. This old and sick man remained in jail for many years. His only crime was that without his knowledge, his sons had kept a small cache of arms in store. As for Murtaza, he declared that both Moeenullah and his father were traitors who had surrendered the arms to the police to sabotage his operation.

With hundreds of PPP workers being hauled in by the police all over the province at the slightest suspicion, Jamal Shah decided to flee Pakistan and managed to reach Thailand, where he approached the Pakistan embassy offering to return to Kabul to work against Murtaza Bhutto. A copy of this letter fell into the hands of the KGB, which passed it on to Afghan intelligence. From them it reached Murtaza.

In August 1979, Murtaza's first cousin Tariq Islam, son of his father's sister, arrived from London. So too did Bashir Riaz.[7] Riaz stayed in Kabul for three weeks, and Murtaza arranged for him to interview Hafizullah Amin. It was odd that the Afghan Prime Minister should have agreed to be interviewed by a publication for exiles which did not circulate more than a couple of hundred copies.

Until October 1979, what was left of the PLA was no more than a Murtaza fantasy. The empty headquarters of this 'revolutionary army' were located in a derelict house in Koocha-e-Murgh Faroshan, the chicken vendors' street. It had no toilets or bathrooms nor any electricity. The few volunteers dumped there had named it Dracula House. In one of its rooms lived the poet Manawwar Masood, who had pinned one of his verses on the wall which said: 'Do not look up to the politicians; it is your sons who will avenge your blood.' The verse was addressed to Zulfikar Ali Bhutto. This poet was to move on from Kabul to India and then to Scandinavia. In October 1979, there were only four PLA 'soldiers' staying at Dracula House. They were Rana Shankat Ali, Tajbar Khan, Sheikh Gul and Zubair Shad, and they had undergone much hardship during their clandestine journey from Pakistan. Food was brought to them every day by Kausar Ali Shah and his wife.

Murtaza did not give up easily, and even when there was no reason to be optimistic, he found or invented enough reasons to feel upbeat. There were days when nothing seemed to be working out, but there he would sit, with newspapers from Pakistan spread all around him. Any snippet he spotted about a fire or an accident was clipped and passed on to Afghan intelligence as his work. Intelligence agencies accept such claims only if they have prior knowledge of the operation or if their own sources confirm their authenticity. Murtaza's claims met neither test, so the Afghans laughed them away. There were even occasions when some incident in Pakistan staged by Afghan intelligence itself was claimed by Murtaza as his. After some time, the Afghans began to supply Murtaza with a list of their successfully staged operations, asking him to feel free to take credit for any or all of them publicly. Many of these 'hits' were claimed by Murtaza in 1979 and 1980 in his occasional cyclostyled newsletter.

In the world beyond, other things were happening. In China, after the death of Mao Zedong in 1976, the new leadership under Deng Xiaoping had decided to concentrate on internal reform rather than slogan-mongering. To him, what mattered was that a cow should give milk: never mind what colour she was. For the first time, the emotionally charged revolutionary polity of China had made way for a more settled style of politics. Mao had been subjected to criticism for the first time. After losing China's financial and ideological support, pro-Beijing communist parties elsewhere in the world had begun to break up.

The pro-China communist groups in Pakistan were equally affected. The Mazdoor Kisan Party (MKP) of Afzal Bhangash had broken up into four factions by the end of the 1970s. The one representing middle-class intellectuals was led by Professor Eric Cyprian. Afzal Bhangash now decided to try his luck in anti-China Kabul, and soon two of his rival groups led by Bacha Khan and Imtiaz Alam also arrived in the Afghan capital.[8] The purpose was simple: to gain the political patronage and ideological support of Moscow and to do each other down. That was what their 'revolution' had taught them. Bhangash was a pastmaster at such factional infighting. However, his old rival Ajmal Khattak, who came from the same generation, had been living in Kabul since 1973. Until 1962, they had been colleagues in the NAP. Here in Kabul, they were now engaged in the old game of constant intrigue against one another. Bhangash would often say: 'This standard-bearer of Pushtunistan won't let me get settled in Kabul. I have asked him several times to let bygones be bygones but he continues to tell everyone that I am an unreformed Maoist. He's afraid that if I hang on here long enough, he will become irrelevant to the Afghans.'

The truth is that Bhangash was his own worst enemy. Emotional and often undiplomatic, he was openly critical of the ruling party in Afghanistan and would talk about Babrak Karmal so critically that members of the Afghan cabinet would disappear the moment even his name was mentioned. Ajmal Khattak, on the other hand, was cool and poetical. He had seen the wind of change blow in Kabul several times, and his experience and familiarity with the scene made it difficult for anyone to uproot a guest who maintained the best of relations with both the government and with the opposing groups. If he was photographed one day with Sardar Daud, the next day you would find him clapping at a rally by Nur Muhammad Taraki. He was among the favoured when Hafizullah Amin was in power, and at Karmal's arrival he was among the celebrants. He called Najibullah his 'nephew'. In 1983, when Najibullah's father died, Khattak sobbed loudly at his funeral (which I too attended) and even read an elegy. It is another matter that he later went to Pakistan in 1988, leaving Najibullah surrounded by his enemies. If he lived in Kabul today, he would be on cordial terms with the dominant Mujahideen groups, having shed his former Marxist persona. As long as Ajmal Khattak lived in Kabul, he operated on the valid assumption that given the old game of Pushtunistan which every Afghan government had played against Pakistan, they would need someone like himself to stand in the middle of the city's main square and celebrate Pushtunistan Day every year. He was not going to lose this position to Afzal Bhangash.

After the arrival of the Red Army in Afghanistan, many Pushtun nationalists had begun to dream about 'liberating' Pushtunistan with the help of Russian tanks. Of the two men, Khattak's right to this dream was better deserved. Bhangash was a born schismatic. Instead of trying to reunite his party, he was fonder of setting up meaningless 'united fronts' with like-minded elements. He spent the last ten years of his life doing that in exile. One of his dreams was to ally with the PPP. In March 1980, supposing Murtaza the true heir of his father's party, he formed a joint front with him. Perhaps he was thinking that an alliance with Murtaza in Kabul would somehow translate into a marriage with the PPP in Pakistan. As for Murtaza, having sacrificed his troops to wildcat ventures, he was keen to use Bhangash in his vendetta against the Zia regime. He was indifferent to the factional politics of the MKP, and cared nothing for its history or ideology. The alliance between the two men was programmed to self-destruct. The only benefit that Murtaza was able to derive from their short-lived association was that he managed to use some of Bhangash's tribesmen to smuggle arms to Pakistan.

In the formation of the Bhangash–Murtaza alliance, a Major Iftikhar Ahmed played an enthusiastic role. In fact, the initial understanding between the two took place at the Major's house in London, which both Murtaza and Bhangash were briefly visiting. It was there that they decided to mark the first anniversary of Bhutto's death on 4 April 1980 by planting bombs and causing disorder in Pakistan. Both of them were bluffing because neither had any organized force to carry out the blitz they boasted of. Bhangash sent a letter to his people in Peshawar informing them of the new alliance and asking them to mark 4 April as a day of mourning. This letter was not sent to Pakistan direct but through Major Iftikhar to Bhangash's son, who was living in Kabul. Iftikhar was booked by Murtaza to fly to Kabul from London on Ariana Afghan Airlines' sole aircraft on 20 March 1980, flight number 702.

But who was Major Iftikhar? In 1978, he escaped to London after deserting the Pakistan army and obtained political asylum. At that time, Murtaza was running the 'Free Bhutto Movement' from London and Major Iftikhar soon made himself welcome. The two men became quite close to each other, and were to remain so for the next few years.

The story Iftikhar told about himself went something like this. By overthrowing the Bhutto government, Zia-ul-Haq had been guilty of violating the constitution of Pakistan. Iftikhar had therefore decided to dissociate from this anti-democratic army. While this may not have been the first instance of a soldier deserting because his chief had acted in an unconstitutional manner, the story was a little hard to swallow, especially because it contained no elements of blind love for Bhutto or devotion to the PPP. Shahnawaz, for one, would not buy it. He considered Iftikhar a plant of the army, and never missed an opportunity to needle him.

Iftikhar was serving in East Pakistan when the break-up of the country came, and he and ninety thousand companions surrendered to the Indians. Obviously, he saw no future for himself after repatriation, as most of those who returned were either passed over for promotion or forcibly retired. He was more inclined toward law and literature. Later, he obtained a law degree in London. When Major-General Imtiaz Ali declined Murtaza's offer to head the military wing of the PLA and returned to Dubai in 1979, Murtaza appointed Iftikhar instead. In other words, Major Iftikhar Ahmed was the commander-in-chief of Murtaza's army of revolution.

Ariana Afghan Airlines' flight No. 702 took off from London on 20 March 1980 but was unable to land at Kabul because of bad weather. It was diverted to Kandahar but conditions over that city were even worse and since there was no other airport in Afghanistan that could accommodate a large-bodied aircraft, the pilot had to seek permission from the Pakistani authorities to land at Karachi. Not only had Major Iftikhar been declared a deserter by the Pakistan army, he was also the commander of the anti-Zia force being raised by Murtaza. He was travelling on a UN refugee passport that bore his real name, valid for travel to all countries except Pakistan. In his pocket was Afzal Bhangash's letter for his son in Kabul. Had he been arrested at Karachi, there would have been hell to pay.

According to Iftikhar, when the plane landed at Karachi he was convinced that his end had come. He tried to stay cool as all passports were collected from the passengers and given to immigration. However, since the immigration officials did not stand to make any money from this visit, nobody looked at the documents too carefully, and this was odd, because in those days Afghanistan or anything connected with it triggered every alarm bell in Pakistani intelligence agencies. Four agencies controlled airport security: the Federal Investigation Agency, Inter-Services Intelligence, the Intelligence Bureau and the Airport Security Force. So it was strange that no one paid any attention to the passports collected from Ariana Afghan's diverted flight. On the other hand, simple inefficiency cannot be ruled out, for only one year later, from this very airport, a PIA plane was hijacked to Kabul. Anyway, Iftikhar along with the other passengers was taken to the Hotel Intercontinental, Karachi, where they spent two nights before being finally flown out to their original destination.

Bashir Riaz, one of Iftikhar's opponents, interpreted this incident as conclusive proof that he was on the payroll of Pakistani intelligence. Such allegations were printed in the local press in London, some say at Riaz's behest.[9] The Major was wise enough not to move to Kabul permanently. London remained his base. When the PIA plane was hijacked a year later, Murtaza put Iftikhar in charge of press statements at the 'London bureau'. In March 1984, when Benazir landed in London, he became part of her inner circle and was appointed director of the Bhutto Academy formed by her in 1988. This academy did not live very long, and is not even remembered today. (Since 1993, Iftikhar has been practising law in Pakistan and is said to have a good working relationship with the PPP.)

Meanwhile, Sheikh Gul and Tajbar Khan made various trips to Pakistan in 1979 and 1980 but were unable to raise more troops for the PLA. As for the Bhangash–Murtaza alliance, it remained confined to paper because neither party was sincere. Bhangash was in no doubt that Murtaza, after losing his men, was seeking to collect somebody else's. Gradually, the two drew apart. Murtaza, never at a loss for new diversions, soon got involved in something that may well be called the Tori revolution.

The Toris, a sub-branch of the Bhangash tribe, are settled in the Kurram Agency in Pakistan's tribal areas. Shi'as by faith, they are always at loggerheads with the neighbouring Sunni tribes. Politically, they were inclined to favour the PPP. They were also fervent supporters of the Afghan revolution. They came to Kabul every other week, to pick up arms for use against the Mujahideen. In fact, though, they were selling them on Pakistan's open market. In November 1979, Murtaza met a Tori youth in Kabul by the name of Muhammad Hussain Nashha. By this time his men had been arrested in Pakistan, and in Kabul Bhangash had failed to oblige, so it was natural for him to turn for help to the Toris. He had Nashha put up at Dracula House, and since he considered the Toris practically members of his party, he hoped to enlist them to do away with Zia and a few judges.

Muhammad Hussain Nashha was an educated young man who could almost be called the public relations agent for his tribe's interests in the Afghan capital. When Murtaza asked if his people would carry arms to Pakistan he readily agreed, seeing that this arrangement would double the tribe's profits from arms sales over the border. The Toris were inventive: each time a consignment went out, Nashha would return with news of heroic clashes with the local militia or even with units of the Pakistan army itself. The 'field commander' of this daring group was a man named Karim, and he spun Murtaza so many yarns about his fighting powers that he had him convinced that if there was one man who could get to General Zia, it was he. I feel sure that there were nights when Murtaza went to bed quite confident of waking up next morning to the news of Zia's killing.

So close had the Toris come to Murtaza that they could now see him without an appointment. Sohail Sethi was not too pleased with this informality, and once said to Murtaza: 'Baba [affectionate family name for Murtaza], unless you keep people at a distance they will not see you as their leader. If they come close to you, all distinction will disappear.' Murtaza took the advice, and from then on remained aloof. He was still hopeful of the Toris, failing to realize that tribal people are not as simple as they may choose to appear, nor are they seasoned hired assassins. They fight their own fights, settle their own vendettas, and see to their own interests. For the last couple of centuries, they have managed to retain their independence in territory sandwiched between two countries, British India and Afghanistan. Every tribal person is a born and bred diplomat.

Nashha was a graduate of Peshawar University, and should have gone to Pakistan and started a career, but he seemed to prefer lounging around on the sagging beds of Dracula House in Kabul, half-believing in Murtaza's tall claims and high hopes. One day he told Murtaza:

We have had word that the Political Agent in Pakistan has offered millions of rupees to Karim in order to sabotage our efforts, and they have also promised to drop all the murder cases they have registered against him. But there is no cause for alarm. I have already taken steps that will ensure that he does not enter Afghanistan again.[10]

The fact was that there was no need for Karim to return to Afghanistan because the arms he had taken from Murtaza would sell for good money in Pakistan.

For me it was a shocking disappointment that contrary to our earlier decision, Murtaza did not even mention to the PPP workers about installing the radio station and setting up a working-class revolutionary organization. He was so consumed by the idea of his so-called 'revolutionary struggle' that he would not accept that it is always easier to pick up a gun than to get rid of it. So far, Murtaza's planning had cost the freedom of several good men, lost all the shipments of weapons dispatched to Pakistan, made a few tribesmen rich, and struck not a blow against the Zia regime.

Murtaza's confidence was always hard to puncture, but he badly needed to make his mark on events. Under these circumstances, I tried to convince him to leave Kabul and go back to London, where he could open up a central office for the PPP in exile. Being naive I further suggested to him that from London he should try to ignite a democratic struggle against the military regime in Pakistan. If he listened to my advice, I thought, undoubtedly he would be a leader of his father's party and a contender for the office of prime minister. However, my advice proved to be disastrous for me. To him, everyone who tried to dissuade him from committing political suicide was worse than a traitor.

Though we were still on friendly terms, living under the same roof, eating, drinking and enjoying our evenings together, under the calm surface of a dormant volcano magma was building up. It was only a matter of time before it erupted and the lava flowed over each and every trace of our friendship.

6

The Indian Link

Elections in 1977 brought ill luck not only to Zulfikar Ali Bhutto in Pakistan but also to Mrs Indira Gandhi in India. Bhutto was removed in a coup staged by a cabal of generals, and Mrs Gandhi had to step down after suffering the worst defeat of her career. The results of the Indian election showed that the poor and economically deprived people of India had not forgiven the Prime Minister and her son Sanjay, the heir apparent, for making a mockery of democratic institutions by declaring a state of emergency in 1975 and suspending rule of law. It was to Mrs Gandhi's credit that she accepted her defeat graciously and left office with her dignity intact. By exhibiting respect for the popular verdict, she had also demonstrated that she could return to power in the future through the same door by which she had left. As it was, the Janata Front papered together by her political opponents did not last more than two years. Open conflict between the motley alliance of parties that had ganged up against Mrs Gandhi led to the appointment of Chaudhri Charan Singh as caretaker Prime Minister with the sole task of holding fresh elections in 1980.

Plainly it was only a matter of time before the political pendulum would swing back in favour of the former Prime Minister. Disappointed after the abortive experiment with the PLA, Murtaza therefore decided to link his future plans with her expected return to power. Her response to this was positive, and on 15 December 1979 they met at her residence in New Delhi. Back in Kabul, Murtaza told us that Mrs Gandhi had kept criticizing Chaudhri Charan Singh through most of the meeting, saying it was an insult to the people of India to be represented by so ignorant and light-weight a figure. As the daughter of the aristocratic intellectual Jawaharlal Nehru, she could not bring herself to accept a down-to-earth politician like Charan Singh as her social or political equal. Like all politicians born into the ruling classes, she felt that only she and her kind were qualified to rule.

Murtaza said that he had waited until she had had her fill of deriding Charan Singh when he said to her: 'The army has not executed my father; it has executed what was left of Pakistan after 1971. These generals are also a threat to your security, and the only way we can be rid of them is to

70

divide Pakistan into four parts.' If the untried Murtaza had thought that his words would make Mrs Gandhi jump out of her chair and start dancing, he betrayed his status as a novice in politics and diplomacy. How could she take seriously a young man who was offering to dismember his own country at his very first meeting with her? The vastly more experienced Indian leader did not respond to Murtaza's gambit, and instead changed the subject. Murtaza tried again: 'It is obvious that any such movement should originate in Pakistan – and that is the entire object of our struggle.' What Mrs Gandhi made of the phrase 'our struggle' she did not say; but Murtaza was representing the whole Bhutto family here, and he never did reverse the poor first impression she formed of him, despite his later efforts. She did not accord him political patronage, but used him later to perform acts of terrorism.

Ultimately, the responsibility for pushing an angry and immature young man like Murtaza to extremism must lie with Pakistan's military rulers whose only conquests since 1958 have been those inflicted upon their own people. What these small-minded Bonapartists thought of constitutional rule, parliamentary government and politicians was best expressed by General Zia-ul-Haq:

> What is a constitution? It is a booklet with twelve or ten pages. I can tear them away and say that tomorrow we shall live under a different system. Today, the people will follow wherever I lead. All the politicians including the once-mighty Mr Bhutto will follow me with tails wagging.[1]

These words dictated his country's destiny for the next eleven years. Not only did Zia utterly subvert the constitution, but a pack of politicians came sniffing at his heels. The only man who stood up to him, Zulfikar Ali Bhutto, was hanged.

Men like Ayub Khan, Yahya Khan and Zia-ul-Haq did not rise to power because they were reformers or revolutionaries, or great war heroes like de Gaulle and Eisenhower, but because they exploited the Cold War to grab power by toeing the American line. It is a long-standing shame that democratic America has seen nothing wrong in pushing the poor and powerless people of the Third World under the heels of military dictators in order to safeguard its superpower interests. Today, now the Cold War is over and the United States less in need of ruling generals, the institution of martial law has grown unfashionable. Few countries are ruled by generals; strange as it may sound, that same Pakistani army was decorated as the guardian of democracy by Benazir in 1989.

The offer of breaking up his country to bring down the ruling junta typified Murtaza's confused state of mind and his naiveté. He was proposing to cure the ailment by destroying the patient. It was the same solution that Sheikh Mujibur Rahman had contrived – and with Mrs Gandhi's help had succeeded in implementing – in 1971. Ironically, only four years later Mujibur was murdered by his own nationalist Bengali army. The situation in 1980 was oddly symmetrical. What used to be East Pakistan was being ruled by General Zia ur-Rahman, while the former West Pakistan – now the entire nation – lay under the boot of General Zia-ul-Haq. If what remained of Pakistan was to be further split into four parts, as proposed by Murtaza, it would only have meant promoting four more General-Presidents. While Sind would have been ruled by a Sindhi general, Punjab would have had a uniformed Punjabi overlord. So the answer lay in changing the oppressive system. A geographical change would bring no solution to the problems of the toiling masses, it would only change their masters.

After Murtaza's return to Kabul, he and I had long and sometimes heated discussions on the implications of what he had told Mrs Gandhi. I told him that Pakistan was not an alien territory annexed by a general. The generals might rule it today, but it could have a democratic government tomorrow. The country belonged to all of us. Our ancestors were buried in its ancient earth and our personal survival and that of the generations to follow was linked with it. To place Pakistan at the feet of Mrs Indira Gandhi would violate history, as well as betraying our country. Eventually, Murtaza agreed that he would never repeat his 'one-to-four' thesis, as he began to see that it could spell the end of his political career. He also agreed that in his future meetings with foreign government representatives, he would always take one or two colleagues. Given his lack of expertise about Pakistan and its government and politics, he conceded that more knowledgeable companions would be an asset at such meetings. I told him that no captain could win a match off his own bat. I also felt sure that with other people around he would not repeat such a fatal prescription for Pakistan's ills.

Although he had accepted my view, he saw it as restrictive, if not humiliating. Like most men born to riches, he was convinced that he was congenitally more intelligent and far-sighted than those of less fortunate descent. He saw history as a princess with flowing black hair waiting for him to beckon her. Not only had Murtaza been unable to complete his education, but he had very little experience of or insight into politics. He could imitate his father, but only in the most superficial way. It was my idealism or naiveté or both that caused me to confront him. I took the view that if we were to embark on a social, economic and political revolution, we should first set our own house in order. Murtaza saw my attitude as a challenge to his authority as leader, and bided his time until he could dispose of me.

At this point, it is relevant to examine an episode in the career of Benazir

Bhutto. From March 1984 to April 1986, her political activities centred on London, where a number of her father's political companions were also based. As was to be expected, before long a conflict developed between the 'old guard' and the new leader. Would she bow to the decisions of the central committee, or would it take orders from her? One section of the party began to demand party elections, so that instead of a nominated central committee, decision-making should pass to a representative elected body. As Benazir saw it: 'There was an undeclared war for party leadership. The old guard in London realised that if they accepted me once, they might have to accept me forever.'[2]

The Western-educated Benazir did not take long to learn the golden rule of Pakistan's feudal politics, namely that a leader must not be answerable to his or her party. It was for the leader to issue orders, for the party to unquestioningly obey them. A leader might call for national elections in order to come to power, but elections within the party were out of bounds. Benazir thought the safest course was to liquidate the old guard altogether, and in two years, she managed to purge the PPP of Abdul Hafiz Pirzada, Mumtaz Bhutto, Mustafa Khar (who has had a number of re-entries and exits since), Ghulam Mustafa Jatoi, Dr Ghulam Hussain, Qayyum Butt and Sardar Mazhar Ali Khan.

In January 1985, when Bhutto's birthday was being celebrated in London, great tension prevailed between his daughter and Bhutto's old colleagues. Murtaza was in France and decided to intervene. Using two former operatives of Al-Zulfikar, the brothers Agha, he sent unsigned threatening letters to Qayyum Butt, while the elderly and much respected Sheikh Muhammad Rashid was sent a bottle of cough mixture. Some were sent bottles of Scotch whisky. These 'gifts' were reportedly laced with poison supplied by the Syrians, and if any of the recipients had imbibed the stuff, he would surely have either died or been taken severely ill. In Murtaza's book, anyone who dared rebel against 'The Family' invited punishment. He also wanted to convey to those who dared question that it was he who was his father's rightful heir and whoever defied Benazir was indirectly defying him. At that time, he considered his sister no more than a weak girl who was filling in for him. The old guard of the PPP should be thankful to Benazir that she only eased them out of the party. Had they fallen foul of her brother, it might have been their lives they left behind.

We can now return to 1980 and Mrs Indira Gandhi's dramatic though expected electoral victory. Murtaza celebrated her return in Kabul because he was sure that his proposal about breaking Pakistan into four parts would still be ringing in 'Mother India's' ears, and soon he would be summoned to New Delhi. No such invitation materialized. In April 1980, Vasant Sathe, Joint Secretary of India's Ministry of External Affairs, visited Kabul and Murtaza called on him through the good offices of the Indian embassy, requesting an appointment with Mrs Gandhi. Still no invitation came. Finally, Murtaza decided to try his luck in New Delhi personally, and in keeping with his pledge about meetings with foreign leaders, after a great deal of discussion it was decided that I should be his companion.

In June 1980, Murtaza presented himself at the Indian embassy in Kabul and was greeted by an officer called Malhotra, a graduate of Government College, Lahore, from pre-independence days. After the opening courtesies and preliminaries, he said to Murtaza:

> At your recommendation, I issued a visa to Manawwar Masood, that poet, although under our law Pakistanis can only obtain Indian visas if they apply from their country. As soon as he arrived in Delhi, he began propagating Punjabi nationalism, which brought me a reprimand from my lords and masters. The man has now been sent to Scandinavia, but I have been told in clear terms that I am not to issue any more visas to Pakistani citizens.

Malhotra was right about Manawwar Masood's Punjabi chauvinism, as I knew from experience. Murtaza said: 'But I am holding an Afghan passport.' 'In that case, you need no visa,' Malhotra answered. 'Visas will be stamped on your passport at the airport. What I can do is not inform the Indian Home Ministry about your arrival, and that should suit everyone I think.' As for myself, I had a Pakistani passport in the name of Sarfraz Khan, as Malhotra was aware.

When we arrived in New Delhi, I could see that Malhotra had kept his word. It was obvious that we were not expected. Had he been nice to us because he was born in what was now Pakistan? Such attachments are often stronger than one thinks. The immigration desk officer wanted a bribe of $50. In everyday life in India and Pakistan, whoever has to deal with government officials, especially on the lower rungs, knows that palms must be greased before you can get anywhere. This came as no surprise to me, but it outraged Murtaza whose background had given him no idea of how the rest of the people lived. He hit the ceiling. 'Get me Mrs Gandhi's office. I'll see about your little *bakhsheesh*. Give me the phone. You will soon find out who we are.'

Murtaza could be a perfect actor. The moment he mentioned Mrs Gandhi's name, all colour left the official's face. Not only did he immediately stamp visas in our passports, he even escorted us out of the restricted area right up to the street. He must have thought we were VIPs, though he should have realized that had it been true, we would have been officially received. A few reporters who were out there, and who obviously knew the immigration official, put two and two together and decided that we were important visitors arriving from Kabul. Because of the Afghan war, New

Delhi's Palam airport had become a conduit of sorts for news flowing out of Afghanistan. Any flight arriving from Kabul was scouted by reporters for first-hand or inside information.

Taking us for Afghans, they fired the usual questions. Had such and such a minister been shot? When had we last heard gunfire in Kabul? Were there KGB at Kabul airport? I told one of them: 'When you have a revolution, there is always the sound of gunfire.' Among the reporters was the BBC New Delhi bureau's Satish Jacob, who claimed: 'The exodus of millions of Afghans from the country proves that the people have rejected both the Afghan revolution and the Soviet intervention.' Murtaza's reply was: 'The majority of the Afghan people still lives in Afghanistan, which shows that the people of that country have accepted the revolution.' Murtaza told the journalists, who by now were quite sure that we were Afghan officials on a secret mission, that his name was Dr Salahuddin and I was Sarfraz Khan.

I thought it was time to have some fun. 'We're here on a very important mission,' I said. 'What mission is that?' asked one of them excitedly. 'We've come to try our luck in the Bombay movies. This six-foot-tall young man wants to be the Amitabh Bachhan of the future, so why don't you write a few nice words about us that might make some kind-hearted director give us a break?' The journalists laughed and went away, leaving their calling cards with us. Satish Jacob, however, was smart enough to know that we were not Afghans – he even told us that when he gave out his card. What he did not know was that one of us was the son of Pakistan's executed Prime Minister, seeking the help of Mrs Gandhi to avenge his father's murder. He did not know what a story he had.

We stayed at a hotel on New Delhi's Janpath where a large number of members of India's parliament, the Lok Sabha, were also staying. Outside the hotel were scores of poor people, all in search of employment or justice or a piece of land. Whenever a member stepped out of the hotel, his constituents would rush towards him waving petitions. It was exactly like Pakistan. The next day's newspapers had some exciting and quite fictitious stories about 'two important mystery visitors' from Afghanistan. I suppose it is a newspaper's obligation to keep its readers happy by serving up their daily diet of lies and half-truths. In the world of the media, conjecture, truth and falsehood are meaningless terms with no dividing line, either for those who produce news or those who read it.

Murtaza phoned Mrs Gandhi's secretary and left his name and number. Two days later her office called back giving a time for the requested appointment. No car was to be sent for him: there was no intention of treating him as a guest of the state. It was clear that the appointment had been granted out of courtesy and that he was expected to see it as no more than a formal call. It was 20 June 1980, and so hot that you could have fried an egg on the footpath. We found a rickety taxi which dropped us at Mrs Gandhi's residence on Canal Road. Once her father's house, this was where she had chosen to live as Prime Minister. The essence of her political strategy perhaps lay in just such gestures designed to convey to the people a sense of continued traditions. Many political careers in the subcontinent have been built on the past achievements of others.

An unruly crowd of supplicants was blocking the front wrought-iron gate of the house, all of them trying to push their way closer to the entrance, which was bolted shut anyway. A group of women was on a hunger strike against the city authorities, while hotel and restaurant workers marched back and forth waving a red flag and shouting 'Release our leaders'. We were trying to weasel our way through the crowd when the famous Indian film comedian, Mahmood, emerged from the Prime Minister's house. Once spotted he was quickly surrounded by fans demanding that he declaim famous lines from his hit movies. He had no option but to shout at the top of his voice so that everyone could hear him.

Eventually we broke through to the office of Mrs Gandhi's secretary, who turned out to be a Muslim from Uttar Pradesh by the name of Khurshid. At 11.30 am, Murtaza was sent for (he had told me that if he needed my advice during the meeting, he would bring me in.)

As Murtaza set off to Mrs Gandhi's office, I could not help thinking of a line from one of Bhutto's speeches: 'O Mai Indira, you can keep my sons as hostages but return us our prisoners of war.' During 1972 and 1973, he often used to say this at his public meetings. While his admirers said that it showed how intensely Bhutto felt on the POW issue, his detractors considered it nothing more than deceit from a clever politician who was cheating the people because such practices lay buried with the old Mughal kings. Perhaps Bhutto considered himself the king of Pakistan, they went on, and wanted to revive that archaic tradition. Now, only seven years later, I was watching Bhutto's prophecy come halfway true. The difference was that Mrs Gandhi had not had to take his son hostage: he had gone to her of his own free will.

Murtaza stepped out of Mrs Gandhi's room a few minutes later, accompanied by a young man wearing drainpipe Delhi-style cotton pyjamas and a knee-length shirt. Without a glance at me, he followed him into the adjoining room. 'That was Sanjay ji,' the Prime Minister's secretary volunteered. Mrs Gandhi had passed Murtaza on to her son, and her declared successor, citing a heavy workload. Since Murtaza was Bhutto's unproclaimed heir, it was only natural that both men should discuss the future of the subcontinent. In order to hide his embarrassed disappointment, Murtaza told Sanjay that he was on his way to Greece on an important mission, but had decided to stop in Delhi to congratulate Mrs Gandhi on her brilliant victory. Sanjay thanked him, and expressed concern about the safety and well-being of the Bhutto ladies. A cup of tea was served before the two came out of the room. Sanjay smiled, shook hands with the other heir apparent, and walked away. It was a scene of confident security. Yet in a few days' time this delicate-looking young man would be dead in a plane crash. Years later, the other heir apparent would die on the streets of Karachi still seeking for his vanished patrimony.

Sanjay did not trouble to ask Murtaza where he was staying, or how he had got to the Prime Minister's house. Outside, it took us half an hour before we could flag down a rickshaw. Murtaza was wearing a new suit that day, despite the heat, and was sweating profusely. He looked mystified, and clearly felt insulted. Mrs Gandhi had taught him his first lesson in politics: this was a world where friendships and family did not always count. She had no use for young Murtaza who had mistimed his knock at her door. Mrs Gandhi was sitting pretty. Kashmir seemed peaceful and the Punjab crisis that ended in the bloody storming of the Golden Temple of the Sikhs at Amritsar had not yet erupted. In 1983, when the Sikh rebellion broke out in the Punjab and she detected Zia's hand, she would waste no time in taking Murtaza under her wing.

When we reached our hotel that afternoon, Murtaza fell in a heap on the bed, and then, to cheer himself up rang room service for something to drink. I suggested to him that we should hold a secret news conference in Delhi and denounce the Zia regime before disappearing. Zia would interpret it as a move made with the backing of Indira Gandhi and open a diplomatic front against her. Mrs Gandhi would try to clarify her position but wouldn't be believed. This was one way to pay her back for her offhand attitude towards Murtaza. India–Pakistan relations have always been blighted by a mutual lack of trust. The news conference would be perfectly in tune with the conspiratorial brand of politics practised by the two countries and their governments. Murtaza's first reaction was enthusiastic, but he changed his mind later – 'If I do that, Mrs Gandhi would be forever annoyed with me, while General Zia would brand me an Indian agent.'

In his state of exile and alienation, Murtaza did not wish to lose the possible friendship of Mrs Gandhi. We therefore decided that while he should indeed address the press, he should do so as Raja Anwar. We had met the correspondents of the *Washington Post*, Australian radio and the London *Times* at the airport and had taken their cards. When we phoned and invited them to lunch, they turned up even earlier than expected. Murtaza introduced himself as Bhutto's former adviser on student affairs, Raja Anwar, and passed me off as his secretary. We requested that no pictures should be taken for the sake of our security, and that no stories should be filed in the next four days.

During lunch Murtaza felt in his element and told them a lot of the cock-and-bull stories at which he excelled. One journalist asked him: 'How many of you are here?' 'I have a delegation of seventeen with me,' he replied without batting an eye. Had he met Mrs Gandhi? His answer implied that he was here at her invitation. He also gave out pamphlets on his non-existent People's Liberation Army. As we stepped out to see them off, a couple of Russians emerged from the lift. 'Are these Russians also with you?' one journalist asked. 'I am not at liberty to speak. Please ask him,' I replied. He concluded from my answer that we were travelling in Russian company. Such nonsense often formed the basis of news stories during the Cold War.

On 23 June, Murtaza took off for Athens to meet his friend Daila. When after seeing him off, I returned to Janpath, I saw strange scenes. People were running everywhere, their faces wrung with fear. At first I thought Pakistan and India had gone to war, and it sent a shudder down my spine. In the lobby of our hotel I asked a waiter what was going on. He told me that Sanjay Gandhi had died. He was flying solo in his single-engine Cessna over Delhi when something went wrong and the plane came crashing down, killing him on the spot. In a dual tragedy, Mrs Gandhi had lost her son as well as her heir. She had paid a heavy political price to ensure his succession to power. It was Sanjay who had been the principal cause of her 1977 election defeat when the opposition accused him of corruption and high-handed behaviour. One by one, she had rid the party of her father's friends and companions in order to pave the way for Sanjay, and now he was gone.

It is a tragedy of history that the Indian National Congress which once had in its ranks liberals such as Mohammad Ali Jinnah, non-communal nationalists such as Abu Kalam Azad, revolutionaries such as Subhas Chandra Bose, and brilliant intellectuals of the stature of Jawaharlal Nehru, had become a handmaiden of the naive and brutally ambitious Sanjay Gandhi. Khan Abdul Ghaffar Khan, 'the Frontier Gandhi', was once constrained to comment: 'The party which we had set up by giving it our blood, has been destroyed by this girl [Indira Gandhi].'[3] Since Mrs Gandhi had come into the leadership of the Congress because of who she was rather than what she had achieved, she considered the party as much a family heirloom as her father's house.

Sanjay's death hit India like an earthquake. Streets were suddenly deserted and funereal music played on radio and television. Official India was mourning the loss of Mrs Gandhi's son – the same India where young girls were burnt to death because they were too poor to be married with a dowry, millions with curable illnesses died for the lack of facilities and where eighty per cent of the children could not go to school because there were no schools to go to. But none of these tragedies were mourned. Sanjay's death was tragic, but the high life he lived had been made possible by the sacrifices of those millions of nameless Indians who had no one to cry over them or to fulfil even their most elementary needs. Why were the people crying over the thrill-seeking prince who would soar over Delhi every morning in his own plane? Did the poor cry over the rich in order to make sense of their own barren lives?

Although the simple and trusting Indian people had conferred the title of Bharat Mata – Mother India – on Mrs Gandhi, she had proved to be mother to only two people, her sons. After Sanjay's death, she could find not a single man or woman, young or old, in a country of seven hundred million worthy to succeed her as leader of the Congress Party and, eventually, of India. She only had eyes for her son Rajiv, and it was Rajiv she anointed as her successor – a man whose involvement with India can be gauged from the fact that after marrying an Italian, he had practically lived abroad. He had no interest in politics, but he had been summoned, and there he now stood beside his mother, wearing coarse Congress cotton and the Nehru cap. Already the electronic media had begun to pour out sycophantic stories about Rajiv's brilliance and suitability for his new role.

On 23 June, Murtaza phoned from Athens and asked me to visit Mrs Gandhi on his behalf. Next day I took a cab to the Prime Minister's residence, and when I sent word to her secretary that I was here to convey the personal condolences of Murtaza Bhutto, he remembered that I had come here some days earlier. After a while, he escorted me into the presence of Mrs Gandhi. A group of important Indian politicians was with her. Her secretary whispered in her ear, but either he failed to convey on whose behalf I had come or she misheard what he said, because she assumed that I had come to condole with her on behalf of the Bhutto ladies. It did not seem proper to say that I had not. She asked me how they were. As I was about to say something, there was a surge of activity outside and someone said that Khan Abdul Ghaffar Khan had arrived. Everyone stood up. Like a child, Mrs Gandhi threw her arms around the old Pushtun leader and broke down. The Khan bent over her, his chin resting affectionately over her head. (In Pakistan, Khan Ghaffar Khan's title, the Frontier Gandhi, is a term of abuse; in India an expression of the highest respect.)

Delhi is the central reference point of Indian history, and it would have been unthinkable for me to return without walking through it. It is said that Delhi has been ravaged seven times, and seven times rebuilt. These periods mark the seven chapters or ages of India's history. When I climbed to the top of one of the minarets of Shah Jahan's great mosque, the Jamia Masjid, I found the names of visitors scratched into the wall. Many of the names suggested that they had come from parts of the country that was now Pakistan. One of the men who had visited in 1932 was Adalat Khan from Gujjar Khan, a town near my village. For hundreds of years, this mosque and the land on which it stood was part of our common history and heritage. Now here I was, standing on one of its minarets as a stranger.

79

As far as I could see, old and new Delhi stretched out in every direction. Suddenly I felt overcome, and tears welled up in my eyes. In that moment I understood the tragic dilemma of men like Maulana Abu Ala Maududi, Maulana Hussain Ahmed Madani, Syed Ataullah Shah Bukhari, Khan Abdul Ghaffar Khan, Allama Mashriqi and Abu Kalam Azad, who were unwilling to abandon their old history and geography in favour of a new country called Pakistan. Just as India is unable to do away with these great symbols of its past glory, so these men were unable to wean themselves away from this sweet earth that once belonged to them as it had belonged to others in an earlier time.

After my return to Kabul, the Foreign Minister of the martial law regime in Pakistan, Agha Shahi, arrived in the Indian capital. He was the first Pakistani official to come to India after Mrs Gandhi's return to power. After the Soviet invasion of Afghanistan, Pakistan had assumed a new importance, especially for the United States and China – a development that Mrs Gandhi did not welcome. While only Agha Shahi can tell the full story of his visit, it was reported in the Pakistani press that his mission to Delhi had failed because of my presence in the Indian capital. The press conference given by Murtaza posing as Raja Anwar had been reported by the *Washington Post*, and the army regime in Pakistan alleged that Murtaza Bhutto had formed a government-in-exile of which I, Raja Anwar, was Foreign Minister.[4] The Zia regime also lodged a written protest to the Indian government about my being allowed to hold a news conference in New Delhi. Mrs Gandhi denied that she was in any way connected with the government-in-exile. She was right, though few believed her.

7

Pul-i-Charkhi

Pul-i-Charkhi is the notorious prison in Kabul where I spent the two and a half years between October 1980 and March 1983. Murtaza had done me a favour by locking me away there during Al-Zulfikar's heyday as a terrorist organization. None of its members survived those years unscathed. I have pieced together its history from talks with the survivors, and I don't know how I would have responded to Murtaza's tactics, his choice of targets, his callous treatment of our recruits, his readiness to kill almost at random, and in short his conversion of Al-Zulfikar from a movement of revolutionary resistance into a puppet organization for his personal wishes and hatreds. Anyone who dared to confront Murtaza publicly during his brief reign of terror took his life in his hands, and I doubt that had I been free I could have altered the course of events that I saw unfolding from the comparative safety of an Afghan prison cell.

To explain how I arrived there I will return to 1979, when Murtaza established an intelligence cell of the PLA even before the group had been formally announced, and put his younger brother Shahnawaz in charge of it. He was copying Hafiz Asad of Syria, whose younger brother Rifat Asad was his security chief. The first task he gave to Shahnawaz was to fish out army commando agents from among the volunteers who had arrived from Pakistan. Later, he appointed Shahnawaz as his bodyguard. The poor young man had suffered a near nervous breakdown, and it was cruel to have him standing behind 'Mir Sain' with a trembling finger resting on the trigger of a Kalashnikov. With so much sophisticated technology and surveillance equipment available to our enemies, while we had neither the technology nor skills to use it, and lacked all but the most elementary tradecraft, what could a nervous and inexperienced twenty-year-old former college student do as head of intelligence? However – and probably at Murtaza's advice – Shahnawaz recruited half the PPP workers into his intelligence outfit. The rest were told to perform counter-intelligence work. In effect, everyone was now spying on everyone, and here we were not dealing with large numbers but just the handful who had trudged across the border from Pakistan to 'carry on Bhutto's mission and to punish his murderers'. All this notwithstanding, Murtaza never felt reassured about his men, or even safe from them.

PPP's party workers hailing from non-industrial labour and lower middle classes have often been called *jiyalas*, an eloquent Urdu word which means a man who is committed, enthusiastic, unafraid and even somewhat reckless. For the first time in Pakistan's history, people of this type were elected to the assemblies in 1970 on PPP tickets. Although in the next election in 1977, the party allowed only a handful of them to run again, they had tasted political power once and were not able or willing to forget that heady experience. After the fall and judicial murder of Bhutto, his feudal and landowning supporters fell away. The vacuum created by their departure was quickly filled by the *jiyalas* who had felt generally ignored. Thousands of them spent the better part of Zia's rule lying in jails and interrogation centres undergoing harsh physical and mental punishment and lamenting the fate that had befallen the Bhutto family. Each one of them was hopeful that because of his or her loyalty to the Bhutto family, when elections came around the next time, they would be given PPP tickets to run.[1]

In 1979, just after Bhutto's execution, emotions were still running high and loyalty to the family was only worth the name if it was blind and total. In such a black and white world, there were those who were loyal and those who were traitors. Gossip was commonplace, speculation led to mud-slinging, and no one's reputation was safe. Anyone who got close to the family set in motion a chain of intrigue. Given the social, political and psychological background of the *jiyalas*, it is not hard to imagine the kind of accusations Shahnawaz's excitable agents would have made against their companions and comrades. On the basis of unsubstantiated reports, Murtaza eventually began to denounce, imprison, and finally order the execution of certain individuals falsely accused of being traitors. Things reached such a low point later on that his men would avoid even greeting one another.

Shaukat Ali Rana was the first man to declare that Murtaza was paranoid. This happened in May 1980. Rana had a master's degree in psychology. He noticed that when Shahnawaz was not around, Murtaza behaved like a slightly scared but affable person, but the moment the younger brother came back, his personality underwent a transformation. It was clear that he suffered from acute insecurity. Once Shaukat Ali told him in Shahnawaz's absence that according to the BBC, the Mujahideen could enter the city of Kabul whenever they pleased. It so scared Murtaza that he spent the night in Shaukat Ali's room in Dracula House, although his residence was located in Kabul's most secure area.

In 1978, after the High Court sentenced Bhutto to death, some of his PPP workers decided to sabotage the railway track near Lahore to register their protest. Had this plan worked, hundreds of innocent men and women would have lost their lives. The action was to be carried out near the town of Wah, less than twenty miles from Rawalpindi. They were working on the track when a retired army subedar happened along. One look and they ran, but not before he had caught one saboteur, whose name was Ashraf Ali. According to his statement to the police, the author of the plan was Kausar Ali Shah, an old PPP worker from Lahore. Ashraf was arraigned before a military court which awarded him twenty-five lashes and sent him to jail for fourteen years. Kausar Ali Shah, meanwhile, had managed to escape to Libya. It was to his and my subsequent misfortune that I persuaded him in 1979 to move from Tripoli to Kabul with his wife and children.

On 4 April 1980, the first anniversary of Bhutto's death was celebrated in the Afghan capital. Both Bhutto brothers were out of the country. At the memorial meeting, Shah's wife said that had Bhutto not made a compromise with the United States and the feudal classes, he would not have met the end he did. The Americans were known to eliminate those who had once been their associates and agents when those people were of no further use or had become an embarrassment. While it is true that these were bitter words, bear in mind that this woman had been several times beaten by the police on the streets of Lahore between 1977 and 1979 while marching in support of Bhutto. However, when Murtaza returned and was told what she had said, he at once declared her husband a traitor. It was only with great difficulty that poor Shah was able to cool – but not to extinguish – his leader's wrath.

I became Murtaza's second victim. To this day I do not understand why he accepted the flimsy evidence that drove him too easily first to have me jailed and then to try to have me shot. It is not possible to believe that a normal, reasonably balanced person would want his best friend and comrade killed for the sake of a false report or to appease a whim. Not only did we live under the same roof for a year and a half, we were on close and open-hearted terms. I had been one of his father's advisers, intimate enough to have been invited to stay in the family homes in Karachi and Larkana. To save his father's life, I had run a movement under the aegis of the People's Action Committee. During those dark days, I had been a close confidant of the Bhutto ladies, his mother and sister, and used to write the speeches they made. The first political speech Benazir ever delivered was written by me, for a public meeting she addressed at Dhobi Ghat, Faisalabad, in September 1977. He knew all this, just as he knew that in response to one brief message from him I had left Europe to enter the hellhole of Kabul. Soon after that I had also risked my life by travelling to Pakistan and arranging for the first group of party workers to cross over and join him.

Had trust and reason counted for Murtaza, he had every reason to trust me. I belonged to that generation of idealists which had dreamt through

Bhutto's eyes the dream of bringing about fundamental political, social and economic change to save Pakistan, which had known little except the jackboots of military dictators. I had left my home, my family, my country to chase the dream that I had first seen with Bhutto.

In order to save Murtaza from future accusations of terrorist involvement, I had to invent childish stories and explanations on several occasions. In February 1980, when he planned an operation in Rawalpindi, it was only after lengthy pleading that I managed to persuade him to call it off because I knew that it would end in the injury or death of many political workers. The only success I had before our split was that I did not let him commit any act of violence or terrorism. As he had failed to set up a working-class, revolutionary organization, I tried to convince him to go back to London, where he could set up an office to guide the movement for the restoration of democracy in Pakistan. Later, this suggestion provided his evidence to the Afghans that I had tried to persuade him to 'betray the revolution' and return to London.

On 20 October 1980, Murtaza, his cousin Tariq Islam and I returned to Kabul from London after a short visit. Three days later, one of the *jiyalas* whispered to Murtaza that about six months earlier I had said in his presence that by hanging Bhutto, General Zia had removed half the obstacles that had blocked the people's way. No revolutionary change could come in Pakistan until the Bhutto family was eliminated from the political scene. The word 'martyr' was the best suffix to the name Bhutto, I was supposed to have declared. My betrayer had recorded every word, he assured Murtaza, and would soon retrieve the tape from its secure hiding place. He also told Murtaza that Raja Anwar's sole purpose in life was to seize the leadership of the People's Party. Any sensible person would have laughed off such obvious nonsense. It was clear to all the world that the leadership of the party was secure in the vanity bags of the Bhutto ladies, and even if, for the sake of argument, they were to say goodbye to politics, there could be no question of my becoming Party Chairman. That job was much bigger than I was. At that time, there were just seven or eight of us in Kabul. What leadership position was I going to grab from among this handful of men, Murtaza should have asked himself.

On 23 October 1980, I was put under arrest in a melodramatic scene. Murtaza's face was distorted with fear and nervousness. This was not the man I knew. He would have shot me dead, but he had not yet crossed over the psychological barrier that keeps most of us from taking a human life. He later told Qayyum Butt how much he regretted that, because of his lack of experience with murder, my life that evening had been spared.[2] (From then on, those who fell foul of him did not live to tell the tale.) After mulling over the situation for some hours, he finally had the Afghan government put me in prison to investigate the charges made against me. Keeping Murtaza's ego massaged was one of Najibullah's political tasks. Although it was not a crime under Afghan law to criticize Murtaza or the Bhutto family, he did not hesitate to jail me. The head of Afghan intelligence was so generous in such matters that thousands of Afghans were enjoying his hospitality without the legal formality of a trial.

On 24 October 1980, Murtaza had Shaukat Ali Rana also packed off to jail on the charge that he had criticized one of the press statements of Begum Nusrat Bhutto and called her a 'reactionary'. Murtaza accused him of criticizing the Bhutto family, and sentenced him to death. Rana was an old friend of mine, and by moving against him, Murtaza was trying to kill two birds with one stone. It was conveyed to him that if he testified against me, his death sentence would be commuted. Murtaza asked Najibullah to have him locked up in a separate cell where he was interrogated on a number of occasions by Tariq Islam and Sohail Sethi and told that he must testify against me. However, Rana was not prepared to perjure himself. One day Tariq Islam said to him: 'You know that your wife is a diabetic and she is expecting her first child. If you continue to resist, your wife will bear no child and you will lose your head too.' As soon as he had left, Rana went on a hunger strike and wrote out four demands on a piece of paper which he stuck on the wall of his cell. They were:

1. If it is a crime under the Afghan constitution to criticise the Bhutto family, I should be tried.
2. If I have committed no crime, I should be released.
3. If I cannot be released, my wife should be jailed with me.
4. If this is not possible, my wife's life should be guaranteed.

Rana's demands disconcerted Najibullah. Jail officials who had interrogated him also took the view that he should be released because he had told them that Murtaza wanted to blackmail him into testifying against Raja Anwar. Afghan officials now knew that Murtaza had not only had innocent comrades thrown in jail, but that his trusted lieutenants were visiting the facility to interrogate prisoners.

When Rana was jailed, his wife Fakhra was told that he and I had been sent to Jalalabad on an assignment. Now Murtaza told her that Rana wanted to marry a certain woman in Jalalabad. He then made her write a letter to her husband which was sent to Rana through Sohail Sethi. The letter begged her husband to carry out Murtaza's wishes and get home as fast as he could. This letter devastated Rana. Then, Fakhra's mounting anxiety affected her diabetes, and she grew ill. Finally she had to be taken to a hospital, where Murtaza told the doctor that she was married to a friend of his who was away from Kabul, and because she was diabetic it would not be safe for her to give birth. He claimed that her husband had told him on the phone that in order to save her life, the child she was carrying should be aborted.[3]

The Afghan doctors were mercifully not political pragmatists like Najibullah, and they told Murtaza that an abortion could only be performed if either the wife or the husband were to ask for it in writing. Next day, Murtaza brought along Shahnawaz, who signed the paper, posing as Shaukat Ali Rana. The Afghan doctors were suspicious and waited for Fakhra to come around, as she was having fainting spells. When they asked her what she wanted, she began to cry and told them the real story – not only had Murtaza probably had her husband killed by now, but he even wanted to destroy her unborn child.[4] Fakhra, though born in Lahore, came from a family that was originally Afghan and spoke fluent Persian as many Afghan families do – even those long settled abroad. The doctors called a meeting which even included some Russians, whom they asked to get Fakhra KGB protection.

Sensing the changed situation, Murtaza sent a letter to Fakhra inquiring about her health. That very evening, four policewomen arrived at the hospital and remained with Fakhra until her husband's release, which Murtaza was now forced to agree to.[5] He was reunited with his wife on 20 December 1980. (In January 1981, the couple was sent by Murtaza to Libya. Shaukat Ali Rana is still there. He has no Pakistani passport and has had two heart attacks. One of these days he may become one with the eternal sands of the great Sahara desert. Will posterity remember what his reward for his devotion to the Bhutto family was? The child that Murtaza wanted eliminated before its birth is a young man now. I saw him in 1986 and it brought tears to my eyes. It was by chance that he was alive. Fakhra put her hand on his head, and what she said about the Bhutto family is not for me to repeat.)

But let me return to Kabul's Pul-i-Charkhi prison where I was locked up. My adversary had failed to produce the incriminating tape, and Shaukat Ali Rana had refused to testify against me. The Afghan authorities were now satisfied that I was innocent and had decided to set me free. A decent man would have come to the jail, withdrawn his charges and admitted that he had made a mistake. Murtaza was not that kind of man: he could not admit that he had made a mistake. To his feudal way of thinking, my release with honour would be a personal defeat. He opposed my release and Najibullah went along with him because he wanted to keep on his right side. In any case, it was no loss to Najibullah. He could happily oblige Murtaza, if it was only a fellow countryman he wanted punished. So I was left to suffer in Pul-i-Charkhi, being ground down by both sides.

8

Drawing the Sword

By sending me to prison, Murtaza severed one of his last links with the traditional political process, and took a further step towards transforming himself into a warlord. With hindsight, it is clear that any appearance of democratic leadership or consultation had always been a sham. After Bhutto's hanging, a Murtaza seething with rage and determined at all costs to avenge his father's death arrived in Kabul in 1979 with a promise of PLO arms and no programme beyond causing harm to the rulers of Pakistan and any of their servants or associates. He wanted to do damage, and the more he was frustrated in that aim the more dangerous he became to anyone, friend or foe, who stood in his way.

If ruthlessness was the key to leadership, Murtaza would have made a notable leader. Unluckily for many of his followers, he was as ruthless with the lives of his own men as he was with those of his opponents, and quite uninhibited by his ignorance of any kind of warfare. The first recruit to return uncaptured to Pakistan and put Murtaza's planning into action was Lala Asad, a student from Karachi University. When he reached Kabul in November 1980 it pleased Murtaza that he was the first Sindhi to join him. He was billeted in Dracula House, still the headquarters for the troops, and one afternoon Murtaza arrived unannounced, parked himself on the veranda, and completed Lala Asad's commando training by lecturing him for thirty minutes on how a time bomb worked. There had been no arrangement for properly training the men. Murtaza had learnt a few stock phrases about weapons and their use which he intoned with great authority. He did not seem to realize or even care that he was asking his volunteers to risk their lives when the only skills they pitted against the formidable Pakistani state machine would be those that he himself provided. Little wonder that most of them did not survive their first serious encounter.

In January 1981, Lala Asad was sent to Pakistan, armed with no more than a few time bombs that looked like pieces of stone, the kind you might find lying by the roadside. The bombs had come from Afghan intelligence's counter-insurgency section. Lala Asad was assigned to place them at different points in Karachi. The first person he recruited on arrival was his cousin Lala Aslam. On 5 January, to mark Bhutto's birthday, the two cousins, plus a couple of their friends, set off one of the bombs in the Sind High Court. The next operation involved the destruction of a DC-10 aircraft, the property of Pakistan International Airlines (PIA), at Karachi airport on 15 January. Because of the strict censorship exercised by the martial law authorities, these incidents did not receive much media coverage, and this was unbearable for Murtaza, who wanted the people to know that he had declared war on the Pakistan army. He longed to stage something big and dramatic which would express his need for vengeance against the regime.

Such an opportunity presented itself in February with the announcement that Pope John Paul II was to visit Karachi. Murtaza sent word to Lala Asad that he should detonate a bomb during the Pope's address at the local stadium. What possible goodwill or benefit might derive from an attack on a religious personality like the Pope, only Murtaza knew. No doubt he did not think very far beyond the obvious fact that exploding a bomb in the Pope's public meeting would draw the attention of the international media to his cause. Since he would have liked to convince the world that as long as Zia-ul-Haq ruled Pakistan, the country should be considered an international pariah, he may have believed that it was Zia's Pakistan he would discredit.

It was 17 February 1981 when Lala Aslam arrived at the stadium, accompanied by two friends. The bomb was in a bag he was carrying. At the entrance, the security people asked him what he had in there. Nervously, he put his hand in the bag and triggered the mechanism by accident. A tremendous explosion killed Lala Aslam and a police officer on the spot, while two men standing close by were seriously injured. Lala Aslam was the first victim of Murtaza's blundering war. A photograph of the first martyr of the movement hung thereafter on Murtaza's wall. He knew how useful martyrs were in Pakistan's politics. But ever since coming to Kabul, he had been nursing a much more ambitious plan to focus world attention. Right from the start, he was convinced that he should stage a hijacking to further his cause – the most spectacular of all media events. The idea was in keeping with the reckless nature of youth, and in tune with the current revolutionary concept of struggle, which considered such methods normal and legitimate. In July 1979, only two months after his arrival in Kabul, Murtaza presented a plan to Asadullah Sarwari, then head of Afghan intelligence. The plan involved the hijacking of a PIA passenger aircraft from Istanbul to Kabul.

Although Sarwari was known for his adventurism, he offered a modification.

As it is, we are the principal target of American imperialism. If the PIA aircraft is brought to Kabul, it could create unimaginably grave consequences for us. However, let me suggest something. We will fly your men and arms to Istanbul on our own airline. You can hijack the plane from there and bring it to Damascus, Beirut or Tripoli. You have good relations with these Arab countries, and surely they will be helpful in every way.[1]

In other words, Sarwari was unwilling to see this dangerous game played out in his own backyard. There was also the possibility that the hijackers might be caught with their arms at Istanbul airport. Sarwari's response was intended to cover all bases. He wanted Murtaza to go ahead, but without burning Afghan fingers in the process.

While Murtaza was still weaving his dreams, President Taraki was overthrown and with him went Asadullah Sarwari. Power was now in the hands of Hafizullah Amin, who lost no time in appointing his nephew and son-in-law Asadullah Amin his chief of intelligence. Murtaza had barely established contact with the new man when – three months to the day after ousting Taraki – Amin was killed by the Soviet army on 27 December 1979, and Babrak Karmal installed in his place. The new chief of intelligence was Dr Najibullah. He too refused to host a hijack to Kabul, and before my arrest I did what I could to prolong his resistance. The Afghans would not play, and as yet he lacked a leader for the mission, but still the idea kept smouldering in Murtaza's mind. Five months before it actually took place, he told the *Sunday Times* of London: 'PIA is our first target. I appeal to the people not to use this airline.'[2] It should be added that at the insistence of the newspaper, he also wrote down this statement in his own hand.

This raises the question of why Murtaza should have confessed to a crime not yet committed? Why, in fact, did he publicly accept responsibility for every operation after September 1980? Since this was not usual behaviour, many analysts attributed such raw candour to Murtaza's immaturity and youth, but this can only be part of the explanation. After all, Murtaza had been living in Kabul since May 1979, and for a year and a half, he had made no public pronouncement on his hijack plans. Had it been immaturity that opened his mouth, it should have done so sooner. But there were other reasons that led him to accept full responsibility for every event and terrorist operation after September 1980.

It was Pakistan's domestic and strategic situation that brought about a dramatic change in Murtaza's thinking. While on the one hand the Red Army was practically knocking at Pakistan's northwestern door, Mrs Gandhi had returned to power in India. Given Pakistan's troubled relations with Moscow and New Delhi, General Zia's Afghan policy was bound to further alienate both countries. After the Soviet occupation of Afghanistan, Murtaza believed that it was only a matter of time before India or the Soviet Union would move decisively to settle their old scores with Pakistan and cut it down to size.

89

Murtaza had concluded that the Soviet occupation of Afghanistan was merely a first step towards reaching the warm waters of the Arabian Sea. The United States and its media had been propagating this baseless theory for years, with a view to creating a Red scare in the region and thus forcing Pakistan, Iran and the Gulf states to seek US protection.[3] Murtaza's background had endowed him with a boundless confidence in his new powers of judgement and command. Given his limited experience, partial education, and assumption that he knew all there was to know about international affairs, he decided that the Red Army could only reach the warm Gulf waters by marching through Pakistani Baluchistan and Sind. We had several sharp clashes, in which Murtaza insisted that the Red Army had not come all this way to camp across Pakistan's frontier at Torkham, but intended to move on down to the coast. He was convinced that the independence of Baluchistan and Sind was around the corner, and felt certain that while Pakistan's Northwest Frontier Province (NWFP) would be reabsorbed into Afghanistan, Punjab would be annexed by Mrs Gandhi.

In Murtaza's view, the United States, bloodied in the Vietnam conflict and powerless even to free its hostages in Tehran,[4] was now no better than a cripple. He was convinced that the international role of the United States was over once and for all, and that it would not risk a nuclear conflict for the sake of saving Pakistan. If the destruction of Pakistan was a foregone conclusion, it was only natural for him to reckon that he would never have to answer for the claims he was now making, least of all in Pakistan, which would cease to exist before long. Who would keep records of a nation in collapse? That was the euphoric mind-set that made him thump his chest and accept full responsibility for every single action and operation. The delusion persisted until the murder of Mrs Gandhi. In other words, the mask of valour that he wore from 1980 to 1984 resulted from his mistaken analysis of the situation. The idea of Sindhu Desh, a free Sind, on which basis he fought the 1993 election in Pakistan years later, also flowed from this tragic political and intellectual fallacy. Of course, he saw himself as the natural leader of a free Sind.

The political fallout of this wishful thinking also affected the Punjabi, Mohajir and Pushtun members of Al-Zulfikar, the new organization he was going to set up at the time of the PIA hijacking in 1981. These young men had arrived in Kabul to bring about a revolution in Pakistan. In Murtaza's view, Pakistan was already in its death-throes, so his non-Sindhi members could have no place in his dream state of independent Sind. His solution was to treat them with such lack of concern and compassion that most were either killed or ended up in torture cells. Those who survived, he labelled as agents of the Pakistan army and expelled them from Al-Zulfikar. These stateless political orphans could neither return to Pakistan nor travel anywhere else.[5] In the end, only Ehsan Bhatti and Sohail Sethi remained with him: one a Punjabi, the other a non-Pushtun resident of Peshawar. They both lived in Bangalore, India, until 1993 and returned to Pakistan when Murtaza did.

In November 1980, Salamullah Tipu sought refuge in Kabul after attempting to kill a Bhutto opponent in Karachi.[6] He was the man Murtaza had been waiting for – daring, streetwise, a proven killer, ready for anything. Murtaza knew him for what he was. Tipu stayed in Kabul for two months, and during this period the hijack plot was hammered out in detail between them. While the Afghans were willing to bear the financial costs of the operation, they still would not play host to the aircraft to be hijacked from Karachi. Murtaza therefore decided it should be flown to Damascus or Tripoli, which he believed were safe and hospitable. There is reason to assume that he had received the go-ahead from high-level quarters in both countries. Tipu assured Murtaza that he would himself recruit the two helpers he would need as soon as he returned to Karachi. He was confident that he would be able to find enough loopholes in the security systems at the Pakistani airport to smuggle the arms required for the hijacking.

After finalizing every detail, Tipu began his journey back to Pakistan in the first week of January 1981, crossing the Afghan border at Kurrum Agency. Ironically, though he had escaped to Kabul to save his life, his desperate bid now took him back to the same city of Karachi where he was wanted by the police. He had taken no money from Murtaza for this mission. Instead, soon after his arrival in Karachi, he carried out two robberies, which raised all the cash he expected to need. Who can say if it was the adventurist streak in Tipu's character or his fatal devotion to the Bhutto family that were uppermost in his mind when he took these enormous risks?

Who were the fellow hijackers he recruited, and how did he find them? One of them was Nasir Jamal, a student at Karachi University. In May 1983, after my release from prison, he told me:

> On 25 February 1981, I was appointed president of the PSF in Karachi. I was introduced to Miss Benazir Bhutto by Masroor Ashen [later a PPP member of the Senate], and it was at his recommendation that this office was given to me. It was a wonderful political opportunity so it was my ill luck that on 26 February 1981 there was a clash outside Karachi University between members of the PSF and the Islami Jamiat-i-Tuleba (IJT). There was firing from both sides and one IJT worker was killed. Although I was not responsible for it, my name along with the names of six of our members was listed among the accused. The charge was murder. Under instructions from the local martial law authorities, the police began raiding different places

in an attempt to arrest us. I knew that if I was picked up, I would be executed. It was also clear to me that I would neither be able to return to the campus nor complete my education. The only chance of my survival was immediate escape from Pakistan to another country. Then I heard that Tipu was in town from Kabul looking for volunteers. He was distantly related to me, and when we met he immediately took me in confidence about the hijacking. At first I refused, but after the 26 February incident, I suppose I had to take a chance by joining him. That was the only way I felt I could get out of Pakistan. Had certain death not been staring me in the face, I would never have passed within miles of this quixotic idea of his.

When Nasir Jamal spoke to me, he was already rid of the illusion of Murtaza's revolutionary struggle. He had realized that the head of Al-Zulfikar had used him and others with merciless cynicism and then dumped them like so much rubbish. When I met him, he appeared to have embarked on a long journey of regret over his past actions. However, even then he was perhaps not capable of believing that in return for all that they had done for Murtaza, Tipu would be shot, and he himself imprisoned in a foreign land.[7]

The third hijacker, Arshad Ali Khan Tegi, I first met in 1986 in Tripoli, Libya, where he was living, recently married to a Pakistani girl. He was one of Tipu's childhood friends, but it was a union of opposites, because there was no similarity in their characters and temperament. He was one of those people who can never make up their minds and whose indecisiveness will often get them used by others. Tipu told me in Kabul:

> We not only hijacked the aircraft but we also hijacked Bhai [he always called Tegi Bhai, or brother]. He had not realized until we were at the airport that we were going to hijack him too. He wanted to say goodbye to us and then return to work. He was even carrying his lunch-box with him.

Tegi worked at the Karachi steel mills, and it is ironic that an apolitical young man like him turned out to be Tipu's ideal companion. When he returned from Kabul to set the stage for the hijacking, Tipu stayed at his house. It was through Tegi that he was able to recruit Nasir Baloch, a bus driver at the steel works. Throughout, in fact, Tipu used him in a most heartless way. In Tegi's words:

> I have never had anything to do with politics. That idiot Tipu it was who dragged me into this hell. Even during the hijacking, I was not sure if Al-Zulfikar was an organization or a literary name Murtaza had

taken. After the hijacking when we met Murtaza, I told him that since I had no interest in politics and was just a simple working man, I should be sent to a country where I could get a job and earn a living. One month after the hijacking, I was shipped to Libya, where I have been working since. I never took part in the activities of Al-Zulfikar. I was such an unknown that even after the hijacking, the government of Pakistan did not know who the third hijacker was. When we released the aircraft at Damascus airport, my face also appeared on Pakistan television. When my father saw me, he ran to the Deputy Inspector-General of Police in Karachi and told him that the third hijacker was his son who was completely non-political and he simply could not believe that he had anything to do with the hijacking. However, since my father had identified me, the police registered a case against me.

One meeting with Tegi and it was clear to me that his role in the thirteen-day hijacking could only have been secondary. His non-aggressive manner was noticed by the passengers of that unfortunate aircraft too. According to my investigation there was no case registered against him before the hijacking, but later on he was accused of having snatched guns from policemen on duty. The summary military court which heard this case in 1982 in absentia awarded Tegi a year's imprisonment and fifteen lashes. To return to Tipu, he got down to work in earnest as soon as he arrived in Karachi. Those who helped him, and who later suffered arrest and severe punishment, were Nasir Baloch, who was hanged, Malik Ayub, pawnbroker, and Saifullah Khalid, student, both sentenced to fourteen years, Allah Bakhsh, grave digger, and Muhammad Isa. What punishment the last two received I have been unable to ascertain. Tipu recalled:

Someone told me that Irshad Rao, a well-known journalist who knew me and whom I had met once, was laid up in hospital with a stomach ailment. Although it was not safe for me to venture out, I decided to go and see him. Rao was so taken aback at seeing me that his colour changed. He raised his eyebrows to ask what I was doing there. I bent over him and said: 'I was told that you had a stomach ulcer which had burst and I felt that I must look you up.' Rao turned on his side, and it was quite clear that he was in much pain, but he managed to keep his sense of humour: 'Not so far, but now that I have seen you, there can be no doubt that my ulcer will start bleeding.'

Why did Tipu who knew Rao neither for long nor very well, take the risk of visiting a public hospital to see him? Tipu's was a shallow but impetuous personality. He resented his inferior status and was ready to trade it for notoriety. After his return from Kabul, he came to see himself not as a useless, unemployed nonentity, but as a certified revolutionary. He was in no doubt that he had taken the first decisive step towards a brilliant political career. In particular, he felt confident that after the hijacking, he would begin to be seen as a virtual member of the Bhutto family. That being so, it was a good idea to get to know important journalists like Irshad Rao who would soon be writing his profile and recording his interviews for their papers.

When I met Tipu in Kabul in May 1983, he was so full of himself that he kept assuring me that the people of Pakistan worshipped him like a hero, and that whenever he ran for parliament from Karachi he would win by a landslide. While Tipu did not live to try his chances, his leader Murtaza did, and was equally convinced that he would sweep the board in the 1993 elections. The results brought his dream to the ground. It is one of the tragedies of Al-Zulfikar that its leaders and adherents were unable to draw a line between the ballot and the bullet.

9

The Hijack to Kabul

In Karachi, Tipu's plans were underway. It was useful that the incident of 26 February 1981 at Karachi University had forced Nasir Jamal to join him. At 1 pm of 2 March he made three separate reservations in the names of Nasir Baloch, Malik Ayub and Saifullah Khalid on a PIA flight leaving Karachi for Peshawar.[1] That day he rode to Karachi airport in a Pakistan Steel Mills bus with Nasir Jamal and Arshad Ali Khan Tegi. The police and security personnel on duty at the airport had no way of knowing that the familiar-looking bus parked around the corner contained three men who were soon going to commit the most dramatic crime in Pakistan's history. The hijackers on their part were assailed by last-minute fears. Would some policeman recognize them? Would they be able to board without being caught with the weapons? When they walked into the terminal, they were mortified to hear that the flight had been delayed for two hours by a technical problem. Their suspense had been prolonged.

Tipu, who had not yet told Tegi that he planned to make him part of the hijack team, now said to him: 'Why don't you come with us as far as Peshawar? You could leave the aircraft with some of the other passengers and no one will ever know that you were with us. We will take over the plane afterwards.' Tipu's purpose in bringing Tegi along was to use him as the patsy to prevent their being caught at Karachi airport with the arms that Tegi was carrying. By the time the police got the truth out of Tegi, Tipu was sure he would be in Kabul. Tegi was taken in once again. He failed to see that there was no way he could get off the plane at Peshawar because if it was to be hijacked, it was going to be hijacked in the air, along with all its passengers. He could not have realized that by agreeing to Tipu's suggestion, he was cutting himself off from normal life for years to come. There is no shortage of people willing to be fooled, nor of the means to fool them easily. Tegi was fooled by Tipu, Tipu by Murtaza and Murtaza by his ambition to become a leader.

By one of those accidents that so often prove decisive, that day the baggage and passenger X-ray unit at Karachi airport was out of order and the three got through without any difficulty to join the hundred and fifty passengers who walked towards the green and white PIA plane. One of those passengers was Tariq Rahim, his eyes still swollen because he had been crying at the sudden death of his father. It was this tragedy which had brought him to Pakistan from Tehran, where he was serving as first secretary at the Pakistan embassy. One of his fellow passengers was also his assassin-to-be. Once he had boarded the plane, his feet would never touch Pakistan's soil again.

Minutes after the plane became airborne, it suffered a bird strike but luckily for the hijackers there was no damage and the flight continued. As it reached cruising altitude, Tipu became obsessed with the thought that there were plain-clothes commandos on board who would blow his brains out the moment he made his move. His first hour in flight was spent in a state of acute anxiety. However, as the plane flew over Mianwali he informed his companions that they should now address him by his code-name, Alamgir. Nasir Jamal was Siraj and Arshad Tegi was Khalid. As soon as he rose to go towards the cockpit, they were to take their positions. A few minutes later Tipu got up and walked forward. He entered the cockpit without any difficulty.

According to Tipu's account, he opened the door of the cockpit and announced: 'This aircraft is now under my command, and if anyone makes a threatening move I'll shoot him dead. I want the plane flown to Damascus.' The startled but very calm captain answered that he did not have enough fuel. 'Then take it to Tripoli,' Tipu ordered, but the captain informed him that Tripoli was even farther than Damascus. Tipu told the me later: 'I was left with no alternative but to go to Kabul.' Had Tipu known any basic geography, he would have hijacked the plane as soon as it took off from Karachi because Syria was closer from that point. It was probably his first air journey. That explains why the plane was taken to Kabul and not Damascus as Murtaza had ordered.

Tipu landed in Kabul because the aircraft was running short of fuel, but what was it that induced the authorities in Kabul to change their minds and play host? Not only did this reckless step expose the Afghans to massive international criticism and pressure, but later it cost them heavy financial losses.

As the plane began to taxi, Tipu informed the control tower that he was connected with the Pakistan People's Party and wished to make immediate contact with Dr Salahuddin – Murtaza's code name. Najibullah was immediately informed. He phoned Murtaza, who was taken aback by the unexpected arrival of an aircraft intended to be taken to Damascus. He told Najibullah that he had issued no orders to bring the plane to Kabul. Before he could say whether they were his men or not he would have to meet the hijackers. Murtaza was actually unsure whether it was Tipu he would meet at the airport or someone he did not know.

96

Tipu meanwhile had already issued a statement declaring that he represented the armed wing of the Pakistan People's Party, the People's Liberation Army, which was determined to avenge Bhutto's blood and spread Bhuttoism. The hijack was aimed at the restoration of democracy in Pakistan and the release of all political prisoners.[2] Tipu's statement was played big by the Afghan media and picked up worldwide. It took Murtaza three days to shift the spotlight from the PPP to Al-Zulfikar, which until then had not even been a paper organization.

When the hijacked PIA plane reached Kabul, I had been in prison for four and a half months and could only catch glimpses of the ongoing drama on Afghan television. The way the Afghan media played the hijacking gave the impression that this single event had shaken Pakistan to its foundations. It was beyond my comprehension that the Afghan government should have permitted Murtaza to use Kabul airport. Confined as I was, I began to think that perhaps international politics had undergone a radical change since I had been put away. Perhaps the Soviet Union wanted to use this provocative act as a springboard to invade Pakistan. Could Murtaza have been right all along? What was it that led to the murder of Tariq Rahim, and what role did the Soviet advisers in Kabul play in the hijacking? These were questions I wanted answered once I was out of prison.

It was two years since the hijacking and I had a feeling that the Afghans would be prepared to talk about it with less reserve than previously. They felt bitter about their former honoured guest now living at ease in Delhi, totally unconcerned with what they had had to go through on his account. The boycott of Afghanistan by international airlines in response to the hijacking had started to bite, and by 1983, it did not need much effort on my part to make various Afghan officials open up about Murtaza and help me assemble a composite view of what happened.

On 2 March 1981, when the PIA plane landed in Kabul, the twenty-sixth Communist Party Congress was in session in Moscow. This was a major occasion for the internal politics of the Soviet Communist Party, since it only took place every four years and was attended by observers from ninety communist parties from around the world. It also marked the holding of elections to the post of Communist Party General Secretary and membership of the Politburo and the Central Committee. Political leverage and survival within the Soviet and communist system required attendance at the Congress. All key Soviet and KGB officials based in Afghanistan had therefore flown to Moscow. No one of consequence, from Red Army general to political commissar, was present in Kabul. Babrak Karmal too was absent as leader of the Afghan observer delegation, leaving behind him Dr Najibullah, the head of Afghan intelligence, as acting head of the administration. When the plane entered Afghan air space and its captain asked permission to land at Kabul, the Russian adviser posted at the airport was a captain and the Afghan officer in charge was a Colonel Asmat.[3] They cleared it for landing without asking too many questions.

Back in Kabul, at 10 pm that same day, Najibullah and Murtaza, both dressed as commandos, arrived at the airport to meet the hijackers. They had come late so as not to be noticed during Kabul's customary night curfew. They spoke to Tipu from the control tower and asked him to step down from the aircraft and wait for them under the tail section. This is how Tipu described it to me:

> I did as I was told, and soon Murtaza and Najibullah appeared. This was the first time I had met the Afghan intelligence chief. I came smartly to attention and saluted Murtaza and offered him my congrat-ulations on the success of the operation. Spontaneously, he threw his arms around me and kissed my forehead. Then he asked: 'Why have you brought the plane here and not to Damascus or Tripoli as ordered?' I answered that there wasn't enough fuel. He then instructed me to check the papers and travel documents of all passengers. Still standing at attention, I replied: 'Sir, I have already done that. There are five Europeans and seven Afghan refugees. There is also a Pakistani military officer by the name of Major Tariq Rahim, son of General Rahim. He is carrying a Pakistani diplomatic passport and is currently posted as first secretary at the Pakistan embassy in Tehran.' Murtaza slapped me on the back and said to Najibullah, 'It seems we've netted a big fish. Surely, this man is the son of General Rahim, Zia's right-hand man [Murtaza had confused Tariq's father with Gen. Rahimud-din]. Good, now we have that butcher Zia where we want him.' He told me to isolate Rahim from the other passengers. He also told me in press statements not to mention the name of the Pakistan People's Party again.

Tipu told me that, in order to impress Najibullah, he remained at attention all through the meeting. Najibullah did not know that inside the aircraft as they spoke was a 'commando' who was holding a gun for the first time in his life. To impress the passengers with the disciplined military character of hijackers, Tipu had instructed Nasir Jamal and Arshad Tegi to address him as sir. What he had lost when expelled from the Pakistan Military Academy, he was now trying to regain at Kabul airport. Even after it was all over, Tipu would always come to attention when Murtaza appeared and salute him in military style.

In the past, Najibullah had thought little of Murtaza and would often refer to him derisively. Now everything had changed. He looked at the young Bhutto with undisguised admiration and said: 'Now that the plane is here, why take it to Damascus or Tripoli? As for the senior comrades, I know how to deal with them.' Najibullah, who had been educated at Peshawar, then said to Tipu in Urdu: 'Let me have the names of the Afghan renegades. It's possible that they include one of the big shots we have been trying to catch.' The names were duly passed on to the Afghan spy chief but, to his disappointment, none of them was on his 'wanted' list. Najibullah's reference to 'senior comrades' meant Soviet advisers, who ran everything. It was their absence that had encouraged him to give a welcome to the hijackers. Najibullah must have thought it would strengthen his position if he could take credit for the hijack and claim Tipu as one of his boys.

The hijack was unique in the sense that it was not staged to achieve a specific objective or satisfy a set of demands. That alone proves that Murtaza wanted violence for its own sake – a brick through Zia's window. The plane was hijacked first: demands were thought up later, when he asked for the restoration of civil liberties and release of political prisoners. It is a revealing irony that Murtaza had no list of the prisoners he wanted released from Pakistani jails. Actually, he did not himself know a single political prisoner, and never took much interest in such details. When the government of Pakistan asked for names, he could only offer five, all of them students picked up by the police after the Karachi University incident of 26 February, and whose names had been provided by Nasir Jamal. As for his demands, they were as old as Pakistan itself, the whole history of political struggle in the Islamic republic had consisted of efforts made since 1947 for fundamental rights and civil liberties. These demands were neither new, nor so immediately urgent as to require a hijacking.

It was also ironic that Murtaza's first demand – restoration of civil liberties – would have counted as an 'imperialist conspiracy' if made in Kabul or Damascus. It was only natural, therefore, that both countries played down this aspect of the hijack for fear that it might give the Afghan and Syrian people ideas. The same part of the story was also blacked out in Pakistan by Zia's information machine. At a special press briefing, General Rahimuddin, who was in charge of the Defence Ministry, claimed that no demand for the restoration of democracy and civil liberties had been made by the hijackers, and such reports had only been spread by the anti-Pakistan foreign media.[4]

Murtaza was being pressed for details, and after much running around and frantic calls here and there, three lists were prepared. The first contained forty-nine names, and was based on what the Kabul-based workers of the PPP knew or believed they knew. This was handed over to Tipu, who communicated it to the Pakistani negotiating team. Meanwhile, to augment the list and oblige other exiled political groups, Murtaza asked for more names. By the time this exercise was completed, the total number had risen to sixty-nine. On 5 March, this revised list was given to the Pakistani team led by the director of the country's Civil Aviation Authority. The next day, more names were supplied by Murtaza. These additions represented the jailed members and workers of the pro-Moscow groups based in Pakistan, taking the total to ninety-two. Ten of the names had been supplied by the Pushtun nationalist leader, Ajmal Khattak, who was living in self-imposed exile in Kabul. Included were the names of Hamid Baloch from Baluchistan and Jam Saqi, the Sindhi nationalist. Khattak was a member of the central committee of the Communist Party in Pakistan, which was led by Nazish Ali, one of the oldest communists in Pakistan who has had the singular honour of remaining 'underground' all his life. I do not know whether, after the fall of Moscow, he also followed the example of Ajmal Khattak and went to Mecca to seek divine forgiveness for his sins, or whether he now lives in some far corner of the former Soviet Union ruminating on the past. In the end, there were four lists.

It was the hijack that brought Al-Zulfikar into being.

(Al-Zulfikar, by the way, was the title of a pamphlet written in August 1980, before my arrest, by Shaukat Ali. This pamphlet was an attack on General Zia and was to be distributed in Pakistan. In other words, Al-Zulfikar had no existence before the hijack: it was named on the spot by Murtaza from a pamphlet. Thus, it was not Al-Zulfikar that hijacked the aircraft, but the hijack that created Al-Zulfikar. The baby had preceded the mother.)

For the first two days, it was the People's Liberation Army in whose name Tipu spoke and issued statements, adding always that it was the armed wing of the Pakistan People's Party. Because of this, the publicity came to focus upon the PPP and the Bhutto ladies, Nusrat and Benazir. For Murtaza, the hijack was a great revolutionary achievement whose credit he would not assign to his mother or sister. He wanted to be the sole claimant to the fame he had in store. Murtaza was temperamentally incapable of conceding even a fraction of what he thought was his by right. To him the plane parked at Kabul airport was a symbol of his power, the fulfilment of his dreams and the starting-point of a revolutionary career. He had instructed Tipu to give all credit for the hijacking to Al-Zulfikar. All future statements must declare that Murtaza Bhutto was the organization's revolutionary leader and general secretary – a title he chose as a gesture to the Soviets in preference to the Chinese practice of calling the head of their Communist Party the chairman.

To trumpet the past achievements of Al-Zulfikar, Murtaza proudly accepted responsibility for the earlier attacks led by Lala Asad – the bomb blast at the Karachi High Court, the destruction of a DC-10 at Karachi airport, and the bungled bombing of Pope John Paul's rally in Karachi. By making these claims, Murtaza wanted to create the impression that Zia's law and order regime in Pakistan was based on force and fear, and that his men were everywhere. He also wished to please the Soviets, who believed that the Pope was behind the formation of Solidarity in Poland in September 1980.

Not only did Murtaza invent an organization as he stood beneath the tail of the hijacked Pakistani aircraft, he also acquired the services of a spokesman identified only as Wolf, whose daily briefings began to be provided to London and Delhi papers. In a few days, the name became well known. The Pakistani intelligence agencies opened dossiers on this unidentified spokesman of Al-Zulfikar. Even today, there must be cases waiting to be heard in Pakistani courts against Wolf. Few people know that Wolf was the name of Murtaza's specially imported Alsatian. Murtaza was fond of saying: 'Don't call him a dog. He is a founding member of our revolution.' When I heard the name Wolf in Afghan TV broadcasts in my Kabul jail, I felt sorry for Murtaza. Najibullah only found out after the hijacking ended who Wolf was, and forbade the use of his name.

Wolf was no ordinary dog. He was treated like a prince, and one of Murtaza's close companions, Sardar Salim, had the honour and duty of bathing him regularly. His quarters were far more luxurious than the hovels in which the majority of the people in Asian countries are forced to live out their lives. In 1980, Wolf got lost, and so distraught was Murtaza that he rushed to Najibullah and asked him to use his intelligence apparatus to find the dog. However, Wolf returned on his own three days later. From that day on, Najibullah and his staff began to refer to Murtaza as Khwaja Sag Prasat, a character in the *Arabian Nights* who prefers the company of his dog to that of human beings. One of Najib's deputies, Farooq Yaqubi, asked me:

> What kind of a man is this son of your leader? In Afghanistan, a man who can get a meal a day considers himself lucky; and here is this fellow who has servants tending to his dog. There is a war on. Men disappear every day and no one even bothers to go looking for them. And here he is, asking us to find his dog! Can a man like that bring a revolution?[5]

Tipu and his companions had taken over the aircraft with the help of revolvers, but one day after their arrival in Kabul they were equipped with state of the art close-combat weapons. This hardware had been supplied at Tipu's request by Murtaza and Najibullah. Recalling that moment, Tipu told me:

> Because I was a former army cadet, I had some idea about the use and type of light weapons. In any case, what I did not know, Murtaza

101

explained to me, such as the locking and firing systems, when we conferred under one of the wings of the aircraft on the first day. However, Nasir Jamal and Arshad had never seen such weapons in their lives. I had set up my 'revolutionary command office' in the first class section of the aircraft and I asked them in one by one and tried to explain to them, at least in theory, how these weapons worked, but I could not get very far. I wasn't sure what they would do if it came to using them.

We seldom learn from history until it is too late to profit from the lesson. It is ironic to think, for example, that three years after Tipu received those weapons from Murtaza and Najibullah that night, he would be shot dead in that very city, at the orders of the men who had armed him. It did not occur to Murtaza that his actions might force him into many years of exile or that one day he would have to ask pardon from the same Pakistan Army against which he was now taking up arms. Could he have believed that one day he would publicly dissociate himself from the hijacking itself, disowning it completely?

Tipu told me that on Murtaza's instructions he announced to the passengers that they would soon be addressed by Murtaza in person. It was only when Najibullah vetoed the idea that the address was called off. However, in order to heighten the revolutionary sentiments of the passengers, Murtaza gave a couple of audio cassettes to Tipu, who recalled:

> I can't express to you what effect these 'revolutionary songs' had on the passengers. Forget the passengers, I myself developed a headache after listening to them. In all my life, I've never heard such crude, unmusical, off-beat, mindless drivel. All of us had to undergo this tuneless torture day after day. At the end of the hijacking I asked Murtaza where these cassettes had come from, but he avoided an answer.

Tipu did not know that the singer, composer, lyricist and musical arranger of these 'revolutionary songs' was none other than Shahnawaz, Murtaza's younger brother. This young man had two hobbies: exercise, and rehashing Indian film songs and then singing them in a flat voice while drumming on the table. His creative efforts were free from the discipline of normal poetical compositions. For instance, one of the songs which he had based on an old Indian film number ran like this (only the original words can convey its numb absurdity):

> *Fauj se tum na ghabraya karo*
> *Balke bandooq le ke pahar par churr jaya karo.*

(Fear not the army.
Just pick up your gun and run up the mountain.)

With the utmost seriousness, Shahnawaz had recorded a number of cassettes of these jingles, all of which I had had to suffer many times before my imprisonment. Since this handsome youth had earlier suffered a nervous breakdown, it had always been my intention not to cause him the least emotional disturbance. One day, I had suggested to him that after asking some accomplished poet to make what revisions he considered necessary, we could have these numbers properly recorded by some known Afghan singer. Shahnawaz loved the idea. In August 1980, he, Tariq Islam (his cousin, who was known as T.I.) and I went to meet the Afghan singer Fauzia, who agreed to sing them for a small fee. The following month, Shahnawaz and I went on a tour of Europe. On 23 October 1980, three days after our return as mentioned earlier, I was arrested and sent to jail, and thus the recording project remained unimplemented.

Forty-eight hours after the plane landed in Kabul, as a show of their humanitarian instincts, the hijackers ordered that the women and children were to be released. According to Tipu, Murtaza told him:

The Afghan government has come under severe criticism because of its support for the hijackers and wants the women and children set free in response to its appeal, so that the imperialist press can be silenced. Tomorrow, one of the Afghan ministers will make an appeal to you from the control tower which you are to accept.

Tipu wanted to go one better. As he explained to me,

I thought the women and children are going to be released anyway, so why shouldn't I let the head of the Pakistani negotiators' team claim this credit? Accordingly, I told him that in order to show my good will, I was prepared to release the women and children, but in response the Pakistan government would have to put an end to its propaganda barrage against the hijackers. The leader of the team, who saw it as an advance on the situation, promised to convey my offer to the authorities back home.

According to the prearranged programme, the Afghan Minister for Education and President of the Afghan–Soviet Friendship Association, Anahita Ratebzadeh, went into the airport control tower on 4 March, which happened to be International Women's Day, surrounded by TV cameras. After expressing sympathy with the 'just demands' of the hijackers, she asked them in a poignant voice to release the women and children in honour of the special nature of the day being celebrated worldwide. Tipu, like a well-behaved and respectful child, replied that he would be happy to do so. I saw this drama taking place on TV in the Pul-i-Charkhi prison. At the very moment when the Afghan minister was speaking of respect for women and children, eight women and six innocent children from the family of the deposed President of the country, Hafizullah Amin, were in the same jail as I and had been there for a year and a half. One of the children was only eighteen months old.[6]

And what was the situation in Pakistan? Until he rid himself of Zulfikar Ali Bhutto, General Zia-ul-Haq kept the right-wing parties as partners in government. As soon as his formidable rival was dead and buried, he threw these men out of the ministries they held, declared all political parties defunct, and ruled out the possibility of general elections. To consolidate his power, General Zia pulled out the magic casket of Islam from his bag of tricks and declared that his sole objective was the 'implementation' of Islam in Pakistan. To get even with Zia, the rightist parties, though nursing bitter memories of their treatment at the hands of Bhutto, decided to join hands with the PPP leadership to revive democracy. The multi-party alliance chose to call itself the Movement for the Restoration of Democracy (MRD). Public support was warm and spontaneous. Then, just as the campaign was starting to gather momentum, Murtaza Bhutto hijacked the PIA plane in the name of 'the restoration of democracy'. By issuing a statement in favour of the hijackers, Begum Bhutto only helped put brakes on the movement against Zia that was growing in strength and popularity every day. Ironically, both Murtaza and his mother thus equipped Zia with a weapon which he immediately used to smother the MRD. For the General, the hijack was to remain like a gift from heaven for several years. Incidentally, when the hijack took place, General Zia was in Saudi Arabia for 'spiritual' reasons, having earlier announced that he would soon nominate an 'Islamic' cabinet.

When the head of the Pakistani negotiating team sent to Kabul turned out to be the country's director of civil aviation, Murtaza took it as an insult and instructed Tipu to harden his attitude. For Tipu, even a hint from Murtaza was sufficient. After giving the Pakistani negotiator the rough edge of his tongue he told him to get somebody with the authority to take decisions. In Murtaza's eyes, that person might be one of the three or four generals close to Zia. He was in a state of runaway excitement at the time, and behaved as if what he had hijacked was not an aircraft but General Zia-ul-Haq himself. The military government, contrary to Murtaza's wishes, now nominated a joint secretary of the Ministry of Foreign Affairs as head of the negotiating team. The Pakistanis wanted face-to-face talks with the hijackers, but Murtaza and Najibullah ruled that out. The hijackers now set 5 pm on 5 March 1981 as the deadline for meeting their demands. Otherwise they would start to execute passengers.

Meanwhile, General Zia, back from Saudi Arabia, rejected out of hand even such a minor demand as the release of political prisoners. He was giving Murtaza time to walk into his own trap. If Murtaza went ahead and killed one innocent Pakistani passenger for every twenty-four hours that the General did not meet his naive demand, he could not make a better gift to the dictator. If Murtaza released them without his demands being accepted, it would be proclaimed in Pakistan as proof of Zia-ul-Haq's iron will. Murtaza did not appear to be aware of his precarious situation: he could not see that all the paths of retreat were closing on him. From now on, the game would be played according to the General's rules.

Zia was keeping his cool. It was clear that the deadline would pass and an innocent man be condemned. By now, Najibullah had become party to the drama, but before things came to a head, he wanted insurance: he wanted Babrak Karmal in the capital. If something should backfire, he did not wish to bear the sole responsibility and have to answer to the Soviet advisers. An urgent message was sent to Karmal in Moscow to return immediately.

At 2 pm on 5 March, Karmal landed at Kabul and drove straight to the control tower where Afghan TV cameras were already in position. From the tower, he directly addressed Tipu, and while strongly supporting his 'just demands', asked him to extend his deadline by twenty-four hours. The way Karmal spoke seemed to suggest that, like Najibullah, he too believed that Tariq Rahim was a close relation of General Zia-ul-Haq. While Murtaza had come to know that it was not so, he was continuing to assure Najibullah that in Tariq Rahim they had one of Zia's key men.[7] He felt that if he confessed to the Afghans that he had misled them or made a mistake, it would play havoc with his image as leader. Justice came second to vanity. Tariq Rahim must die to prove Murtaza right.

The conversation between Karmal and Tipu was being broadcast live. A road-runner like Tipu, who had spent much of his adult life being chased by police, could not in his wildest dreams have imagined that one day a head of state (let alone Babrak Karmal) would be speaking to him directly, and that this exchange would be beamed around the world. Unable to deal with the enormity of the occasion, the hijacker began to stutter. His responses were barely intelligible. In a trembling voice, he declared that Karmal was the greatest man in Asia, and stammered that he would extend the deadline by twenty-four hours, as asked.

How you receive and understand a piece of information or news often depends on the circumstances in which it is presented. If circumstances change, so does the meaning and perception of what you see or hear. Had I heard the exchange between Karmal and Tipu in a normal environment,

I might not have been conscious of the irony of history that was its backdrop. At the very moment when Karmal was talking so movingly about political prisoners in Pakistan, his own jails were packed with thousands of his countrymen whom he had locked up without any legal trial. While Karmal was bewailing the lot of the poor in Pakistan, General Zia was shedding tears over the privations of the Afghan masses. Both men had set up kangaroo courts to deal with their political opponents. In both countries, the mere mention of human rights amounted to treason. One was smothering the people in the name of socialism, the other in the name of Islam. One was in power by virtue of Soviet tanks, the other, by courtesy of American dollars. In a few years' time both men would be disowned by their one-time patrons.

Meanwhile Tariq Rahim, who had been declared a 'big fish' on day one and separated from the other passengers, sat alone brooding over his fate. I questioned the hijackers about it.

In the beginning, you thought he was the son of General Rahimuddin, Zia's close confidant and relative. When you discovered that he was actually one of Zulfikar Ali Bhutto's former ADCs, who was travelling from Iran to Pakistan to attend his father's burial, what was your reaction?

Tipu replied:

At first, Tariq Rahim kept very quiet but when I announced that the aircraft had been hijacked on Murtaza Bhutto's orders, he took out a pen, scribbled a note on a newspaper, handed it to Nasir Jamal and requested him to have it taken to 'Mir Baba' [Murtaza's pet name]. That evening, I passed on the message to Murtaza who told me: 'The night the army staged the coup, we were told that Tariq Rahim was part of the conspiracy, and this confirms it. Had he not been a traitor, the General would have imprisoned him instead of putting him in the foreign service. Don't believe a word of what he says. He is using his father's death as an excuse to save his life. His father must be the martial law administrator of some area in Pakistan even today. Remember the army is only loyal to the army. General Zia was supposed to be loyal to us, but look what happened! This Tariq Rahim is loyal to us in exactly the same way. He should be taught a lesson for his treachery to the Shaheed ['the Martyr' which is how Zulfikar Ali Bhutto was referred to].'

A sick-minded young man like Tipu, who knew that he had Murtaza's full support and free to use the arms he was carrying was bound to act brutally towards the terrified and defenceless people that fate had placed at his mercy. By the time it was all over, every passenger on that flight had had a taste of Tipu's cruelty.

Tipu summoned Tariq Rahim to his 'revolutionary command office' and asked him if he had been the Martyr Bhutto's ADC. When Tariq answered hopefully that he had, Tipu slapped him across the face and screamed: 'Why didn't you say so earlier so that I could have started giving you the treatment you deserve straight away?' Then in harsh, abusive language he denounced his prisoner as a traitor and as Zia's agent. He also pulled out his gun and put it to Tariq's temple, making as if to shoot him. I asked Tipu what Tariq's reaction was when he did that. He told me that Tariq had taken it all very quietly. He did not seem quite to take in what was happening to him. The plane's captain requested Tipu not to kill Tariq. 'As far as I was concerned, I was showing him a sample of what was to come,' Tipu said. After this 'interview', Tariq Rahim was sent back to his solitary corner.

On the morning of 3 March, Tariq Rahim had been isolated by Tipu and it was announced that he was to have been executed on 5 March, but due to Babrak Karmal's intervention, his life had been extended by twenty-four hours. It was Tariq's misfortune that in General Zia's eyes, he was a Bhutto man, and to Murtaza, an agent of the regime. Thus he was neither Zia's responsibility, nor could he expect any mercy from Murtaza. Death was crawling towards Tariq as Tipu's twenty-four-hour extension began to tick away. If there is anything more terrible than death, it is the anticipation of death. People have been known to commit suicide rather than wait. We can imagine what went through Tariq's mind as the hours passed. He must have thought of Zulfikar Ali Bhutto, a man for whom he had almost got himself killed once. He knew Murtaza and Shahnawaz well, and he must have wondered why they should want him killed. An hour before his death, he wrote his fifteenth and last letter to Murtaza:

Dear Murtaza and Shahnawaz,
    As I have said in my earlier letters, I am your late father's ADC Tariq Rahim. Both of you know me well. It is a happy coincidence that you are in Kabul. Please tell the hijackers who I am.
    I have already told you of the personal tragedy that has befallen me. A few days ago, I lost my father. I came to Pakistan to bury him. You can imagine how depressed I feel. I have no doubt you will do your best to save me from this catastrophe.
With best wishes,
Tariq Rahim

He handed over this letter, written on the margin of a newspaper page, to Nasir Jamal. His earlier letters were also worded more or less similarly.

After the first two, Murtaza instructed Tipu to tear up such 'rubbish' on receipt. Tariq was at the mercy of an uncaring, unseeing fate where nothing meant anything. The human response for the Bhutto brothers would have been to condole with Tariq when told of his father's death, but such customs are only followed by ordinary people. The Bhutto brothers, scions of the ruling classes, raised on different lullabies, had no time for such sentimentalism, nor did it matter to them whether the Tariq Rahims of the world lived or died.

The evening of 6 March approached and with it death. Tipu scanned the airport building looking for Murtaza, whose instructions were that if Tipu should see him, it would mean he could go ahead and kill Tariq Rahim; but if he failed to appear, Tipu should wait for further orders. Murtaza's caution can only be attributed to his lack of certainty about the Afghan government permitting a cold-blooded murder on its soil. Suddenly, Murtaza and Sohail Sethi appeared on the flat open roof of the terminal building. As soon as Tipu spotted them, he screamed to Nasir Jamal: 'Bring Tariq Rahim to me, but give him a few good kicks as you walk him forward.' Nasir Jamal pulled Tariq Rahim out of his seat and began kicking and pushing him towards the first class cabin. He also hit him with his fists a few times. Recalling those moments, Nasir Jamal said to me:

> The truth is that it was very hard for me to come to terms with the humiliation inflicted on Tariq Rahim. Unconsciously perhaps, I wasn't really hitting him hard. But Tipu noticed, and ascribing my lack of enthusiasm to my fear, he shouted: 'What are you doing? Hit him harder, harder . . .'

Even butchers are gentle to the animal which is about to be slaughtered, but the savagery with which Tariq Rahim was murdered is perhaps without precedent even in the bloody history of hijacking. His murder cannot be explained away as that of a hostage who had to be sacrificed because of the hijackers' demands. Tipu justified his cruelty by his belief that he was avenging the murder of Zulfikar Ali Bhutto by punishing a man who had collaborated with his assassins. He did not know Tariq Rahim personally, neither did he have any enmity towards him, nor had Tariq said or done anything to provoke him or the other hijackers. One of the women passengers, Mrs Hubble, a barrister, told the correspondent of the London *Guardian* after it was over that the hijackers had isolated Tariq Rahim on the first day from the other passengers. For days he sat by himself in the rear section of the aircraft apprehending death.[8] When the hijackers were taking him to be executed and kicking him forward, he offered no resistance.

As Tariq Rahim was given the final push into the first class cabin, he found himself facing Tipu, who was playing with a machine pistol, jauntily waving it from side to side. Tariq was petrified, knowing that only a single step separated him from death. He stood there stock still. Then Nasir Jamal kicked him from behind. A scowling Tipu grabbed him by the collar and shot him at pointblank range.

Tipu slid open the aircraft door and threw the body onto the tarmac. Murtaza waved his satisfaction as he watched the writhing body of Tariq Rahim, sprawled on the concrete below. As Tariq lay there dying or already dead, Tipu screamed: 'Let the world know that I have killed Tariq Rahim.' After the hijacking was over, a victorious Murtaza took responsibility for Tariq's murder. He told the BBC, according to a report in the *Guardian* of 17 March 1981, that the ADC of the Martyr Bhutto had played a role in the imposition of martial law and had been on Al-Zulfikar's 'hit list' of over one hundred names.

Murtaza's boast on day one that he had netted a 'big fish' had sealed Tariq Rahim's fate. Now Murtaza justified his action by assuring the Afghans that the murdered officer was a 'great criminal', already included in his execution list of one hundred. Until the night of 23 October 1980, Murtaza and I were sharing the same house, and I know for a fact that he could not even list one hundred Pakistanis, not to mention listing one hundred hit-list candidates. Had Al-Zulfikar had a hit-list, the attacks on Pope John Paul and Zahurul Hassan Bhopali (see chapter 12) would not have taken place. Murtaza used to vow every evening that if he ever came into power, there were certain people who would be shown no mercy, among them Abdul Hafiz Pirzada and Mumtaz Bhutto – whose names preceded those of Ghulam Mustafa Khar, Ghulam Mustafa Jatoi and the late Maulana Kausar Niazi. How indicative it is of Murtaza's sense of consistency and discrimination that years later Pirzada was his defence lawyer, who helped him fight his way out of the Pakistani court system, and Mumtaz Bhutto became his political guru!

Life is a hotchpotch of unthinkables. For instance, Tariq Rahim and I both worked for Zulfikar Ali Bhutto, and while his duties were ceremonial and mine political, the number of times we travelled together in the same plane I cannot begin to count. Could he ever have thought that one day the sons of the Prime Minister he was serving would murder him, and that his dead body would be dumped out of an aircraft at Kabul airport, the same airport where he had landed with Bhutto as a guest of the state in 1976? As for me, could I have imagined myself jailed in the same luckless city, and watching on Afghan television as Tariq's dead body tumbled down? The ironies do not cease here. The coffin that carried Tariq's body back to Pakistan was crafted in front of my eyes in that very jail! Even today, the death of Tariq Rahim and my own survival are equally incomprehensible to me.

(Major Tariq Rahim was not only an exceptionally handsome young man but bore a fine and impeccable character. This tribal Pushtun was instinctively shy and quiet, but he was completely devoted to Prime Minister Bhutto. Perhaps Murtaza would not have known that perhaps Tariq once saved his father's life. In 1974 Bhutto had banned the National Awami Party and perhaps because of that there were frequent reports of bombings in different parts of the Frontier Province, which was why Bhutto decided to go on a tour of the tribal areas. As he stepped out of his helicopter and began to walk towards the public meeting organized for him, there was an explosion. Like a tiger, Tariq pushed the Prime Minister to the ground, shielding his body with his own. He received shrapnel wounds. Bhutto was safe, but a member of the Senate died in the blast. The spontaneous courage with which he had placed his own life in danger to save the Prime Minister from harm was handsomely acknowledged by Bhutto. When the meeting started, in the presence of thousands of people, Bhutto asked Tariq Rahim to walk up to him. Then in warm words he praised him for his gallantry and his personal sense of loyalty to him and to Pakistan. Bhutto never forgot a good turn, nor for that matter a bad one. What Tariq had done he remembered.

Let me also explain here how Tariq came to join the Pakistan foreign service. This was one of his dreams, and Bhutto was aware of it. In March 1977, before the elections, Bhutto summoned all his personal staff and said: 'It is possible that the results of the election may not go in my favour and I may no longer be Prime Minister. So if any of you desires a transfer elsewhere, I am prepared to issue the orders right away.' His ceremonial military staff, of which Tariq was one, unanimously replied: 'We cannot even think of leaving you at this critical hour, sir.' Four months later, everything changed. Bhutto was overthrown and placed in 'protective custody' at the hill station of Murree, less than forty miles from Islamabad. His military staff was allowed to go with him. The first time General Zia came to visit Bhutto, he said to him while taking his leave: 'Sir, are there any orders which you were not able to issue because of this temporary change? I will be honoured to carry them out.' Bhutto answered: 'Thank you, General, I can't think of anything, but I promised my military staff that once things were back to normal, I would send them to the post they desired. So, if you could—' The General did not let Bhutto finish, 'Sir, consider it done.' After he left, Bhutto asked the ADCs to let him know what they wanted, which was how Tariq Rahim got into the foreign service. Bhutto's other ADC, Khalid of the Pakistan Air Force, was also taken into the foreign service and is now a joint secretary.

This was no ordinary incident. It is not easy to imagine a man of Bhutto's stature and temperament asking the same general for a favour who only seven days earlier had overthrown his government and who now held him in custody. A man like Bhutto could never entertain the thought of asking Zia for a favour, including the crucial one that would perhaps have saved his own life, but he made the request for the sake of Tariq Rahim and others. Had Murtaza known this, perhaps he would not have had Tariq killed for 'treachery'.)

In May 1983, when I told Tipu and Nasir Jamal about Tariq's background, they were speechless for some time. Staring into the far distance, Tipu finally said:

> Murtaza had told me that this man had played an important role in the imposition of martial law and the assassination of Bhutto, and therefore I should kill him. It was for Murtaza to distinguish between the friends and enemies of his father.

Nasir Jamal reacted differently. His face showed signs of anguish. He looked at his hands and said: 'May God forgive me because with these two hands I hit him and hit him!'

After the murder of Tariq Rahim, Tipu announced that unless his demands were fully met, he would kill one passenger every twenty-four hours. Murtaza lacked the decency to realize that no political demand can matter more than a human life. Zia began to stall, knowing that Murtaza had left himself no fall-back position. The deadlock continued. Twenty-four hours had passed since Tariq's murder, and now it was 7 March. To continue the pressure and to tell the world that the hijackers were serious, Murtaza was about to take another life, but the Afghans pulled the rug from under his feet. It is possible that General Zia's meeting in Islamabad with the Soviet ambassador was a factor. However, to save Murtaza's face, on the evening of 7 March, Babrak Karmal appeared on state-owned television and 'requested' Tipu to extend the ultimatum once again. Saying yes to this appeal from 'Asia's great hero', Tipu extended the deadline until the evening of 8 March. This time, Karmal sounded listless and unenthusiastic. It appeared that Moscow had taken a dim view of the hijacking. The hourly reports on Afghan TV and radio suddenly stopped. The anticlimax had begun, and it was the Afghans who were now calling the shots. Murtaza was told that he should fly out of Kabul at the expiry of the 8 March deadline.

General Zia, taking full advantage of the murder of Tariq Rahim, remained unbending despite the 'final' deadline. What better turn could Murtaza do to the General than throw one more dead body into his arms? The deadline came and went and Zia did not release any political prisoners.

10

Flight to Damascus

Murtaza told Tipu on 7 March that the next port of call was Damascus. 'Who will look after us in Damascus, since you are here?' he asked. Murtaza replied:

> First of all, I am going to put Shahnawaz on the plane with you. Secondly, I have already asked Brezhnev for an aircraft and I will be in Damascus before your arrival, and, lastly, General Kholi, head of Syrian intelligence [and an assistant to General Rifat Asad, the brother of the Syrian President], will be waiting for you. There's nothing to worry about.

Two years later, recalling this childish reassurance, Tipu, using typical Karachi jargon, said bitterly:

> The leader made me lick a lollipop. The Afghans didn't let Shahnawaz come with us, and as for Murtaza, it took him several days to get to Damascus via Moscow as an ordinary passenger. I only found out later when I got to know him better that he often made tall claims like that. He fooled us all, and for so long. Whenever we'd go to see him, he was always busy talking to Brezhnev. The calls would come while we were with him and last a long time, with Murtaza giving advice to the Soviet leader. It was only later that we learnt that the 'Brezhnev' at the other end was none other than Murtaza's henchman Sohail Sethi.

According to the main Afghan TV news bulletin on the evening of 8 March, the hijacked aircraft had taken off for 'an unknown destination'. Tipu told me that when the plane entered Iranian air space, Iranian fighters came alongside and stayed with the aircraft till it had cleared it. They did not want the aircraft to land in their country. When it landed in Damascus, General Kholi, the wizened head of Syrian intelligence, was waiting. The first thing he did was to walk up to the plane and take a look at the hijackers. He had set up an emergency control room at the airport which enabled him to be in direct contact with them as well as with Murtaza in

Kabul. He had also set aside an area for Pakistani officials with a hot-phone link to Islamabad. General Kholi presented himself to all concerned as a well-meaning arbitrator. Unlike Najibullah, he did not prevent the hijackers from talking to representatives of the Pakistan government. His experience told him that direct negotiations never produced any result in such situations, and the contending parties often had to rely on an arbitrator. General Zia now discovered that Syria was the host to the hijacked aircraft and sent a personal message to Hafiz al-Asad, the Syrian President, asking for help. The Pakistani government described the Syrian attitude as 'positive', not suspecting that the next episode in this drama was to be directed by Damascus.

No Arab country has ever had an intelligence chief of General Kholi's ruthlessness, experience and cunning. For years he fought successfully on three fronts. He kept the massive Sunni majority in Syria at bay, saw to it that the Ikhwan al-Muslamun, the Muslim Brotherhood, remained on a tight leash, and dealt effectively with the Israeli Mossad and its moves. Both Asad and Kholi belonged to the Alwi sect which believes that Ali, the Prophet's son-in-law, was God. There is hardly an armed group in the Middle East which has not at some point sought General Kholi's help or protection. Even the dreaded terrorist Carlos was forced to come to the General. No expert on terrorism or hijacking, on land or air, could match the Syrian intelligence chief's knowledge, tact and experience.

Kholi had been around long enough to know that while thousands are stabbed or shot as a matter of routine in American cities every year without creating a national panic, if the life of even one American citizen is threatened in a Third World country, alarm bells start ringing in the White House. He calculated correctly that while General Zia would not lose any sleep if every Pakistani passenger on that aircraft was killed, he would do everything to ensure that no harm came to an American. It was Kholi who advised Tipu to declare that all American passengers were CIA spies and would be killed one by one. Had Kholi not played this master card, there is no doubt that as calculated by Zia, Murtaza would have slaughtered another Pakistani with his next ultimatum. The Syrian's move worked, and the US government made it clear to Zia that he must bring the hijacking to an end, no matter what it took.

Zia was taken by surprise, and the next plane from Karachi flew Tipu's father and Nasir Jamal's brother to Damascus to see if they could persuade the hijackers to let go. Owing to American pressure, Zia had been forced to surrender to amateurs. Nasir Jamal refused to meet his brother, but Tipu told me about the encounter with his father.

My father was brought to the plane and he stood under it and called my name. I slid the door open and there he was, looking anxious and

113

fatigued. He told me that as my father he ordered me to release every passenger on the aircraft, and that if I disobeyed him, he would no longer be my father or I his son.

When Tipu reached this point in his story, he was overcome, but collected himself and continued.

What a fool I am because I told him: 'I don't know who you are or what has brought you here. I am not your son. My father's name is Zulfikar Ali Bhutto and my mother is called Nusrat Bhutto. My life is dedicated to the Bhutto family. I advise you to leave.'

All his father could say in reply was: 'You are no longer my son, do what you want.' Then with head bowed, the old man walked away. In his blind loyalty to the Bhutto family, Tipu did not realize that it was the last time he would see his father, and would never have the chance to seek his forgiveness. 'Do you think my father understood what I was trying to say?' Tipu asked me in 1983. 'I wanted him to be spared General Zia's torture cells.' There was great pain in his voice. I replied: 'I think it isn't what you said to him; it is what he saw you as: a man with a gun in a hijacked aircraft. Can a father ever bear to see blood on his son's hands and a noose around his neck?' It was clear to me that in order to assuage his conscience, Tipu was now inventing arguments to rationalize his past actions. Only two years before, he had been proud to be the most loyal devotee of the Bhutto family – a position for whose sake he had killed Tariq Rahim and disowned his own father.

Tipu's father had failed and the Americans were stepping up their pressure. In the end, General Zia was left with no option but to ask the hijackers for a list of the political prisoners they wanted released. That was the only way he could save American lives. Kholi then briefed Murtaza in Kabul, and soon afterwards Murtaza put ninety-two names on Najibullah's desk. He wanted to oblige the Afghans by ensuring that no pro-Moscow prisoners were left in Pakistani jails. The Afghan intelligence chief took one look at the list, then crossed out every pro-Moscow name, including Hamid Baloch's. 'These are our men and we will look after them. There's no need for you to include them here,' he told him. Why did Najibullah do that? Did he want the entire blame for the hijacking to fall on Murtaza? Only Ajmal Khattak can unveil this mystery, especially since it was he who had supplied the names of the pro-Moscow prisoners.[1] The line that Najibullah drew across Murtaza's list led to the death of Hamid Baloch, a young man from Quetta who was under sentence of death from a military court. A few days later, he was hanged in Quetta. Had Najibullah not done what he did, the hijacking would have saved at least one life in return for the one it had already taken.

After Najibullah's culling, only fifty-four names, all from the PPP, were left. These Murtaza read out to General Kholi's control room on the phone. The Syrians immediately notified the Pakistanis. When Tipu heard of Zia's capitulation, he was jubilant. Pointing his gun at an American passenger, he ordered him to get up and dance while he put a pop song on the intercom system. 'I think the passengers must have enjoyed that,' he told me.

To put a good face on what he had been forced to do, General Zia said of the fifty-four prisoners flown to Damascus: 'We have thrown out the rotten eggs and saved lives.' By 'lives' he meant American lives. But Zia's humiliation did not end with the release of the prisoners and their safe passage to Damascus. According to the arrangement worked out with General Kholi, the aircraft and its crew were to be taken to Tripoli and released there. It was Zia's bad luck that as the plane was getting ready to land at Tripoli, the Libyan government refused it permission to do so. This was the first time the Libyans had declined hospitality to a hijacked aircraft, notwithstanding that Colonel Gaddafi personally supported hijackings. An official statement from Tripoli said: 'Whenever we allow hijackers to land here, we are accused of being supporters of terrorism, which is why we have said no this time. Let's see what new name we are given now.' Tripoli was upset that while all the thrills of the hijack had been shared between Najibullah and Kholi, they were being handed the dregs, as it were. Libya was not prepared to be an also-ran in the hijacking stakes.

This unexpected refusal from 'uncle' Gaddhafi created a strange situation. The hostages had already been released, the fifty-four political prisoners had arrived in Damascus, and now that the hijackers wanted to release the plane and the crew, no country was willing to take them. It vexed General Zia to now have to ask Syria to give temporary asylum to the hijackers so that the aircraft and crew could be released.[2] He admitted this 'part defeat' to a correspondent.[3]

The hijack finally ran its course on 14 March. General Kholi had won. He had made General Zia suffer humiliation and it had all been peacefully done. For Murtaza, the hijacking was a 'triumph'. Before, he had had to claim credit for natural accidents and events with which he had had little or no involvement; now here was something real and sensational, and it was he who had led it. Where Murtaza had formerly presented a monthly 'progress report' to the Afghan authorities based on clips from the Pakistani press, he now presented Tipu's one-man show to the world as evidence of his planning and organizational genius.

In an interview with the BBC on 14 March 1981, also lifted by London's

Sunday Times, the Pakistan Press International news agency and the *Pakistan Times*, Murtaza boasted: 'I had been preparing for a hijacking for the last one year.' The hijacking had indeed made a cherished dream come true, but he had neither an organization nor a trained cadre of commandos. It was a sheer accident that a rank amateur like Tipu, assisted by even more amateurish companions, had managed to hijack an aircraft. Had Najibullah and Kholi not been behind him, Murtaza would not have been able to keep the plane and passengers even for a day.

The hijack had happened at the height of the Cold War, and the plane had landed in Kabul, so the world media put two and two together and declared that Al-Zulfikar was trained by the KGB. If Murtaza's dog Wolf was to be included, at the time there were only eight who could be called Al-Zulfikar. However, the hijack brought changes. The Afghan government made over several palatial houses to Murtaza in the city's Karta Chahar residential quarter and Al-Zulfikar's headquarters were moved from Dracula House to one of these houses. The first Al-Zulfikar training camp was opened in India. Murtaza began to be treated as an important person both by Kabul and New Delhi.

For Murtaza, the release of the prisoners from Pakistan had no significance except for the psychological boost it gave him. Those who arrived in Damascus from Pakistan believed quite mistakenly that their leaders had planned the operation to free them from General Zia's clutches. For many days, they waited in their Damascus hotel for a glimpse of the 'sahib' but he took his time. When he came, he told them that he was prepared to kill and be killed. Those who wanted to join the struggle should come with him to Kabul, while those who felt disinclined were free to leave. Twenty-five of the men who opted for Kabul were taken there via Delhi on 22 April 1981. Most of them were later sent on 'operational duty' to Pakistan. The hijack did not bring them freedom but eight years of exile. Had they stayed where they were, they would all have been set free in a year or two. As it was, they could only return to Pakistan after General Zia's death in 1988.

A steady stream of young men who hated the Zia regime now came trickling into Kabul from Pakistan. For the PPP workers, the hijacking had put the seal of legitimacy on Murtaza's leadership. From 1981 to 1983, these men obeyed Murtaza blindly. If he asked them to jump, they jumped. They asked no questions, simply carried out orders. Many were caught in Pakistan and sentenced to death. In their innocence and devotion to Murtaza, they went to the gallows confident of being saved by their leader at the last moment.

A key feature of the hijack was Syria's hostile attitude towards General Zia. There was no historical, ideological, political or territorial dispute between

Syria and Pakistan, nor clashing trade or financial interests. Unlike New Delhi and Kabul, Damascus was not concerned with the domestic politics of Islamabad. Why then did a wise and experienced leader like Hafiz al-Asad provide help and protection to Murtaza? Murtaza's own theory was that since in the Yom Kippur War of 1973 'we' had sent some nurses, doctors and pilots to Syria, it had placed Asad in 'our' debt. This was of course absurd. First of all, what help Pakistan rendered in 1973 was not a personal favour to Asad. It was on a state level between the two armies rather than through the agency of a PPP ward committee. Second, there is no evidence of any deep friendship between Asad and Bhutto that would have induced the Syrian to help the fallen Pakistani leader's son. The only gesture Asad made to Bhutto was in the form of two mercy appeals sent to Zia after his death sentence. It is true that when Zia ignored Asad's appeals against Bhutto's hanging – as he did the appeals of many other foreign leaders – Asad cancelled a visit Zia was scheduled to pay to Syria.

There were more powerful reasons for Syria's antipathy. During the Iran–Iraq war, Zia seemed to favour Saddam Hussein, Asad's worst enemy. Asad was bitter about Zia's permission to a former Iraqi ambassador to open an office in Karachi which recruited and sent hundreds of Pakistanis to fight in the war. Asad is one of those people who believe in maintaining enmities rather than friendships. How much he hated Saddam can be gauged from the fact that in both of Iraq's wars, Syria was the only country to side with Baghdad's adversaries, when even so bitter a foe as Iran almost forgave Iraq during the Gulf War. Even Israel did not react after suffering Iraqi rocket attacks. Asad, however, sent Syrian troops to fight Saddam Hussein even though it was practically under the American flag. If this aspect of Asad's personality is kept in mind, it may not be difficult to understand the Syrian leader's attitude to Zia.

In 1980, General Zia turned Peshawar into the largest mustering point for fundamentalist Arabs keen to take part in the Afghan jihad. These fervent souls, captivated by the rosy vision of a great Islamic revival, came to the Pakistani city in much the same way as revolutionary communists from all over the world came to Spain in 1936 to fight against fascism. It was the CIA that trained these fundamentalists, seeing the Afghan war as perfectly suited to the crusade against Soviet communism.[4] These trained Arabs could also be put to another use. They could be employed against those Arab countries – in particular Syria and Libya – that were trying to sabotage American short- and long-term interests in the Middle East. Eventually these trained fundamentalists were dispatched to carry out many bomb attacks and acts of sabotage, especially in Syria, causing heavy loss of life. That was another reason why the two countries extended support to Al-Zulfikar.

Before finishing with Asad, it is important to mention that in 1995, on the personal instructions of Benazir Bhutto, six new training aircraft costing millions of dollars were presented to the Syrian leader as a gift.[5] This must have come as a surprise to her countrymen, since they were made aware every day of the dire economic straits in which Pakistan now found itself – a country crushed by foreign debt, domestic corruption and runaway inflation. What was the basis of this generous gift? It is well known that Syria has always openly opposed Pakistan in all international forums. On Kashmir, Pakistan's most cherished interest, it has always supported India. Asad took Murtaza under his wing because of his hostility to Pakistan. There is only one explanation for the gift. It was a favour returned. The hospitality provided by Asad to the Bhutto family or some of its members during the Zia years had been acknowledged and repaid, though at the expense of the Pakistani taxpayer. The favour done by Asad was personal to the Bhutto family: it should have been repaid at personal not state expense.

The hijack of the PIA aircraft in March 1981 proved to be the opening chapter in the tragic history of Al-Zulfikar. In only twelve days, this incident brought the new-born organization and its leader to widespread international attention. The moment the aircraft landed at Kabul airport, it became the focal point of worldwide media interest. As it was, the presence of the Red Army had turned Kabul into the world's most sensitive Cold War spot. In Pakistan, because of domestic political factors, the hijack was the biggest-running story of the day. It should be pointed out in passing that the hundreds of thousands of words printed by the Pakistani press about the incident in Kabul were characterized by a total lack of interest in or concern for the facts, a practice that continues to this day.[6]

If the hijack is studied in detail, it can provide a map to the mind of a deluded and angry young man. Murtaza arranged it through a loner called Tipu. Al-Zulfikar came into being on the spur of the moment under the giant belly of the PIA plane as it stood in a far corner of the Kabul airport. Murtaza wanted to address the passengers but was prevented from doing so by the Afghans. Knowing who Tariq Rahim was, he had his father's ADC murdered. These are the truths that Murtaza later tried hard to bury in the backyards of Pakistan's courts.

Yet Murtaza was not alone in claiming or denying this revolutionary victory/murderous atrocity according to the tenor of the times. The subsequent history of the PIA hijack has been one of blatant zigzags by his mother and sister too, and by the Pakistani media. While the Zia regime was in power, its point of view on the subject was treated as revealed truth. As soon as the pendulum of power swung in favour of the Bhutto family, the press, some journalists in particular, came to discover aspects that had so far remained hidden from view. There were even articles that fell just short of saying that there had been no hijack in the first place, and even if such an event had indeed taken place, it had nothing to do with Murtaza Bhutto.[7] In other words, while in the Zia period the blame for the hijack was laid on the Bhutto ladies, when the Bhuttos returned to power, it was Zia-ul-Haq and the Jamaat-i-Islami that were held responsible. Of course, both of these versions were wrong and no more than facile attempts to blame the other side – fabrications cooked up by the Pakistani national press at the service of the country's peculiar brand of politics.

Begum Nusrat Bhutto has taken mutually exclusive positions on the subject over the years. She was the only Pakistani politician who, four days after the hijacking, as mentioned earlier, issued a ringing endorsement in the international press of the demands made by the hijackers. Her statement led to the first outbreak of dissent within the ranks of the Movement for the Restoration of Democracy. The MRD vice-president even threatened to resign. Begum Bhutto, however, refused to change her position.[8]

Immediately after the hijack, Begum Bhutto made an announcement that amounted to a recognition of the Kabul regime. She also declared that the Afghan rebels would be thrown out of Pakistan. With this statement, not only did Begum Bhutto gain merit in the eyes of the left in Pakistan, but the revolutionary reputation of the PPP received a timely shot in the arm. In Kabul, the statement had yielded immediate results. Murtaza was allotted a separate camp and compound that was practically a mini-estate administered and controlled by him with full powers, including the power to sentence its inmates to death.[9] For the next ten years at least, there was no change in Begum Bhutto's position. In 1992, describing the hijacking and all other Al-Zulfikar operations as a reality, she said in a statement: 'Al-Zulfikar is not a puzzle or a fairy tale. It was a fact of life in Zia-ul-Haq's time.'[10] Twelve years after the event, at the beginning of 1993, she said: 'In March 1981, the PIA aircraft was hijacked by the Jamaat-i-Islami. Murtaza only accepted responsibility for it in order to save the lives of the passengers. The nation, instead of calling him a terrorist, should, on the other hand, pay tribute to him.'[11]

In other words, in her keenness to modify facts to suit her requirements, Begum Bhutto turned her son into some sort of a hoaxer who had bragged for years about a great feat that now turned out to be the Jamaat-i-Islami's doing. With this disclosure, she also robbed him of the incidental gain of his being Zulfikar Ali Bhutto's truly begotten son, considering that according to Bhutto's last testament, if his sons failed to avenge his murder, they would no longer be his sons. Another paradoxical consequence of Begum Bhutto's assertion was her description of the very hijackers in whose defence she had issued a statement in 1981 as Jamaat-i-Islami agents. Had she forgotten that it was Salamullah Tipu, the plane's hijacker, who had taken one look at his own father at Damascus airport and in a show of loyalty to the Bhuttos, refused to recognize or acknowledge him?

After the hijack, Murtaza appointed Tipu his deputy commander. He was the only member of Al-Zulfikar whom Murtaza decorated with the 'Bhutto Shaheed Medal', the Nishan-i-Haider of Al-Zulfikar.[12] Tipu received the ultimate reward for his blind loyalty in 1984 in the shape of a bullet. As for his two co-hijackers, for many years now they have been confined to a foreign prison where there is no facility to address news conferences, nor do they have the privilege of special facilities while in custody.[13] Because of their underprivileged origins, their mothers and sisters have no press or public relations outfit that might contrive to get their tear-stained faces splashed across newspaper pages. The bitter truth is that all those who were the standard-bearers of the victimized Bhuttos, are themselves the victims today.

As far as Benazir Bhutto was concerned, she did not issue any press statement about the hijacking. But she was happy to tell her friends about it over the telephone. Perhaps she was farsighted enough to see the family contradictions that were to arise in the future over the question of Bhutto's legacy and who his true successor was. So, while the young lady did provide her brother with a golden cage when he first returned in November 1993, she refused to share her hard-earned golden throne with him.

11

Al-Zulfikar's Hit-List

Al-Zulfikar was neither a political party nor did it have a political, social or economic programme. It was the manifestation of an emotional response by male members of the Bhutto family to the barbarity of martial law and the hanging of the deposed Prime Minister. The sole objective of the organization was to punish those who had played a part in Bhutto's overthrow and execution. It was only natural, therefore, that its popular base remained as limited as its objectives. It was not a national liberation movement, nor did it have anything in common with any of the groups elsewhere in the Third World waging armed struggle for revolutionary or ideological change.

Without making the least effort to set up a political or organizational network in any part of Pakistan, or to relate its struggle to the needs of the people, Al-Zulfikar jumped into the maelstrom of armed action, bringing itself to world attention through the reckless and ultimately suicidal act of hijacking. There was a temporary increase in its membership after it managed to get some prisoners released from Zia's jails as part of the hijack's negotiated end, but even during those years 1981 to 1982 its total strength never exceeded ninety-six.[1] Only a man with Murtaza's limited awareness of politics and simple logistics could have believed that less than one hundred untrained amateurs with no ideology and not even a medium-term agenda could defeat the army of a country with a population of over eighty-five million.

The successful hijack in March 1981 brought Murtaza some extra recruits as well as more practical support from Kabul and New Delhi. The hijacking was entirely the work of a few Mohajir workers from Karachi. Murtaza, declaring these men – while it suited him – as sons of Sind, began to believe that the first success of his organization was to be credited to his home province. He had happily appointed his cousin Tariq Islam the 'commander of Sind', something that never failed to amuse the Mohajir members of Al-Zulfikar. Murtaza also fell into the habit of taunting his Punjabi volunteers to come up with something to match Sind's example. He had no qualms about raising tension and resentment between these two sub-nationalities as long as it helped his operations.

After the hijack and his appointment of Tipu as his deputy, Murtaza declared that from then on only those who had proved their operational valour would be considered fit to hold a post of responsibility in Al-Zulfikar. As for himself, his birth and status exempted him from enduring the ordeals he inflicted on others. In the footsteps of his father – but lacking his father's genuine gifts for cementing friendship and promoting allegiance – he was the leader and that was that. He never got to know the pain and tribulations of his followers because he never embraced their concrete experience himself. He was always safely ensconced somewhere else, and never sought the opportunity to feel the cold hand of death creeping towards him. His ignorance was extensive: he did not even know where exactly Kabul lay in relation to Pakistan. Impossible otherwise to have written: 'Try to sleep as I have many a night on the hard stones of the Hindu Kush mountains in the middle of its freezing winter, and then you will soon dream of our dreams.'[2] Had he ever walked through the Khyber Pass across the Durand Line into Afghanistan, he would have known that historic pass ran across the Suliman Range – also known locally as Spin Ghar, the White Mountain – rather than the Hindu Kush range that lies between Afghanistan, China and northern Pakistan. The man who had set out to change history and change Pakistan's geography, did not know what that geography was.

In November 1981, three Al-Zulfikar men – Idris Beg from Tench Bhata, Rawalpindi, Idris Toti from Dharampura, Lahore, and Usman Ghani, also from the same Lahore locality, all in their teens or early twenties – were ordered to travel to Pakistan from Kabul. Their mission was to assassinate Chief Justice of Pakistan Anwar-ul-Haq. (Murtaza, meanwhile, would disport himself in Kabul with his new-found Afghan bride.) These three youngsters had no experience and hardly any training. Arrangements had been made, but not confirmed, to find safe houses in Rawalpindi. Regardless of the success or failure of their mission, no route back to Kabul had been planned. While the PLO, so respected by Murtaza, spent months training its men before it would send them on dangerous missions, in Al-Zulfikar one lecture by their leader conferred capability. It was in a typically 'Paki' style, imitating the imitations in a negative way.

The three men got through to Rawalpindi, and after some difficulty managed to find a place to stay in the city's Pir Wadhai area. They located Justice Anwar-ul-Haq's residence at West Ridge, a short distance from Pir Wadhai, and made notes of his daily routine and movements. However, before they could try to kill the judge, they ran into ill fortune.

Before the launch of this dangerous operation, Murtaza had sent an operative called Asif Butt from Kabul to Rawalpindi in August 1981 with instructions to organize two secret hideouts and the transport required for the mission. (These two hideouts were also to be used by the group designated to carry out an attack on General Zia later.) Instead of getting on with his mission, Asif travelled to Bahawalpur to look up a former student friend. Asif, who came from Sialkot, felt confident that no one would know him here. He was sitting in full view in a restaurant, enjoying a cup of tea, when the assistant superintendent of the Bahawalpur jail happened to drop by. Asif paid no attention to him, but the jailer knew his face. He recognized him as one of the prisoners released only five months before, under the terms of the PIA hijack settlement, from Camp Jail, Lahore, where the officer was serving at the time. Butt had been part of the group of fifty-four which was flown out of different Pakistani jails to Damascus. It was the height of folly to have sent him back there so soon.

The official slipped out of the restaurant and rushed to the nearest telephone to alert the local suprintendent of police, whose men picked up Asif without any trouble and handed him over in handcuffs to what the Pakistani press likes to call 'the sensitive agencies'. Under intense physical and psychological torture, he must have told them everything he knew. Murtaza's hit squad knew nothing of Asif's arrest, but the facts he spilled to the authorities had Rawalpindi swarming with police and infested with checkpoints.

Checkpoints or not, caution would have required Beg and Toti never to venture out armed, especially if visiting the main inner city. Being untrained, they did not know this. One day they were challenged by a police patrol that wanted to frisk them to see if they were clean. They ran, the police pursued, and in desperation, they turned, pulled their weapons and fired. Two policemen died on the spot. Idris Beg took a bullet in the leg, but they were able to escape.

Fate had offered them an exit from Rawalpindi but they possessed neither the judgement to realize how dangerously they were placed, nor funds enough to travel. Idris Beg could not visit a doctor for fear of being turned in. His wound kept oozing blood. For three days, they slept in a graveyard before shifting into a room arranged for them by a friend. Finally, Idris managed to get in touch with a PPP worker named Abdul Khaliq Khan, who brought him the means to dress his wound. For this act of kindness, he later had to flee the country.[3]

Abdul Khaliq Khan told me years later that Idris Beg had walked all the way to Tench Bhata, the Rawalpindi neighbourhood where he had always lived, and met a cobbler friend of his, but the police had come to know, possibly through the cobbler. There was a raid and all three of the squad were arrested. Yet their morale remained high. They told the police what organization they belonged too, and added proudly that Al-Zulfikar had the means to come and rescue its men. Here they were repeating what the Bhutto brothers had told them: 'Never be afraid of being arrested. We will spring you. Remember that we successfully freed our prisoners through the PIA hijack.' The three young men and many others like them obviously believed what they were told. Why would their leaders tell them lies?

Until their last breath, these idealistic youngsters were confident that Murtaza would come to their rescue, but Murtaza missed his appointment. By the time they were executed by the Zia regime in 1984, he was living in Cannes, the south of France, where Begum Bhutto played the matriarch to a large brood of sons, daughters-in-law and grandchildren. On 6 August 1984, Idris Toti and Usman Ghani were hanged in the Kot Lakhpat jail at Lahore. They were hanged together, by the same noose. Usman Ghani was nineteen and Toti just twenty. Four days later, on 10 August, Idris Beg was hanged at the Rawalpindi jail. He was no more than twenty.

All three were younger than Shahnawaz Bhutto. None of them was married and they had yet to begin life as adults. Toti was the son of a railway worker and had completed school under the most straitened circumstances. None of them had had his father executed by Zia or his mother or sister burdened with the responsibility of leading a political party. These simple young men had confused Murtaza's desperate bid for revenge with their dream of establishing a just order in Pakistan where the poor did not go under. Their delusion not only lost them their lives but destroyed their families too. Much time has passed, but to this day the families of these idealistic young men have not been able to find economic security. When they were hanged, Begum Bhutto did not even consider it necessary to send their families a message of sympathy from her sanctuary on the Côte d'Azur.

In March 1984, the military government allowed Benazir to go to London to have a serious ear infection treated. Her mother had been allowed to leave the country two years earlier for the treatment of her cancer. After Benazir's arrival, Begum Bhutto placed the charge of PPP affairs in her hands. In London *Amal*, an irregularly published magazine brought out under Benazir's supervision, published an article on the hanging of the three boys which said that the family of Idris Beg had persuaded the families of the two murdered policemen to accept blood money but the government had ignored it and pressed ahead with the executions.[4]

The undeniable fact is that both Murtaza and Zia needed sacrificial lambs for their own reasons. While Murtaza was driving his flock of young believers into the slaughter house, for the sake of a personal vendetta and political power, Zia was brutalizing Pakistan in the name of Islam. These young men whose lack of training and experience doomed them to certain death were skilled and dangerous terrorists in General Zia's book.

It needs to be stressed that as far as Benazir Bhutto was concerned, at least in 1985, she considered Al-Zulfikar's armed struggle as an admission of political failure at the people's level. She was right to maintain that without the involvement of Pakistan's vast peasantry, no popular revolution was possible. There were no peasants in the ranks of Al-Zulfikar.[5] Its members were nearly all ill-educated, unemployed lower-middle-class youths, full of enthusiasm, and burning to grab the ultimate prize without having to go through the painful process of a revolution. While she kept herself studiously away from Al-Zulfikar, she never hesitated to confer the title of martyr or holy warrior on any of its fallen members. It was unfair of her to hold General Zia-ul-Haq entirely responsible for the plight of these youngsters. Half the responsibility belonged to Al-Zulfikar's leader, her own brother, who squandered these immature boys without a thought for their safety or survival.

One of Al-Zulfikar's primary targets was Maulvi Mushtaq Hussain. Zulfikar Ali Bhutto and Maulvi Mushtaq Hussain, Chief Justice of the Lahore High Court, had a history beginning in 1963 when Bhutto was a minister in Ayub Khan's cabinet and Mushtaq federal Law Secretary. When Ayub arrested Bhutto in 1968, after easing him out of his cabinet post following the so-called Tashkent Accord in the wake of the 1965 India–Pakistan war, it was Mushtaq in whose court Bhutto was arraigned. It was the same judge once again who less than ten years later tried Bhutto on a murder charge. Both men were egotistical, vengeful and unforgiving of enemies, real or perceived. It was only to be expected that they would clash early on in the trial.

During his prime ministership, for reasons unknown, Bhutto had blocked Mushtaq from becoming the Chief Justice of the Lahore High Court. An explanation, if one is to be sought, would lie in Pakistan's political culture, where every ruler moves people up and down with total arbitrariness, asserting what he sees as his prerogative. Bhutto felt no hesitation in following his predecessors. It was his tragedy that he promoted out of turn a general like Zia-ul-Haq, who was to charge him with murder, and refused to promote Mushtaq who was the most senior judge and should have been appointed by right. It was ironic that he now found himself at the mercy of both. Mushtaq ordered that the case against Bhutto be moved from the lower sessions court to the court of first appeal, the Lahore High Court, thus eliminating one step that would have been to the accused's advantage.

The High Court hearing was the most painful experience of Bhutto's life. Mushtaq let no chance pass to needle Bhutto. It is a convention that unless the judge takes his seat, the accused does not take his. In order to keep Bhutto standing, Mushtaq would take all the time in the world to sit down. Bhutto would turn it into a farce by making faces and even laughing at the charade. The truth is that the court proceedings were often no more than a clash between two massive egos.[6] General Zia had cleverly transferred his animosity towards Bhutto to Mushtaq. Throughout the trial, the judge continued to irritate and insult Bhutto. During one such encounter, Bhutto lost his cool and threatened to 'fix' Mushtaq, a threat that was made the basis of another case against the former Prime Minister. It was the kind of emotionally charged threat that Bhutto had once made against Ahmed Raza Kasuri, for the murder of whose father he was now being tried.

The hearing of the murder case against Bhutto was completed with amazing speed, and it came as no surprise when the deposed Prime Minister was found guilty and sentenced to death by hanging. The judge's prejudice was evident by his description of Bhutto as a 'Muslim in name only', a congenital liar, and not fit to hold any public office in Pakistan. The case against Bhutto was not about his being or not being a Muslim, but that was how he had been dealt with.

Soon after the hijack, Murtaza picked out two young men named Abdul Razaq Jharna and Rehmatullah Anjum to kill the judge who had sent his father to the gallows. Anjum was the commander, with the code-name of Dr Mussadaq. As usual, the training of these two assassins consisted of a lecture or two by Murtaza. They were given no arms and no funds. Instead, he told them to enter Pakistan, rob a bank, buy their weapons and carry out their task. He told them that even Stalin had robbed a bank for the sake of revolution. It was not that Al-Zulfikar was short of funds, given the generosity of Libya, Kabul and New Delhi: it was just the way Murtaza was.

On arrival in Pakistan in August 1981, Jharna and Anjum got in touch with Lala Asad, still at large after his activities in Karachi earlier that year (see chapter 8). Lala had recently been joined by a young man from Karachi by the name of Javed Akhtar Malik, who like Tipu had the reputation of being a past-master at prying any car door open. He and Lala began by stealing a Toyota Mark II which the four of them used to rob the Muslim Commercial Bank's Manawan branch near Lahore. Without wasting time in the city, they drove to the tribal areas, dodging the many checkpoints on the way, and there they bought hand-grenades and sten-guns. They stayed at the student hostel of the King Edward Medical College, Lahore, located Maulvi Mushtaq Hussain's house in Model Town, and familiarized themselves with his routine.

On 25 September 1981, Maulvi Mushtaq arrived at his residence after his Friday prayers, accompanied by the lawyer M.A. Rehman and by Chaudhri Zahur Elahi, the maverick Punjabi politician and arch Bhutto foe. They had a plan to visit a mutual friend, Chaudhri Amin, to offer condolences for the death of his mother. At about 2 pm they drove out of the Mushtaq residence in Zahur Elahi's car. Zahur Elahi was riding in front with the driver, while the other two were in the back seat. Just before they got into the car, Zahur Elahi said to the judge: 'Asif Butt, one of the Al-

Zulfikar boys caught by the police, said during interrogation that you, Justice Anwar-ul-Haq and Ijaz Batalvi [the prosecution lawyer in the Bhutto murder trial] are on the group's hit-list.' Soon, he himself would be a target.

The car had hardly moved two hundred yards when it was overtaken by the Al-Zulfikar vehicle. Jharna lobbed a hand-grenade, while Anjum and Lala opened up with sten-guns, killing Chaudhri Zahur Elahi and his driver Nasim on the spot. Mushtaq and Rehman escaped, though not unhurt.

Zahur Elahi had spent time in jail during Bhutto's rule, indicted on the false and ridiculous charge of having shipped arms on camel-back to Baluchistan's rebel tribesmen. He was only released from prison after the overthrow of Bhutto's government, when Zia rewarded his hostility towards Bhutto by making him Minister of Labour and Manpower. After Bhutto's execution, newspapers had reported that the pen with which General Zia had rejected Bhutto's clemency appeal had been given to Zahur Elahi at his request. Had the story been leaked at Zia's instructions, because he wanted to give the impression that his rejecting the appeal was a great and historic decision, or was it that he wanted to leave Zahur Elahi no way out? The fact is that Zahur Elahi died by accident since he was not the target of the Al-Zulfikar team. He had just happened to be at the wrong place at the wrong time. However, Murtaza claimed his murder as proof of his elaborate advance planning, and not only celebrated the event in Kabul but told the BBC in an interview recorded on 26 September 1981 that he was responsible for the operation. According to Benazir Bhutto: 'Mir [Murtaza] did not help when the day after the assassination, he took credit for it in the name of Al-Zulfikar in a BBC interview.'[7]

It is worthwhile to note that Benazir wrote this six or seven years after the murder of Chaudhri Zahur Elahi. During this period, she met Murtaza many times and their meetings involved political discussions about the situation in Pakistan. It was also during this period that her brother Shahnawaz died in Cannes. The statement is an open admission that Benazir placed the responsibility for the murder of the Punjabi politician on Murtaza's shoulders. Had she considered Murtaza innocent, in keeping with honoured Pakistani political tradition, she would have denounced the BBC interview as a baseless invention.

It was the misfortune of poor, unemployed and rootless young men like Jharna that instead of doing something for themselves, they wasted their pity on the aristocratic leaders who had pushed them into this deadly vendetta while living in luxury themselves in their Kabul palaces. To embark on such a dangerous mission, armed with home-made weapons and without the benefit of any military training, was little short of suicide. They were lucky to have escaped through the thick traffic, driving straight to a flat in Lahore's cantonment which they had been using for some time. It stood on Shami Road and faced the house of a Professor Jahangir, at the back of which lived a brigadier. Lala Asad and Javed Malik later abandoned the stolen car in Gulberg's K block and took off for Karachi. Jharna and others moved out of the cantonment, shifting to house No. 53 in Gulberg's L block.

Death in the guise of poverty stalked Jharna. He came from a poor family in Bhakkar, and though he had had two years of college – something his father had managed to do for him at great sacrifice – he had not been able to finish, and earned his living selling odds and ends on a street barrow. At one time he decided to go abroad in search of employment because the money was good. It was around then that he came into contact with Tanvir Begum, who was married to a wrestler from Gujranwala. She was on her way to Kabul, and talked him into coming along. That was where he ran into Murtaza, who had no interest in his poverty or the poverty of his parents, whose only hope in the world was their son. Murtaza pushed him back into Pakistan to kill and destroy.

After the Maulvi Mushtaq operation, Jharna thought of raising some money for his parents. Al-Zulfikar had already taught him how. His decision to rob a bank turned out to be the cause of his arrest and hanging. Had Murtaza had the humanity to give Jharna what he spent on his dog Wolf's food every day, he would not have thought of robbing a bank.

On the day chosen for the robbery, around the end of October, Jharna and Yusuf Khattak, another Al-Zulfikar operative (probably dragged into the organization through Ehsan Bhatti) went to a friend's house in Lahore, a fellow nicknamed Kairi, to pick up the arms they had earlier stored there. They had taken a rickshaw back to 53-L, Gulberg, and were driving along the canal when they noticed a police unit that was stopping vehicles and searching them at the bridge that they needed to cross to get into Gulberg. Soon they would have to turn right to cross the bridge. Jharna asked the driver to slow down, then flung a gunny bag containing a sten-gun into the canal. What Jharna did not know was that because of a silly mistake made by Kairi, there was a piece of paper in that gunny bag carrying an address that would ultimately lead him to the gallows. The gunny bag was found next morning and handed over to the police by the municipal staff that cleaned the canal every now and then. The sten-gun was examined and found to have been fired recently. There were also some papers, some of them legible despite being waterlogged. One of them contained an address in Rawalpindi that eventually led the police to Jharna.[8]

It could not have taken long for the police to extract a confession from Jharna. Keeping his arrest secret, the interrogators obtained Lala Asad's whereabouts from him, and on 20 November 1981 they closed in on his fourth-storey flat in block 54-F of Karachi's Federal B-Area. Asad tried to get away, there was an exchange of fire, and when it was over he and a police inspector lay dead. An assistant inspector in the raiding party also sustained an injury. Lala Asad was the second young man from the family of Lala Aslam to become a victim of Al-Zulfikar's game of death.[9]

Jharna was tried in Martial Law Court No.50 presided over by Brigadier Ijaz Ahmad. Since there was insufficient evidence, the brigadier wanted to release him, but he was transferred.[10] Chaudhri Zahur Elahi's family is said to have met Jharna alone and asked him if he was part of the assassination team. Jharna answered proudly that he was. The new president of the court heard the case again and sentenced Jharna to death. On 15 January 1983, he was marched in fetters to the gallows and hanged. It is said that until the very end, he waited for Al-Zulfikar commandos to spring him.

When Jharna was hanged, Murtaza was in New Delhi. He told the BBC in an interview that from now on every plane flying over Pakistan would be a target for his commandos' missiles. The BBC did not broadcast the story.

12

Zia Escapes Al-Zulfikar Attack

If it was bravery alone that made the difference, Al-Zulfikar could be counted as a successful underground organization. Hasan-i-Sabah, the leader of the sect of Assassins that terrorized the Muslim world in the twelfth century, is said to have inspired his followers by visions of Paradise induced by the use of hashish, and the promise of Paradise for agents martyred in his cause. Murtaza guaranteed rescue for his captured agents, and was fortunate enough to bear a name that inspired his unfortunate followers to risk their lives. But whereas Hasan-i-Sabah and his successors wielded real power from their mountain fortress of Alamut, Murtaza did not wield it from Kabul or New Delhi. First, his aims were too personal: in the end he represented nothing much beyond the right of himself and his family to have their way. Second, he was never able to implant centres of organization inside Pakistan: he wanted no lieutenants working on their own initiative. Third, he acted like some random urban sniper, firing off at opportune targets: spite was a poor rationale. Fourth, he relied on bravery unaided – other men's bravery. When he could be bothered to make plans, they were simplistic. When his allies gave him weapons, he found no hard-bitten sergeants to train his fighters in their use. Al-Zulfikar did make an impact in Pakistan, as any group must that contains men ready to die for a cause. The history of the attacks on General Zia-ul-Haq shows how much more formidable the group could have been, even as a mere instrument of terror, had its leader respected his followers enough to maximize their chances to succeed and to survive.

After the PIA hijacking, the three targets chosen by Al-Zulfikar were Maulvi Mushtaq Hussain, Justice Anwar-ul-Haq, and General Zia-ul-Haq. The men chosen to carry out the operations were all Punjabis. The first strike at Zia was finalized in November 1981 and the men assigned the task were two former Punjab University students sprung from jail in the hijack settlement. Ten years later, Murtaza claimed with pride: 'I had two attacks carried out against General Zia. Once the computer of the missile fired at him malfunctioned, and the second time, he had a hair's breadth escape.'[1]

The first operation to eliminate Zia was successful to the extent that for a split second he was made to see his death staring him in the face. The two young men who carried out the operation bore the code-names of Faisal and Aamir. This is how they recall that event.

The decision to liquidate Zia was taken in November 1981, but it was not till the middle of January 1982 that we left Kabul for Rawalpindi. Our guide was known to us by his code-name of Rahim Shah. We never discovered his real name, nor he ours. In underground organizations, only code-names are used: no one asks you who you are or what your real name is. Rahim Shah belonged to Pakistan's tribal area, and because of his membership of Afzal Bhangash's Mazdoor Kisan Party he was a committed socialist, so we felt sure that he would prove to be a reliable guide. From Kabul to Jalalabad, we were part of a military convoy. Because of the Mujahideen guerrillas, convoys were preferred to travelling singly. Even civilian transport was often escorted by tanks or military vehicles.

The road from Jalalabad to Torkham, the Pakistani border post, was impassable because of heavy fighting between the Soviet army and the Mujahideen. We waited four days for things to improve, but that was not to be. Finally, Rahim Shah told us that we could reach the Pakistan border by another route: a thirty-kilometre trek along the river at night. After crossing into Pakistan, we were to walk another twenty-five kilometres through the tribal belt. The whole way, we were to be carrying two crated SAM-missiles that we were to use to shoot down General Zia's plane. We chewed over Rahim Shah's suggestion for quite some time, because it was hard and dangerous. In the end, despite our misgivings, we agreed to go along. It was dangerous because we were to walk through an area which was already the scene of fierce battles. Today, when we look back, we are astonished at our courage.

We left that day quite early in the evening and began to walk along the river towards the Afghan border with Pakistan. The cold was intense but we were sweating. It was dark, we were carrying those heavy missiles, and we were plagued by fear. Although we were in a kind of backwater as far as the main fighting was concerned, it was known that the Afghan rebels were in full control of all the hills in this area. They often moved at night, because during the day they were at the mercy of Soviet helicopter gunships. After eight hours, we paused for breath. Our shoulders were sore, but we were relieved that so far we had not run into trouble. We were now only about four hours away from the Durand Line, and it was good to know that we were well away from the battle area.

Rahim Shah was a smoker. At one point, as we sat down to rest, he lit a cigarette. Within minutes, the stillness of the night was shattered by the terrifying sound of bullets flying everywhere. We'd caught the attention of rebel snipers who had seen the glow of the lighted cigarette. We fell to the ground, then crawled to our left to shift our position and returned the fire, hoping that whoever was shooting would end the exchange at 'one all'. We were not sure we would survive. Had we died, our families would never have known what happened to us. Had we been taken alive, we would have been shot, because in the book of Afghan tribal justice, executions are preferred to prisoner-taking. Or we might have been delivered to the Pakistani authorities for a reward. Every Al-Zulfikar man handed over to Pakistan was worth one hundred thousand rupees in reward money. However, none of those things happened and we resumed our journey. Our destination was Rahim Shah's village which was twelve or thirteen miles inside Pakistan's tribal area. When we finally got there, we were a sight. Our feet were bleeding and our shoulders were sore and swollen. Lack of sleep had worsened our condition.

Village and country people, unlike those born and brought up in the city, are used to a harder life physically and can walk long distances over rough terrain. These men spoke only Punjabi or Urdu, not a word of Pushto, nor had they ever carried any kind of weight, let alone the donkey-load they had had to lug across rough ground and hilly country. Now that they were in Pakistan, they fretted about betrayal or arrest. The punishment awaiting Al-Zulfikar men was swift and merciless. Nothing can make up for the pain, fear and mental torture they must have undergone. Instead of luxuriating in the safety of his fortress in Kabul, had the leader of Al-Zulfikar ever joined his men on such a journey, he would have known something of the ordeals they endured. I doubt that it occurred to him. In Pakistani culture, if you go to someone's house to condole a death in the family, they consider it a favour. Here were young men who laid their lives on the line for the murder of Murtaza's father – a responsibility and an obligation that it was up to him to fulfil. An honourable man would have washed the blood off the feet of these brave men with his own hands. Murtaza's world did not contain such sensitivities. To him, these men were counters in a game he played by right of birth. Later, he branded many of them as traitors. Therein lies our great social tragedy. The higher classes that wield political and financial power consider it their divine prerogative to lead and the duty of the lowly to follow. To them there is little to choose from between the earth they own and the men who walk it with bare feet.

After resting for three days in Rahim Shah's humble tribal dwelling or *hujra*, the two young men began the second leg of their journey towards Rawalpindi. They left their host the address of a house in Rawalpindi's Satellite Town neighbourhood where he was supposed to deliver the

SAM-missiles and Kalashnikovs they had brought from Kabul. True to his word, Rahim Shah appeared at their door after a few days and handed over the weapons.

To move the consignment from the tribal area to Rawalpindi, Rahim Shah chose a simple but clever method. He put the SAM-missiles and guns in a wooden box, boarded a goods truck and brought them to their destination. Throughout 1981 and 1982, everything that Murtaza entrusted to Rahim Shah for delivery to Pakistan came through safely and without interception, mainly because he was a man of conviction who felt a commitment to things higher than money. In that, he differed from some of his less scrupulous compatriots from the tribal areas. By contrast, all the arms sent by Murtaza between 1979 and 1980 through Afghan intelligence operatives were either seized by the Pakistani police or security, or else kept by the tribesmen themselves.

Aamir and Faisal were ready for Zia, and had chosen a spot to the east of Islamabad international airport at Rawalpindi. Now they had to wait. In January 1982, they read in the papers that Zia would be returning from Saudi Arabia in the early hours of the morning. The plane due to land at the airport would also carry General K.M. Arif, Foreign Minister Sahibzada Yaqub Khan and several other generals. This was the target the two Al-Zulfikar men chose. They had an old car in whose boot they placed the missile, and as night fell, they drove towards Islamabad airport. Rawalpindi was a heavily policed city in those days. To avoid the checkpoints they took a roundabout route before parking in their chosen spot and walking to a hillock that gave a clear view of the airport. All night long, they sat there watching the sky.

At four in the morning, they saw a plane approach the airport from the east. Aamir placed the missile on his shoulder and got ready to fire. He wanted to be sure that it was Zia's Falcon jet and not a passenger aircraft. The plane had begun to lose height, and was now flying at no more than two hundred metres from the ground. It was the President's Falcon. Aiming the missile at the plane, with the light in the viewfinder still red, Aamir pressed the trigger.

Nothing happened. He had fired too early. The inexperienced and nervous Aamir had pressed the trigger without waiting for the heat-seeking missile to lock on to the aircraft's engines, when the light in the viewfinder would have turned from red to green. The computer on the Russian-made missile had not malfunctioned. It was another indication of the meagre training given to Murtaza's men. Had Aamir waited just a few seconds, there would have been no chance of the missile missing the target. The plane landed safely after a couple of minutes. Zia-ul-Haq never knew that on a morning in January 1982, only seconds had separated him from certain death.

The two men carried the SAM-7 back to the car as they needed a new computer eye to launch it, and as they got in they heard a police car siren wailing. It was General Zia being driven to his residence in Rawalpindi. They were greatly disheartened but they still had another working missile at their hideout, and they consoled themselves with the thought that they would get their man the second time.

It was not safe for these two to be living in Rawalpindi. Asif Butt, who had been sent ahead to make arrangements for the mission in Rawalpindi, had already been picked up by the police. Only a few weeks earlier, Idris Beg, Idris Toti and Usman Ghani had been arrested. Razaq Jharna too was in the torture cells of the Lahore fort, having been held soon after the attempt on Maulvi Mushtaq's life and the murder of C.Z.Elahi. There was every likelihood that the agencies of the government were aware of the plan to shoot down Zia's plane. They must also have known about Aamir and Faisal. This was how the two described the situation to me:

> When we left Kabul, we were not told that Asif Butt had been arrested, nor anything about the jailing of Usman Ghani and others. We had said that in view of the dangerous nature of our mission, no other Al-Zulfikar operation should be undertaken in Rawalpindi as it would create a special security alert, but to those who had sent us over, our lives didn't matter more than insects crawling on the ground. We had chosen a road from which there was no turning back.

It was not Murtaza's problem if the mothers of his young soldiers were to spend the rest of their lives wailing over the dead bodies of their sons. Nor did he care if scores of mothers should die without setting eyes on their absent children. In his defence, though, it should be said that Murtaza did nothing new: this was exactly the way that Mughal princes used to treat their subjects. The history of India was full of such stories.

Back in Rawalpindi, the two Al-Zulfikar men lay in waiting for another crack at Zia. They did not have long to wait. Newspapers said that General Zia-ul-Haq would be arriving in Lahore on board his personal plane at 9.45 am on 7 February 1982. This meant that his Falcon would take off from Islamabad airport any time between 8.30 am and 9 am. They decided to act. They must have known that regardless of the success or failure of their attempt, their chance of escaping alive was limited. These young men, as university graduates, would have been holding good jobs somewhere safe if fate had not intervened in the form of Al-Zulfikar. Instead, here they were, tempting death to claim them. In ordinary day-to-day life, such actions would have been unthinkable for young men like them, but they had been caught up in an extraordinary and awesome situation. Perhaps gallantry is a melange of emotions, circumstance and a certain state of mind.

On the bright, clear morning of 7 February, Aamir and Faisal arrived at the public park that lies close to Chandni Chowk on Murree Road. Every plane taking off from Islamabad airport for Lahore flies over this park. Quite a few people were in there, enjoying their morning walk. They parked their car in a side lane, wrapped the missile launcher in a sheet and placed it on the grass in a corner. No one paid any attention to them. They were staring at the sky in the direction of Islamabad airport. They had done some homework and they knew that for half an hour before Zia's VIP flight, no other plane would be permitted to fly in the vicinity.

Around 8.45 am, the General's Falcon raced down the runway and was quickly airborne. Faisal ran towards the car, started the engine and then picked up his Kalashnikov, draped in a piece of cloth, with his finger on the trigger, so as to cover his friend in case of an emergency. Aamir unwrapped the missile launcher, set it on his right shoulder and pointed it at the plane. His right eye was glued to the eyepiece, where he could see a red light. He was not going to botch it this time, and waited for the light to turn green, when he would know that the heat-seeking SAM-7 had locked on to its target. The light turned green. Aamir pressed the trigger, his heart racing with excitement. The missile left the launcher, gushing a cloud of smoke in its wake. Faisal screamed from the car: 'Run Aamir, it's a hit.'

As Aamir ran towards the car he looked up and couldn't believe his eyes. The missile had missed the Falcon by several yards. Aamir did not know that the pilot of Zia's aircraft had seen the missile coming and made a sudden manoeuvre, almost losing his balance. Even so, his skill should not have saved the Falcon. Once again, the SAM-7 had missed because Murtaza disregarded technical training.

The SAM-7 was a lethal weapon but there were things you had to know before you used it. Murtaza had skimmed through the manual, picked up a smattering of information, and passed it to his soldiers. As far as he was concerned, they were now fully proficient militarily, fit to be launched into what takes professional commandos years to train for. He did not look closely enough at the manual to learn that the person who fired the missile should keep his eye on the target through the computerized sights until it had been hit. Nor had he lingered over the passage that explained that when the missile was fired it emitted a cloud of smoke, and the man who fired it must put on special goggles so that the smoke should not affect his eyes. Aamir had no goggles. When he felt the smoke in his eyes, he jerked his head to avoid it and in the process shifted the computerized guiding launcher resting on his shoulder. The missile could only have missed.

It was just General Zia's luck that he escaped death a second time. No less lucky were the two men who ran away from the scene without being noticed. They drove straight to Lahore, and stayed there for about a week before returning to Kabul via Torkham. Years later, when I asked them what their reaction had been when they realized that they had missed Zia once again, they said: 'Our first thought was that now the Al-Zulfikar people arrested in Rawalpindi earlier would not be allowed to survive.' They were right, because all three men were hanged after a summary trial.

The story of the missile attack on Zia's aircraft quickly spread all over Pakistan, but because of the regime's draconian censorship it did not make the newspapers. What Zia's own reaction was we will never know, as he is no longer alive, but I have heard from various people that when the captain of the Falcon told his chief that they were under missile attack and asked if he should abort the flight, Zia ordered him to gain altitude fast, in order to get out of range. Whether that would have been the right decision if there had been another missile aimed at him, it is hard to say.

The police report of the attack was filed exactly one year after the incident. Zia had not panicked. No widespread arrests had occurred. He believed in selective repression, and was keen to identify the men who had staged the attack. He did not want the energies of his agencies to be frittered away on wild goose chases. The police, after thorough interrogation of anyone and everyone connected with Al-Zulfikar or aware of its operations, did manage after a year to correctly identify Aamir and Faisal. It would have unearthed their names in any case, since the leader of the organization in Kabul was claiming responsibility and credit each time that Zia stubbed his toe.

(By 1984, Al-Zulfikar, such as it was, had disintegrated. Murtaza was in the south of France with his family, and his soldiers were either rotting in the camps of Kabul and Delhi or suffering torture and interrogation at Lahore's notorious fort, the Shahi Qila. The two missile men, Aamir and Faisal, managed to get to Europe in 1985. To my surprise, one of them began to openly attack Murtaza's opportunism and the pro-American policies of the PPP. I was surprised because normally the tradition had been to shower blind praise on the Bhutto family and to hang around in the hope of being rewarded for loyalty shown. Perhaps it was his impending death that cleared the scales from his eyes, for one day he was shot to death in Holland where he had settled. When this happened, the entire Bhutto family was living in Europe, but no one came to his funeral, or helped to send his body home for burial. No word of sympathy was spoken. The real name of this unfortunate, honest and brave young man was Azam Chaudhri.[2] His other companion continues to live in exile to this day.)

In those days, the moment you left Kabul you were at large in open country where the writ of government did not run. Those who ventured out in a bid to get to Pakistan exposed themselves to double jeopardy: if they managed to escape the marauding Mujahideen, they were almost certain to be collared by the Pakistani security agencies. Murtaza lived in luxury and comfort. He could sit back in his Kabul palace and dream up daredevil schemes that other men would hazard.

In 1982, Murtaza decided to mount a further SAM-7 attack on Zia's aircraft. This time he chose two young men from Lahore, gave them their single 'training' lecture, and shipped them to Pakistan in July 1982. The code-names of these two brothers were Akbar and Asghar.[3] Once again, Rahim Shah was assigned to smuggle two SAM-7 missiles to Pakistan. The method the tribesman chose this time was quite original. He had a special ornamental top designed for his goods transport wagon – something common in Pakistan – so that the case containing the two missiles was built into the brightly painted framework. He delivered the missiles to the address in Lahore that he had been given.

The two brothers belonged to a family known to be sympathetic to the PPP, and as such were kept under general surveillance – such were the times. To minimize the risk of exposure, the two missiles did not remain in the same place for too long. First they were shifted to a safe house in the Lahore cantonment, and then to the home of the famous former Pakistani cricketer and lawyer Aftab Gul. He told me later that he had nothing whatever to do with Al-Zulfikar and did not even know what the two wooden crates left in his custody contained.

Aftab Gul was a well-known and popular figure with a wide circle of friends and acquaintances. He was opposed to martial law, but was not prepared to join an outfit involved in acts of sabotage, arson and murder to destabilize the regime. It shocked him when the police staged a raid on his house around the end of the year and the missiles were found and taken away. Aftab Gul's father, a retired military officer, was imprisoned, and the entire family suffered untold hardship. Gul eventually escaped to London, where he stayed for several years. He only returned to Pakistan after the death of Zia-ul-Haq.

As for the two brothers, in December 1982 they found their way back to Kabul and immediately claimed that they had fired one missile at Zia's plane at Lahore's Walton airport, but had somehow missed. As for the other SAM, they claimed that it had been captured by the police in a raid because of Aftab Gul's indiscreet talk. The Walton attack story was false, as many Al-Zulfikar people later confirmed. The Pakistani police received the SAM-7s as a gift, the same way they had come to Murtaza from the PLO, and to the PLO from Moscow. There were some who maintained that the two brothers 'Akbar' and 'Asghar' had themselves tipped off the police because they did not want to risk their lives by trying to shoot down Zia's plane. However, it should be borne in mind that allegations of treachery, like professions of blind loyalty, have been an integral part of the lower middle class-culture of the PPP.

In August 1982, Murtaza moved to New Delhi. There were two reasons for his leaving Kabul. First, because of the pressure and entreaties of various international socialist organizations, the Kabul government had been trying to persuade him to agree to my release from prison. He could not however accept the idea as it amounted to a defeat. A year and a half earlier, Murtaza himself had announced that I was dead. He did not want it known to anyone, and especially to Al-Zulfikar and PPP workers and sympathizers, that he had told a lie. Second, Murtaza, afraid of Zia's peace initiative, which was actually meant to milk the USA, had wrongly become convinced that the Afghan government would hand him over to General Zia-ul-Haq in exchange for Gulbadin Hikmatyar, a rebel leader based in Pakistan. He felt that his safest option was to pack up and leave for New Delhi. In order to delay my release Murtaza told Najibullah that he would return to Kabul from time to time and would thus maintain a base there. So Najibullah once again agreed not to release me, in order to appease Murtaza.

The Indian Reseach and Analysis Wing, RAW, was the prime espionage agency of the country, and far more efficient than the amateurish KHAD, its Afghan counterpart. As Al-Zulfikar men began to arrive in India from Pakistan and Afghanistan from the beginning of September 1982, RAW set up a reception centre and camp for them in the city's Surya Nagar locality. It was under the charge of Sardar Salim, a PPP worker from Rawalpindi. Every new arrival was fingerprinted and photographed by RAW and given a code-name that was always Hindu. The agency did not want the junior training staff to know that these men were Pakistanis or Muslims. Sardar Salim's name was Kashi Ram, while Yaqub Cheena was Ashok and Umar Hayat was Deepak. Sohail Sethi was Prakash and Murtaza Bhutto the leader was Kumar.[4]

RAW was not only careful with the code-names; it took security seriously. For instance, it knew that some of the men would eventually be caught by Pakistani agencies such as Inter-Services Intelligence (ISI), and so it took steps to prevent them from knowing where they had been trained in India. These men were transported to and from their camps by helicopter. Where the training camp was located they did not know, except that it was in a hilly area about three to four hundred miles from New Delhi. Actually the training centre lay in the city of Bhuj. What they learned there included the use of light weapons and techniques of sabotage, including bomb-making. When they were ready, the men were brought back to the Surya Nagar facility in the Indian capital, where they were always met by Murtaza, Shahnawaz and Sohail Sethi. They were organized into groups of four and smuggled across the border into Pakistan to carry out different missions. All Al-Zulfikar affairs were controlled and guided by a RAW officer named Chawla.[5]

In September 1982, two RAW-trained Al-Zulfikar groups were sent across the border to Pakistan to assassinate two leading members of the Majlis-i-Shoora, General Zia's hand-picked advisory council. The group sent to Sialkot and Lahore was led by Rehmatullah Anjum and included Umar Hayat and Talat Jaffrey. The fourth member, according to some accounts, was Afzal Razzaq – code-name Dr Trailo. The other group went to Karachi. It was led by Ayaz Sammu, and also included Yaqub Cheena, Ilyas Siddiqui, and Javed Malik. Siddiqui and Anjum were among those who only a year and a half earlier had been brought to Damascus by the Pakistan government in return for the hijacked PIA plane, its crew and passengers. Both Rehmatullah Anjum and Javed Malik were wanted for the murder of Chaudhri Zahur Elahi. Murtaza knew that if either man was recognized in Pakistan it would cost him his life.

Anjum's party crossed the border near Sialkot, stole a car from the city and on the night of 2 September Umar Hayat and Talat Jaffrey headed for the house of the respected veteran politician Khwaja Muhammad Safdar, armed with hand-grenades. One Al-Zulfikar man recalled in 1990 that Khwaja Safdar's three-storey house was located in an old part of the city. There was a lot of overhead wiring in the street and around the house and the two operatives were afraid of lobbing a grenade into the house because it could easily hit the wiring and rebound on them. In fact, though, the grenade exploded on the flat roof of the old-fashioned house, and the two made an easy getaway.

The attack on Khwaja Safdar's house was meant to be a symbolic warning, because it was Murtaza's view that if fifty to sixty generals, judges and politicians who were cooperating with the regime were murdered, all of Pakistan's problems would be solved. He was sure that the ruling clique and its undemocratic supporters would run for their lives after the murders, while the generals would be so terrified of what had happened that they would just relinquish power. This was the analysis of an inexperienced and naive young man who had yet to learn that no Pakistani ruler had ever forfeited power voluntarily: all of them had had to be dragged away or kicked out.

The car stolen in Sialkot by Anjum was abandoned at Daska, a small town about twenty miles away. Here they stole another car and drove to Lahore, where on the night of 5 September, they threw a hand-grenade at the residence of Justice Saeed-ur-Rehman, killing a security guard by the name of Murid Ahmed. Two months after this incident, the judge resigned his post, something Murtaza must have added to his trophies. The group's luck held, and the four made it safely back to Delhi.

139

Zahurul Hassan Bhopali, Al-Zulfikar's next victim, was born in Bhopal, India, in 1946. The family moved to Pakistan in 1947 and settled in Karachi. After taking a master's degree at the University of Karachi, Bhopali began life as a journalist. In 1970, he ran for the Sind Provincial Assembly and was elected. He took an active part in the anti-Bhutto movement of 1977 and was jailed for over two months. He was well known in Karachi as a social worker, and it defeats conjecture as to why Al-Zulfikar chose to kill this harmless man who also had a physical disability. He had, after all, played no role in the imposition of martial law or the hanging of Zulfikar Ali Bhutto. Why was he picked out? Was it because he was a soft target, and by getting him killed Murtaza would consolidate his credentials with RAW? Murtaza was not one to retreat from even extreme action if it would promote his reputation for bravery and leadership. It broadened his scope that he believed himself incapable of making a mistake.

The group led by Ayaz Sammu detailed from Delhi to kill Bhopali. Javed Malik drove the car used during the operation, as he had during the attempt on Maulvi Mushtaq Hussain that resulted in the death of Chaudhri Zahur Elahi and his driver Nasim. Javed came from Karachi and knew every inch of the city. As soon as the group arrived, he stole a Datsun-120 by springing its lock, much as his old friend Salamullah Tipu would have done.

On 12 September 1982 at midday, the Datsun carrying the four of them braked in front of the small office that Bhopali kept in the city's PECHS area. Javed let the engine idle while Cheena stood outside watching the street. Siddiqui and Sammu walked towards Bhopali's office. Siddiqui kept Sammu covered as he burst into the legislator's office, where he found him talking to two visitors. Without a word, Sammu opened up with his Kalashnikov and killed not only Bhopali but his two visitors also. As Sammu turned back, to the horror of those who could see him from the street, he emptied the rest of the Kalashnikov magazine into the body of his companion Siddiqui. His body could only be identified many days later. The local newspapers published heart-rending pictures of Siddiqui's mother crying over her dead son.[6] Had she known that he was only being freed and flown to Damascus to be later brought back to Karachi, his home town, and killed, she would have prayed for her son's continued imprisonment. At least in Zia's prison he would have remained alive.

The young Siddiqui was a student at the Urdu Science College, Karachi, and a great supporter of Bhutto. He was also an active member of the PPP-backed People's Students Federation. He had been sentenced to a one-year jail term by a Karachi military court, but had been sprung by Al-Zulfikar as part of the PIA hijacking settlement. Of the fifty-four prisoners flown to Damascus from various Pakistani jails, twenty-five, as mentioned earlier, had made the fatal mistake of joining Al-Zulfikar. Siddiqui was one of them. In April 1981 he had been moved to Kabul, and in June 1982 he had been transferred to Al-Zulfikar's headquarters in New Delhi. Three months later, only eighteen months after his release, he lay dead. One newspaper offered this explanation for his inexplicable execution-style murder:

> It is believed that this terrorist group, after having carried out its mission, had no further use for Ilyas Siddiqui. It was for this reason that he was ruthlessly eliminated by his own companion.[7]

There were various theories about Siddiqui's murder among Al-Zulfikar members. Some said that Ayaz Sammu was a die-hard Sindhi nationalist and hated Mohajirs because they had come and taken Sindhi land and Sindhi jobs. To him, Siddiqui was as much to be hated as Bhopali because they were both non-Sindhi Urdu-speaking Mohajirs. Others said that he wanted to be the sole claimant to the fame of killing Bhopali. Al-Zulfikar people used to believe in those days that those of them considered to have offered the biggest sacrifice would be made cabinet ministers when times changed. Sammu told two Al-Zulfikar people in Delhi, whom I have since met, that he had killed Siddiqui in accordance with standing orders, because he had shown vulnerability during an operation. If Siddiqui lost his life because of this rule, nothing more unjust can be imagined. Sammu was unable to explain where or how exactly Siddiqui had shown cowardice.

Murtaza let Sammu stay in Delhi for some time and then ordered him to return to Pakistan. There are some who say that Sammu was betrayed by Al-Zulfikar itself, which tipped off the Zia regime about his presence in Pakistan. He was picked up, tried and hanged in Karachi on 26 June 1985. The next day's newspapers carried pictures of his wailing mother.[8]

The balance sheet of 'Operation Bhopali' was chilling. It took five lives, including that of the assassin. How can such callous adventurism be justified? However, in London Benazir Bhutto made several appeals to Amnesty International to save Sammu's life – not that the Zia regime was going to listen to Amnesty or anyone else, as its record showed. The day Sammu was hanged in Karachi, in an interview with the BBC, Benazir held General Zia-ul-Haq responsible for what to her was unjustified punishment.[9] Did she really believe that Ayaz Sammu was innocent? Or was she putting a politician's face on events?

Eleven years after Sammu's hanging, Benazir Bhutto, as Prime Minister of Pakistan, named a new bridge in Karachi constructed with state funds after Ayaz Sammu Shaheed, Sammu the Martyr. She announced that she was going to perform the inauguration of the bridge herself, an act that the Mohajirs of Karachi could only have viewed as an insult. To them, Sammu was the outlaw who had brutally murdered four innocent men, namely

Zahurul Hassan Bhopali, Ilyas Siddiqui, and two visitors who happened to be present in Bhopali's office when the gunman burst into it. Those killed had done nothing to earn the wrath of the Bhuttos. It was not they who had deprived Zulfikar Ali Bhutto of power or hurt his family. If Benazir to this day remains unaware of Sammu's past, it can only be attributed to her refusal to know the truth. If she knows and is deliberately distorting the truth, it is an unforgivable act of dishonesty.

Was Benazir trying to prove to Sindhi nationalists that she was the real leader and representative of Sind, a mantle that her brother Murtaza tried to claim? Was Sammu a useful martyr in the pantheon of Sindhi nationalism? Young men like Khokhar and Ajiz, who burnt themselves to death in Bhutto's name, and Usman Ghani, who paid for his loyalty to his leader with his life, failed to have even so much as lip-service paid to them by the Bhutto family. No bridges were named after them, no effort made to resurrect their memory. Or was it that, being Punjabis, they were second-class martyrs? The post-Bhutto PPP culture has decayed into a culture of mausoleums, not of living masses. It was not an accident that Benazir and Murtaza came to see eye to eye on what constitutes martyrdom.

In 1983, when the opposition parties were still attempting to work together in the loose alliance of the MRD, Murtaza too decided to chip in but according to his own ungoverned methods. This time it was Rehmatullah Anjum, Yaqub Cheena and Umar Hayat who entered Pakistan near Sialkot with the help of Indian security. On 13 September 1983, they opened fire on the Lancers officers' mess in Lahore cantonment killing two non-commissioned officers, Arshad Ahmed and Islamuddin. They also placed a time-bomb in the Al-Falah building on Lahore's Mall Road.

The next day, 14 September, proved to be the last for Rehmatullah Anjum. While placing a time-bomb in the lavatory of the city's famous Rattan Cinema on Mcleod Road, he was blown to bits when the device exploded in his hands.[10] After Lala Aslam, he thus became the second Al-Zulfikar man to be killed while planting a bomb. Had he succeeded, hundreds of innocent people would have been killed or maimed for life. The following day, the police were able to identify his almost unrecognizable body. From the clothes he was wearing, they even traced the tailor in Faisalabad who had stitched them.[11]

Anjum had fallen a victim to Al-Zulfikar's back-handed logic which argued that the more people Al-Zulfikar blew up or shot, the greater would be the revulsion of the masses against the army. Finally, the masses would march out onto the streets and overthrow the regime. In life, it is the contrary that happens. Terrorism can never be popular because it destroys the very people in whose name it sets out to act.

Anjum was a law graduate of the University of Peshawar and came from a very poor family which had put him through college with great hardship. How pitiful that instead of living on to support his mother and father, he saw it as his duty to carry the banner of the party that sought revenge for the murder of Bhutto. Al-Zulfikar people told me that in his keenness to show loyalty to the Bhutto family, Anjum used to say that if he was asked to strap a bomb to his body and blow himself up, he would not hesitate for a second. Ironically, this was one wish of his that Murtaza honoured on 14 September 1983 in Lahore.

Anjum died believing that when the Bhuttos returned to power, the problems of the poor would be solved. They did return. In November 1988 Murtaza's sister Benazir became Pakistan's Prime Minister and his mother was sworn in as her Senior Minister. Mercifully for his trusting nature, Rehmatullah Anjum was not alive to see it. No one from Islamabad went looking for his poor mother who was eking out a living by doing domestic service. Rehmatullah Anjum's tragedy is actually the tragedy of Al-Zulfikar and of every idealistic or misled young man who joined its ranks.

Al-Zulfikar, which announced in March 1981 with much fanfare that it was going to free Pakistan from the chains of the Zia regime, had failed to fire the imagination of the common people in the country. By 1984, Murtaza's adventurism had brought him back to where he had started. Eighty per cent of his men were in jail, and there were only two courses available to him: either to throw in the towel and admit that he had lost, or to make an attempt to free the captives who languished in Pakistani jails, some of them waiting to be executed. He chose the second option, deciding to throw everything he had into one last operation. There could be no doubt that if this final effort failed, it would be the last nail in Al-Zulfikar's coffin.

Murtaza was still enticed by the thought of a hijack, but there was no Tipu around any more, nor a short-sighted helper like Najibullah. He therefore decided to seize the Pakistan embassy in Athens on 23 March 1984, Pakistan's national day, take hostages, and order the Greek government to provide a Boeing airliner to which the embassy staff would be taken at gun-point. In exchange for its safe return, the Pakistani government would be instructed to release every Al-Zulfikar men it held.

Six Al-Zulfikar men who were stationed in Libya were summoned for the terrorist attack. They were the last Al-Zulfikar people lodged in the Nasir camp near Tripoli, and bore the following names (real ones): Akhtar Beg, Ghulam Mustafa Memon, Sher Bahadur, Muhammad Karim, Sheikh Iqbal and Muhammad Zubair Minhas. From Delhi, 'Kashi Ram' (Sardar Salim) arrived in Damascus with three more sacrificial lambs, namely Umar Hayat, Javed Malik and Yaqub Cheena.[12] Salim had told them that Al-Zulfikar was pulling out of Delhi. This was a lie: he was afraid that if he told them about the Athens operation, they might simply refuse to come.

Leaving them with Murtaza, he returned to Delhi, where he remained a RAW guest until 1989.

Murtaza found no difficulty in persuading the nine men to undertake the Athens operation. Still besotted with Bhutto, these deluded young men still saw his son as the living presence of the departed and charismatic leader. Murtaza had already obtained forged British passports for them from Holland. All that was needed was to attach the pictures of the nine.[13]

Javed Malik took command. The PLO was to provide the arms. The plan called for the team to travel from Damascus in groups of three, and the first group landed at Athens airport on the morning of 8 March 1984. As soon as they passed through customs and immigration, their instructions were to cable Dr Salahuddin, c/o Jeweller Shop, Hotel Sheraton, Damascus. Dr Salahuddin was Murtaza's code-name outside India.

The moment the three men presented themselves at the immigration desk, they were asked to stand aside. Their pictures were pasted so crudely onto the forged or stolen British passports that the forgery was obvious. Immigration phoned the British embassy, and soon an official arrived to investigate. The only question he asked the three was the amount of the passport fee they had had to deposit. How could they know that? In fact, they hardly spoke English. The British official took them to be Pakistanis who were trying to enter Greece in search of work, and advised the Greek officials to put them on the next flight back to Damascus. Later that day Murtaza was not amused when instead of the cable, the three men greeted him in the Syrian capital.

One of Al-Zulfikar's constant headaches was how to procure forged passports. While Afghanistan, India and Syria did not hesitate to provide the necessary papers to the Bhutto brothers themselves, they would not do the same for their followers. They could not be seen to be implicated in any act of terrorism the holders might commit. The poor forgeries that Al-Zulfikar people used for passports often landed them in trouble. Masroor Ahsen along with two others was caught in Dubai in February 1983 because of the third-rate papers he was travelling on.

After his men were sent straight back to Damascus, it occurred to Murtaza to have them apply for Pakistani passports. It did not enter his mind that if they were caught with Pakistani passports, they were likely to be repatriated to Pakistan to face the wrath of the Zia regime. Acting on these orders, Akhtar Beg and Zubair Minhas walked into the Pakistan embassy in Damascus and pretended to be workers in search of employment who had lost their passports. They probably did not know that in such cases the embassy requires a copy of the police report of the loss, as well as a Pakistani identity card. Often the document issued after these inquiries is valid only for a return trip to Pakistan.

The applications made by the two men gave the Damascus Hotel as their local address – a place known worldwide as a haunt for terrorists. The embassy officials grew suspicious and assigned a man to follow them back to the hotel. When he learned that there were as many as nine Pakistanis staying there, someone smelled trouble. So did the Al-Zulfikar men, and they did not return to the embassy after that single visit.

Left with no alternative but to use the forged British passports he had obtained from Holland, Murtaza decided that on 12 June 1984 he would have his men take over the embassy of Pakistan in Rome. The raiding party would travel there by passenger boat. The first group, led by Javed Malik, left Syria on 20 May, the second and third groups on 22 and 26 May. This time none of the groups had immigration difficulties. They assembled at a cheap Rome hotel that had been designated as their rendezvous point. Murtaza arrived a day or two later. Everything was ready but the weapons. The PLO had promised to provide them but had now changed its mind. It did so because it did not want to antagonize the Italian Communist Party and the country's socialist groups, which supported the PLO and its struggle for Palestinian rights. Another version claims that Murtaza had embarked on the operation without first ascertaining whether or not the PLO would provide the group with arms in Rome. Either way, the attack plan had to be aborted.

It was then that Murtaza decided to do in Vienna what he had been unable to do in Rome. Rather than ship his team back to Damascus and then have to move them to Vienna, he handed out fifteen hundred dollars to each of the nine guerrillas and told them to have a 'good time' in Rome. These young men from underprivileged backgrounds in Pakistan had never set foot in Europe and were dazzled by what they had so far seen: the sights, the sounds, the women. They did their best to taste the fleshpots of the Eternal City. However, the rest and recreation period was short-lived. The first group was put on a train bound for Vienna on 25 June, the second a day later and the third on 30 June. 'Dr Salahuddin' flew into the Austrian capital. He met his men, one by one, in one of the Nordsee Fisch food outlets that dot the city, gave them two thousand Austrian schillings apiece – about two hundred dollars – and said with a flourish: 'We next meet in Cuba.' After this operation they would all receive political asylum there, he explained.

What was the Vienna operation? On 1 July, Canada's national day, the Al-Zulfikar commandos were to take a number of ambassadors hostage at a function organized by the Canadian embassy at one of Vienna's famous luxury hotels, the Imperial. Javed Malik, the commander of the mission, had booked himself a room at the hotel on 29 June. Next day the PLO people in Vienna delivered the arms, which consisted of three machine pistols, seven revolvers, five hand-grenades and two kilos of TNT. This lethal package had been smuggled over from Hungary.

According to the plan, Akhtar Beg was to crash into the reception room of the Imperial where the function was being held and fire a burst at the ceiling to terrify the diplomats and the other guests. The other guerrillas would block the exits. Their orders were to pick up the Pakistani ambassador and if he resisted shoot him dead on the spot. Other envoys to be picked up were those of Sweden and Switzerland. All women present were to be released.

Once they had taken control, the operation was to move into phase two, which featured an aircraft (an obsession with Murtaza ever since the PIA hijack). The Al-Zulfikar men were to demand a Boeing from the Austrians. The captured diplomats were to have their hands tied behind their backs, a task given to self-proclaimed 'expert' Zubair Minhas, and then a bus must collect the guerrillas and their hostages and drive them to Vienna's Schwechat airport. Once inside the bus, the armed men had instructions to pull the pins out of the grenades they carried and make it clear that they would blow everything to bits, including themselves, if the Austrian police or commandos tried any tricks. Murtaza had given Malik a list of all Al-Zulfikar men in Zia's jails. Once inside the aircraft, Malik would demand their release by Pakistan.

This was a copy-cat re-run of the Black September operation against Israeli athletes at the 1972 Munich Olympics. What Murtaza had forgotten was that as soon as the Black September men had reached the tarmac at Munich airport with their hostages, they had been shot dead by German commandos. Vienna was no Kabul, and the head of Austrian intelligence was not the Afghan Najibullah but a die-hard professional. Assuming that the Al-Zulfikar men had succeeded in getting to the Schwechat airport, their chances of making it to the aircraft with their hostages were practically non-existent. They had a hopeless task on their hands and would have been no match for Austrian security, which had developed special anti-terrorist skills since 1975, when the Venezuelan terrorist Carlos staged his famous and successful operation against OPEC oil ministers.

The joke was that no Canada Day function was being held at the Imperial on 1 July. Earlier that day, when two of the guerrillas took a taxi and surveyed the Canadian embassy, they found it closed. Murtaza's last fling was a farce. Some idea of organizational genius can be deduced from the fact that his nine men did not even have a map of the city of Vienna and none of them spoke a word of German. They had no contingency plan in case something went wrong, and no means of reaching their leader because he had left Vienna on the day of the planned attack.

The guerrillas blew some of the money they had on cheap cameras and some of it on drinking beer. They spent part of the day taking pictures of the Austrian capital. Since there was no operation, they found themselves with nothing to do. Staying at the Hotel Bergerland, a cheap tourist place near the city's Westbahnhof railway station, they spent the next six days roaming around Vienna. Had Murtaza not gone off to France to be out of harm's way, he could at least have told the men what they were to do next, if anything. He could also have saved them from the long jail terms they eventually received. These men had committed no actual crime in Austria, though they had violated a large number of laws. They could have ditched the small quantity of ammunition they had, and asked for political asylum like hundreds of their countrymen. No one would have known that they were Al-Zulfikar men.

The holiday came to an end on 6 July, when eight of the team were checked by the police on suspicion of carrying drugs. While their passports were British and all of them bore the names of the original holders,[14] only one of them was able to speak English, and none spoke German. The police were not satisfied, so they followed the 'Englishmen' back to their hotel. A search of their rooms revealed not only the PLO ammunition they had failed to get rid of, but also the list of prisoners who were to be freed from Pakistani jails.

The Austrian police could not believe the ease with which they had unearthed a potential terrorist operation and arrested all but one of its commandos. Even then, so artless were they all that the remaining member of the team, who was out for a walk when the police detained the others, presented himself at the police station voluntarily because he did not want to be left on his own.

These luckless exiles were charged in November 1984 with a host of offences, from smuggling weapons to entering Austria for the commission of an act of terrorism. They were convicted and remained in prison from four to nine years, the longest sentence going to Javed Malik, the commander of the operation that never was. The exiled PPP leaders in London, Jam Sadiq Ali and Dr Zafar Niazi, arranged for an Austrian lawyer for the nine men and kept sending them small amounts of money received from Murtaza until July 1985, after which the remittances ceased. In 1985, Murtaza announced the dissolution of Al-Zulfikar. Between 1985 and 1989, the prisoners in Austria had no financial help from anyone, nor was there anyone to visit them in jail. They had been completely abandoned by the man and the organization which had sent them over.

(In 1987 when Benazir Bhutto, accompanied by her mother Begum Bhutto, came to Vienna to receive the Bruno Kreisky award for human rights work, Begum Bhutto raised the question of the Al-Zulfikar prisoners with the Austrian interior minister. In 1989, after Benazir came to power, eight of the men were released, having served half or more than half their terms. Two of them, Zubair Minhas and Akhtar Beg, did not return to Pakistan but managed to stay on in Austria and are there until this day. They may even be granted citizenship. The group leader, Javed Malik, was released after nine years in May 1993 and sent to Pakistan, where he was promptly picked up and jailed. He remained in prison until 1995, when he was honourably acquitted, along with his chief Murtaza, of the murder of Chaudhri Zahur Elahi.)

The fact that the Bhutto brothers had settled in France in 1984 was not widely known. Not until Shahnawaz died there in 1985 did the world discover where he and his brother had been living. Why did the French government allow leaders of a terrorist organization to live in France, and what was it that kept Zia from asking the French for their extradition to Pakistan? Why did the military-controlled Pakistani press carry not a single story about where the Bhutto brothers were?

After Shahnawaz's death, the impression given to the press by those close to the Bhutto family was that it was Zulfikar Ali Bhutto's personal friendship with a former French Foreign Minister that caused the French to grant his sons asylum. That may have been part of the explanation, but there has been a view that other reasons swayed the decision. It is said that after Bhutto's hanging, the Americans decided to keep their lines open to the Bhutto family, and it was at their request that the French agreed to provide asylum and other facilities to Begum Bhutto and her sons. The Zia regime was also pressured by the Americans to permit Begum Bhutto to travel abroad in 1982 for treatment of cancer. Similarly, Benazir was allowed to proceed to England in 1984 to get an ear infection treated, again under US pressure.

In Pakistan, General Zia was making preparations to hold non-party polls to gain a modicum of legitimacy. To keep the new assembly under his thumb, it was necessary to leave the PPP and other political parties opposed to him out of the exercise. The absence of the Bhutto ladies would thus have suited his purpose rather well. The non-party national assembly, or Majlis-i-Shoora, produced by the 1985 elections provided the General with the token democracy he was seeking, and he added a hand-picked new Prime Minister, Mohammad Khan Junejo.

In April 1986, Benazir Bhutto decided to return to Pakistan. She was hoping to take advantage of what liberties were available under Junejo's semi-civilian rule to mobilize the people. It was not an easy task for this young, inexperienced but courageous woman. To begin with, the very idea of a woman leader was anathema to the male-oriented and anti-feminist Pakistani society and its obscurantist mentality. However, Benazir proved to be smarter than all those who were treating her as just a chit of a girl. She eliminated every principal leader in the PPP who had worked with her father and had occupied important offices during his days of power, and brought in her own younger team. It was her good fortune that there was no Jayaprakash Narayan or Morarji Desai in the Pakistan People's Party.

On the other hand, in order to get into the corridors of power, she did not think twice about forging a compromise with those whose hands were stained with her father's blood. Power has a price and she was willing to pay it.

Zia's flirtation even with a sham democracy did not last long. Not only did he hate any kind of representative arrangement, he was also wary of sharing power with anyone. After liquidating Bhutto, it was essential for his own survival to rule alone with all power vested in his person. Soon, the contradiction of the situation in which he now found himself erupted in the form of an open rift between Zia and Junejo. The break came over Afghanistan. While both the United States and the Soviet Union had agreed that the Soviets would pull out, Zia was not happy with the deal. He wanted to see an 'Islamic' government established in Kabul before any formal agreement was reached in Geneva, where the UN sponsored talks on Afghanistan were in progress. Since Junejo was resisting General Zia, he had to be removed. Zia not only sacked him in May 1988 but also dissolved his self-created Majlis-i-Shoora. Without knowing it, he had also sealed his own fate: with an assembly in place, even a poorly represented one, there had been a chance that he would be able to 'civilianize' himself.

13

A Killer for Murtaza

Murtaza Bhutto was the slave of his own latest impulse, and lacked both the will and the instinct to think through his own ideas or to test his plans against possible contingencies. He was seldom inhibited by logic, and was able to jump in a matter of days or weeks from one sweeping conclusion to its direct opposite without doubting that either was correct at the time when he reached it. Because he could not truly trust anyone who possessed the independence of mind to contradict him, it never occurred to him to assemble a group of level-headed advisers and to work out a set of long-term aims. Such as they were, his plans assumed instant returns, personal celebrity, and a ready supply of expendable volunteers, and he was vain enough to take the supply for granted. From this perspective there was no advantage in training recruits to a level where they could act and survive on their own initiative in hostile countries, and no point in devising flexible missions whose instructions required his agents to keep themselves in play.

Such a leader may find a use for political idealists and romantics, but these may have scruples, or ideological disagreements. For blind obedience, he needed men who are both streetwise and naïve, gullible and ruthless – ready killers and easy victims. Murtaza found the ideal follower in the man he chose to lead the Pakistan International Airlines hijack in March 1981, and the brief history of Salamullah Tipu tells much about the man who used and misused him, and who made Al-Zulfikar into the instrument of his personal fantasies and ambitions.

Salamullah Tipu was born in Karachi in a Mohajir family originally from Uttar Pradesh in India. Almost half the family chose to live in India. His sister, when it came time for her marriage, was found a husband in India and went to live there. Tipu's grandfather, Ashfaqullah Khan, was among those anti-imperialist firebrands of his time who took up arms against the British. He was hanged in 1929, and his name is inscribed on the memorial column erected in Calcutta to honour the heroes of India's freedom.

Tipu's early education was in a good school where the language of instruction was English. He was an energetic and naughty child who was always up to mischief, and he grew up into a quarrelsome young fellow who was never too far from a fight. By the time he entered college, he had turned into a regular hooligan. His great hobby was joy-riding – stealing cars, driving them at breakneck speed and putting them through controlled skids. With time, this hobby turned into a profession, and he began to sell the cars he stole to a junk-dealer by the name of Ayub Malik. He was a pastmaster at picking car locks, and on a Kabul street in May 1983 he demonstrated his expertise to me by unlocking four cars in a matter of minutes.

Not too tall but strongly built, this fair and handsome youth won the chance of a good and socially respectable career when after two years of college he was selected for a permanent commission in the Pakistan army. When he reported to the Pakistan Military Academy at Kakul, his parents must have felt immense relief, but it was not for long. He had scores of car-theft cases filed against him at various Karachi's police stations, and as soon as this record reached Kakul, Tipu was drummed out of the Academy. This old British tradition is still followed by the army in Pakistan.

An orthodox career awaited Tipu had he not been thrown out of Kakul, and it is tempting to speculate about the completely different course that his life might have followed. Perhaps he would have been among those who arrested Bhutto or administered lashes to workers of the PPP. As was to be expected, he reverted to his old ways when he returned to Karachi. Most of his time was now spent as an unemployed, purposeless, half-educated drifter getting involved in gang fights and other trouble-making around the university of Karachi. He felt no loyalty to any particular political party; his only objective was to build a fearsome reputation in the university. At first he fell in with some right-wing students, but since he was given to every excess in the book, he soon parted company with those religious conservatives, and drifted towards the student wing of the PPP, the Pakistan Students' Federation (PSF). This was his first contact with the PPP and Bhutto's politics. He soon became one of the top members of the PSF's strong-arm squad in the violent clashes with rival groups that were part of the student politics of the time.

In 1980, Tipu murdered Hafiz Aslam, a member of the Islami Jamiat-i-Tuleba, the student wing of the Jamaat-i-Islami. It was his first political murder, and he could now claim to have earned his 'revolutionary' spurs. He went on the run, and reached Kabul in November 1980. This is how he described these events to me when we met in May 1983:

I came to Kabul in November 1980, three months before the hijacking. I hadn't left Pakistan to hijack anything but to escape arrest. This was what had happened. One day outside Karachi University, I ran into some members of the Islami Jamiat-i-Tuleba who were raising slogans like 'Murderer Bhutto, hai hai'. I got emotional and angry, and as I had a gun I pulled it out and shot one of them. Next I knew, the army and the police were looking for me everywhere. A murder case had also been registered against me. There was no doubt that if I was arrested, I would be hanged. But as soon as news of the incident at the university reached the Bhutto residence at 70 Clifton, Begum Bhutto made arrangements for me to be taken to Kabul. A senior PPP leader was sent with me as my escort.[1]

When Begum Bhutto helped Tipu to escape arrest, she did not realize that what she was shipping to Kabul was a keg of human gunpowder who would destroy the political future of her son. But one cannot blame her. What one foresees does not always happen, and what happens, one often does not foresee.

He was taken to Murtaza Bhutto with an account of his 'services' to date. After the very first meeting, he became the focus of Murtaza's interest, because so far those he had come in contact with had no qualification other than that of having been lashed or jailed in Pakistan. Tipu was the first man who had refused to behave passively but pulled out a gun to kill a man. It was this that made Murtaza decide to entrust him with the most important plan of his life. It did not take him more than a couple of meetings to decide that this former military cadet could turn his dream of a hijacking into reality. Taking Tipu into his confidence, he told him what he had in mind, which was like music to Tipu's ears. Tipu was one of those men who are never able to distinguish between fame and notoriety. Such people are prepared to do anything or go to any length to become known. So far his only exposure to fame had been within the limited confines of his neighbourhood, school and college. But here was Murtaza Bhutto himself, offering to launch Tipu at an international level. Psychologically, Tipu hankered after the prospect of becoming famous, experiencing the excitement of hijacking a plane and in the process gaining Murtaza's close friendship. This heady mixture which he had sought all his life was now his to savour.

The PIA hijack has been described in chapter nine. After the hijack, Tipu returned to Kabul from Damascus in Murtaza's company. A few months earlier he had come there as an unknown political worker. Now he was the internationally known 'Alamgir', his *nom de guerre*, who had earned the distinction of staging a successful hijack which was also the world's longest. With a Bhutto Shaheed medal strung around his neck, he would walk just one step behind Murtaza and his brother Shahnawaz, and why not? Had Murtaza not declared him to be his 'third brother and deputy'?

Because of the hijack, Tipu was now well known, but he found it difficult to handle his new status and concluded that he was now an international personality. His fellow hijacker Nasir Jamal told me later:

Tipu had begun to write his interviews himself, and he would use the most fantastic expressions when listing his qualities. Sometimes he was 'the mountain of greatness', at others 'the sentinel of the revolution'. These mindless pieces would be mailed to Pakistani newspapers which would throw them into the rubbish bin. Of course, you couldn't say that to him and, consequently, he was always waiting to see them in print.[2]

In May 1983, when he and I first met, Tipu spent nearly an hour boasting about his 'great deed' and what the newspapers of the world had written about it. Finally, he asked me a direct question: 'And what do you think about my PIA hijack?' I told him that in my eyes the hijack had been a foolish operation which only helped the military regime in Pakistan. Expecting nothing but the highest praise, he was disconcerted by my comment on the greatest deed of his life. A few days later, he brought me a little-known Indian Urdu weekly which had an article on him and said: 'What you call foolishness, the world sees as a great revolutionary act.' It is not unusual for a man to look for some accomplishment that will make his life meaningful and bring him happiness: since Tipu's greatest feat was the hijack, it was pointless to argue.

The hijack was the answer to Murtaza's prayers and the high point of his own political life. Before it, he had no public image. In Kabul and Delhi, Damascus and Tripoli, he was referred to merely as 'Bhutto's son'. Now he had chips on the table. He was the man who had master-minded the hijacking. He stood acknowledged not merely as his father's son, but as a player in his own right. In that heyday of the Cold War, when both sides backed champions they could not publicly acknowledge, it was the media who decoded such actions and turned them into political performance art. By the standards of the time, Murtaza was now a star. But there was another claimant to that title, and that was Tipu, who in Murtaza's eyes was no more than a hothead he had rented for the purpose. Other than that he had no value. It is not surprising that he only permitted Tipu to live in a separate house for about a month following the hijack. Thereafter he relegated his underling to the Al-Zulfikar camp, with the rest of the rank and file, and kept him deliberately deprived of such facilities as a car. One aspect of Murtaza's personality was that he wanted all distinctions, all favours received to go exclusively to him. His class origins had taught him the elementary lesson that if everyone was to receive the same treatment, it would mean the end of his special status as leader.

After the hijack, as mentioned earlier, Murtaza began to be received like a VIP in Delhi, Kabul and Damascus, but in Tipu's eyes this international promotion was due entirely to himself, and Tipu was not far wrong.

Murtaza's earlier lifestyle was typified by the black 1955 model Chevrolet the Kabul government had given him, an ailing jalopy that required the constant attendance of three or four Al-Zulfikar 'braves' who must push it before it would start. Such embarrassments were bound to confirm Murtaza's view that any special treatment for Tipu would detract from the prestige he needed for himself. Nevertheless, while Tipu returned to the Al-Zulfikar camp in the Karta Chahar quarter of Kabul, he continued to consider his treatment by Murtaza as insulting and unfair. He told me in 1983 when recalling his downgrading:

> The Tipu who had a price on his head set by General Zia was reduced by Murtaza to a position where he had to trudge along the streets of Kabul and run after buses. Had he had any thought for my safety or comfort, he would have provided me with a secure and separate house and some means of transport. The Afghan government was quite willing to give me those facilities but Murtaza would not hear of it.[3]

Perhaps to test his vassal's loyalty, in September 1981 Murtaza chose to carry out his third murder. Murtaza had become convinced that Al-Zulfikar was being infiltrated by agents of the enemy, the military government of Pakistan. He had recruited a group of people as part of a half-baked scheme to supply Libya with mercenaries to fight in Chad. In this group he soon 'identified' one of Zia's 'agents' by the name of Mazdoor Yar Afridi.

Afridi was an unemployed but well educated man who had come to Kabul hoping to be sent to Libya, and from there to Chad. For some months he had been kicking his heels in Al-Zulfikar's transit camp in the Karta Chahar quarter, hoping that luck would smile on him and he would go overseas and get a job. More out of innocent mischief than anything else, one day an Al-Zulfikar man reported that Afridi had been the close friend of a nephew of General Fazle Haq when they were both students at the university of Peshawar. When the report reached Murtaza, he had Afridi put under arrest. He ought to have realized that if Afridi was as well-connected as he had been told, he would not have travelled to Kabul on the off-chance of a job in Libya, but by now Murtaza had grown obsessed with conspiracies, and Al-Zulfikar was not the first underground organization to fall victim to the proposition that the appearance of innocence was itself a reason for suspicion.

Afridi was locked up in a room and Pervez Shinwari was assigned to interrogate him. He told Afridi on Murtaza's behalf that if he confessed that he had been planted by General Fazle Haq, he would be released and sent to Libya, while his statement would be used in the propaganda war against Zia. No one is alive to confirm the story, but it is said that in order to get out of the trouble he was in, the innocent Afridi took up his leader's offer and recorded an incriminating statement.

As soon as the statement reached Murtaza, he pronounced a sentence of death on his follower. After telling others about Afridi's 'confession', he had him brought out on the lawn of the camp with his hands tied behind his back and a black bandage covering his eyes. Qayyum Butt, a former member of the National Assembly of Pakistan and faithful to the PPP, was sitting next to Murtaza. When he showed signs of unease at this cruel show, Murtaza said loudly so that everyone could hear: 'Qayyum Butt, you consider yourself a great revolutionary. Try to sit steadily in your chair.'

Afridi was made to sit in a chair which had its back to a wall. He had no idea who was watching him, nor could he have been aware that Tipu and Shahnawaz, both of them toting Kalashnikovs, were hovering close by. Murtaza said in a loud voice: 'If you confess that you are an agent, I will release you and send you to Libya.' The simple Afridi did so. 'In keeping with my promise, I release you,' Murtaza announced. Eyewitnesses to this callous performance have described to me how, as signs of relief appeared on Afridi's face, Tipu and Shahnawaz both opened fire together, and blew his brains out. He died at once. Then his blood-spattered body was photographed and the pictures sent to General Fazle Haq with the message: 'Your agent's end'. Tipu and Nasir Jamal threw Afridi's body into the boot of a car and drove out of Kabul to an area called Kargha to dump it.

I visited the spot where Afridi had been killed after I got out of jail in 1983, and saw the bullet marks on the wall where his chair had stood. In May 1983, I spoke about this incident to Tipu, but he showed no sense of guilt and continued to insist that the execution had been justified. I have since spoken to a number of eyewitnesses to this gruesome murder, none of whom has been able to erase it from his memory.

Tipu had proved his credentials in the most absolute fashion, but it brought no concessions from his leader. Only nine months after the hijacking, Murtaza's 'deputy commander' had been reduced to the position of a semi-discarded retainer languishing in the labour camp called Al-Zulfikar. To satisfy his inbuilt need to be considered the organization's sole leader, Murtaza had pushed Tipu down from the topmost rung of the ladder and left him to grovel far below. It was a difficult and dangerous time for Tipu. While one of his hijack companions, Tegi, had already moved to Libya, the other, Nasir Jamal, had got engaged to a girl in Kabul. In a bid to escape isolation and loneliness, Tipu too sought a match but was rebuffed by the family of the intended bride. He complained that even there, Murtaza had been of no help to him.

As days went by, Tipu's bitterness began to surface in his conversation.

Inevitably, whoever he spoke to about his resentment of Murtaza would pass the news 'upstairs'. Interpreting his frustration as rebellion, in December 1981 Murtaza formally declared his execution on the charge of indiscipline and disobedience. That he did not think twice about ordering a close companion killed on the basis of hearsay or minor differences, confirms that in Murtaza's book, the dividing line between friendship and enmity was either movable or non-existent. Having opted for the gun, he had convinced himself that therein lay the solution of every major and minor problem, as long as the muzzle was pointed at someone else, and by someone else's hand.

Party workers present when Tipu was informed of the death sentence saw him begin to weep. Knowing that he had burnt his boats when he chose to come to Kabul, he looked into the future, and found death staring him in the face. It had always been impossible to leave; now it was fatal to stay. The truth is that this was the dilemma faced by every member of Al-Zulfikar except its leader and his brother, who had broader options. It was their collective tragedy. Because they had all been labelled terrorists, they could not seek asylum outside Afghanistan: their world had been reduced to the enclave called Al-Zulfikar. This state of affairs suited Murtaza ideally. He felt no obligation to any of his men, yet he retained the power to control their lives and deaths.

However, reports that Tipu was a broken man finally earned him a reprieve. With Murtaza's restless ego temporarily appeased, the death sentence was 'commuted'. All the same, Tipu's continued presence in the camp was seen as likely to infect others with the virus of criticism, and, for his questionably loyal, unwanted and redundant cadres Murtaza had access to a dumping ground in the great desert where he had already shipped much of his unwanted human junk. Libya was Al-Zulfikar's punishment post. It was an austere place, without such diversions as drinking and women. Those whom Murtaza consigned there were placed in a camp called Ma'askar-i-Nasser, run under the control and supervision of Salem bin Aamir, an adviser to Colonel Gaddhafi, who was not only highly educated but a practising Muslim who expected his charges to abide by their religious obligations through regular prayers and fasting during Ramadan. For a spoilt young man like Tipu, no punishment could be more painful than to be banished to the puritanical Jamahariya.

Murtaza had little liking for Salem, and had complained about his attitude several times to 'uncle' Gaddhafi, though without avail. Every time he needed money from Libya, he had to come to Salem, who not only refused to cosset Murtaza like the princeling he was in New Delhi, but would not allow him to treat the Nasser camp as his personal estate. He had refused to let him exercise his authority there, including punishment for his men.

In March 1982, Tipu arrived in Libya. A man more capable of learning lessons from the past, or gifted with a keener sense of self-preservation, would have seen Ma'askar-i-Nasser as a safe haven, but Tipu was besotted with the pleasures of his recent successes. After his brief brush with fame, he had become incapable of living like a normal human being. He was determined to regain his old closeness to Murtaza, no matter what it took, and that is why he began to seek ways of getting to New Delhi, where Murtaza had shifted around the middle of 1982. It took only nine to ten months before fate intervened to fulfil his desire. In January 1983, Murtaza arrived in Libya, nursing a new and dangerous scheme for a daredevil operation.

In February 1983, General Zia-ul-Haq was due to visit India. As a security precaution, RAW had moved the members of Al-Zulfikar training in camps around Delhi to Bangalore, a city several hundred miles away. The Indian authorities had also advised Murtaza to stay away for the entire duration of the general's visit. Instead, he told them that he would rather go to Syria, where he left his family in safety and flew on to Tripoli. Murtaza had decided that Zia should be assassinated in India. Since the Al-Zulfikar men in India were under the effective control of RAW, and the Kabul camp lay derelict, his only hope for bringing off the planned operation lay in the exiled workers of Al-Zulfikar who were mouldering in Tripoli.

At this point, he decided to seek out Tipu, gloss over the past and offer him the command of the 'Delhi Plan'. Tipu jumped for joy. Begum Nusrat Bhutto was also in Tripoli to see her sons, and to steel Tipu's nerve. To seal Tipu's loyalty, Murtaza arranged for him to see her. This had always been Tipu's great ambition: to get as close as he could to the Bhutto family. In June 1983, recalling that meeting, he told me:

> Together with the Bhutto brothers, I arrived at Begum Bhutto's hotel. As soon as she saw me, she came forward and said: 'At Damascus airport you declared that I was your mother. I want to tell you that from this day on you are my third son. You have shown through your conduct what true loyalty is. It is not possible to recompense you for your great sacrifice.' Then she moved closer and placed a gold locket dangling from a chain around my neck. It contained earth from Zulfikar Ali Bhutto's grave. Tears welled up in my eyes, so deeply had her words moved me.

When he told me the story, the locket still hung from Tipu's neck.

Murtaza picked out three men for the Delhi operation, appointing Tipu, the fourth, as their commander. All four belonged to the Mohajir community. Their parents had moved to the new Muslim state of Pakistan in

1950, three years after independence, and half their families still lived in India. According to one account, these men were chosen because they spoke Urdu and would blend with the residents of Delhi. This was hardly a serious consideration since there could be little chance of their survival after the attack on General Zia. But the casualty list for this or any other action was the last of Murtaza's concerns. In his mind, these people came from a class and a community which was colonialist in outlook, very much like those who had opened the great American heartland in the nineteenth century. Although the Mohajirs had not physically exterminated the Sindhis in the tradition of the American settlers, they had effectively deprived them of their lands and their jobs. (He forgot that his own ancestors had also come to Sind from India and done exactly the same thing.) Like the Punjabis, the Mohajir members of Al-Zulfikar were considered loyal, but 'loyal grade two', not 'grade one'.

Tipu was given $15,000 and British passports were bought for the entire group from Amsterdam. Tipu's passport, which he showed me in June 1983, named him as Victor Jones. The first stage was now complete. The four men assigned to the mission were ready to leave Libya, their fake passports in hand. The next task was to smuggle arms and explosives to Delhi, and Murtaza found a quick and practical way. A quantity of arms and ammunition belonging to Al-Zulfikar was still in Kabul in the care of the hijacker Nasir Jamal. Before he moved to New Delhi in September 1982, Murtaza had told Najibullah, the chief of Afghan intelligence, that he would shift this hardware to India at a later date. To carry out the assignment – which was to move the arms to India but ideally without the knowledge of the Afghans – he picked out Pervez Shinwari, his close companion and a tribal Pushtun who would need no interpreter in Kabul.

The shipment was small: only two Kalashnikovs, two revolvers, four hand-grenades and two hundred rounds of ammunition. It would fit into a suitcase and should not be difficult to whisk past customs and security at Kabul and New Delhi airports, which were fully briefed about Al-Zulfikar and its movements and under instructions to cooperate. Murtaza ordered Shinwari to keep Najibullah in the dark, and to spin him a cover story about visiting Kabul to negotiate the reopening of the Al-Zulfikar office there. He should even hold a round or two of talks on the subject with Najibullah. His real job was to secretly remove and conceal the guns and explosives intended for Delhi and then to await a phone call from Murtaza, who would run the operation from Damascus. As soon as Tipu arrived in New Delhi and gave Murtaza his location, Shinwari would be told to move.

Shinwari flew from Tripoli to Moscow and from there to Kabul at the end of January 1983. A few days later Murtaza flew into Damascus, his temporary operational headquarters. Meanwhile, Tipu and his four companions were busy preparing for their move to New Delhi. Murtaza had assured them that they would not be arrested in India after completing their mission. The moment that Zia was dead, power would fall into the hands of the PPP. Tipu and his friends, when they looked into the future, saw themselves transformed into the greatest heroes of the people of Pakistan. The Bhutto family would forever be in their debt. Millions would be waiting with flowers to receive them when they landed at Karachi. All of Al-Zulfikar's workers actually lived and were sustained by similar illusions. Dispensed under the established Bhutto brand-name, they explain how deprived members of the lower middle class, idealistic, confused but longing to do something heroic, became Al-Zulfikar cannon fodder.

Two days after Murtaza's departure for Damascus, Tipu and his friends took off from Tripoli to New Delhi. They were to transit through Dubai in the Gulf and from there by an Air India flight. Since they were travelling on forged British passports, they did not need to obtain a visa for India.

Luckily for General Zia, something happened in the transit lounge at Dubai airport which foiled the Delhi Plan. As Tipu recalled, they approached the immigration desk separately but while he got whisked through, his companions were betrayed by their Indian features yet very British names. The suspicious immigration officer asked them to stand aside, then scanned the passports and concluded that the photographs on the documents were makeshift additions. All three were taken into custody. The Dutch-made passports were a poor forgery, and in any case Dubai was an unsafe transit point, since the vast majority of the residents was of Indian or Pakistani origin and the immigration officials wise to the different tricks they used to gain entry into the Emirate.

Tipu told me that his companions requested the immigration officials to put them in touch with Major-General Imtiaz Ali, Bhutto's former military secretary, who had been living in Dubai since the Zia coup and had excellent relations with the Sheikhs of the ruling family. However, it is certain that even if the team had been able to make contact, someone of his experience and good sense would not have agreed to take responsibility for bailing out Murtaza's commandos. After a brief inquiry, all three were handed over to their homeland's authorities, and suffered the obvious consequences when the notorious interrogation centres of Pakistani intelligence extracted full confessions about the Delhi Plan. They were sentenced and jailed, and were only released when the PPP returned to power in November 1988 after Zia's death. One of them, Masroor Ahsan, was later returned to the Pakistan Senate on a PPP ticket.

As for Tipu, he boarded the next Delhi-bound Air India flight, not sure what had happened to his comrades. Death overlooked him in Dubai, though the reprieve was temporary. Tipu's name, description and other particulars were with Dubai immigration, courtesy of Interpol. To put a forged travel document in his hand and dispatch him on a dangerous operation amounted to an errand to the gallows. What a blessing for Murtaza that he could call on men with no purpose in life but to prove their loyalty to the Bhuttos.

As Tipu flew towards New Delhi, what worried him was the thought that if his companions failed to make it to India, he would lose his chance of becoming a hero. He therefore decided to complete the operation single-handed. On arrival in the Indian capital, he phoned Murtaza in Damascus, informed him of the misadventure and urged him to rescue the three men in Dubai before they were handed over to Pakistan. He recalled the conversation in Kabul in June 1983. 'As for the mission, I can accomplish it without anyone's help', he told Murtaza. 'Even if those three had been with me, I would have had to act alone. Please instruct Shinwari to get me the hardware.'

Murtaza assured Tipu that he should not worry on that count. He himself would have a word with Sheikh Zaid bin Sultan Al-Nahyan, the ruler of Abu Dhabi, and ask him to release the three men. He may even have tried to reach the Sheikh, little realizing that by then the Sheikh viewed Bhutto's son as an agent of the Soviet Union and a communist. The flow of money from Dubai had already dried up. It was only natural for Zaid to side with Zia rather than Murtaza.

However, even now, there still was an outside chance. Murtaza had Tipu, the last arrow in his quiver, and straining to be loosed. What did Murtaza have to lose? He praised Tipu profusely as a great revolutionary, then told him to proceed with the assassination attempt on General Zia, using Shinwari as his back-up. This was a new departure. According to the original plan, all Shinwari was supposed to do was bring the arms and ammunition to New Delhi and then return. Zia was to be killed at the shrine of the renowned saint and mystic Hazrat Nizamuddin Aulia in Delhi, a venue chosen because it was one place the general was going to visit without his host, Indian Prime Minister Mrs Indira Gandhi, whose life was not to be put at risk.

After his conversation with Tipu, Murtaza spoke to Shinwari in Kabul, and instructed him to arrive with the 'medicine' in Delhi, join Tipu and carry out the operation. For many days following, Shinwari made no contact with Tipu. As the date of Zia's arrival drew closer, Tipu's agitation and his anger at Shinwari increased. He kept phoning Damascus and complaining to Murtaza that Shinwari had failed to turn up. However, one evening Shinwari phoned Tipu and told him that he would arrive forty-eight hours before D-day. This was his first and last phone call. Tipu kept waiting but Shinwari never came. After that, the Kabul end went completely dead. This was how Tipu recalled it in the summer of 1983.

Cultivating sycophants and keeping those who have made sacrifices at arm's length is a Bhutto family characteristic. They either hate those who have made sacrifices or maybe they fear them. God alone knows. You see, I always insisted that people like Shinwari and Sohail Sethi would never stand up for anything or anyone, but the Chief [Murtaza] always encouraged them to hang around, and look what happened! At the crucial moment, Shinwari let me down. There I was waiting in Delhi and that man never showed up. Before the general's arrival I had even rented a car and picked out a spot outside the shrine for the operation. My plan was to stand on the roof of my car with a camera, as if I was taking pictures of Zia and his party. The moment he stepped out of his car, I would have picked up the Kalashnikov lying at my feet wrapped in a cloth and shot him. Had he survived, I would blown him to high heaven with hand-grenades. Even though Shinwari did not turn up, I went to my spot with a camera, and when the general emerged from his car he was no more than thirteen yards from me. I could hardly contain my frustration. I nearly grabbed him by the throat. It was a great opportunity lost because of Shinwari. There will never be another.

He could not shoot Zia with a gun, so he shot him with his camera: he took twenty-four pictures from different angles. He showed them to me, and there can be no question that if he had had a weapon that day, he would have killed Zia.

Tipu phoned Murtaza again and asked him what punishment he would suggest for Shinwari's 'treachery'. Murtaza's reply was: 'You were the commander of this operation. You go to Kabul and question him. If you are not satisfied with his explanation, you have the right to execute him.' Every Al-Zulfikar commander had been authorized by Murtaza to shoot any colleague on the spot who in his judgement showed signs of weakness when an operation was in progress. It made no difference to their leader because he never himself took part in any mission. One reason for Al-Zulfikar's failure was Murtaza's lack of operational experience and half-baked bookish knowledge. Its driving force was personal revenge, which is always a poor formula for victory.

The powers granted by Murtaza to his men had already claimed their first victim when Ilyas Siddiqui was shot. This blind law laid down by Murtaza was now Tipu's to implement. It was as if he had been given a knife and told that he was free to go and slash Pervez Shinwari's throat. That Murtaza did not speak up for Shinwari is further proof that in the ruthless power game he was playing, everyone, even a friend, was expendable.

I have described how in June 1979 Shinwari was caught smuggling arms at Jamrud, the principal post on the Pakistan–Afghanistan frontier. He was among those who were sprung from prison as part of the PIA hijack settlement with Zia. He and Sohail Sethi joined the inner sanctum of Al-Zulfikar and became Murtaza's mouthpieces in all matters involving intrigue and infighting in the organization. While it is true that Shinwari failed to reach New Delhi, had the mission involved only the shipment and delivery of arms, he might not have hesitated. However, to take up arms himself was beyond him. Being close to Murtaza, he must have known that the wheel had come full circle. Al-Zulfikar's game was over, and to join the battle now would be suicide. Shinwari was also married with children. He may have reached his personal limit. It was his misfortune that under Murtaza's rules, his failure to obey orders was treachery for which the punishment was death.

And what if the Delhi Plan had succeeded? To the government of India, it would have come as a stab in the back, and in order to prove its non-involvement, RAW would have rubbed out every trace of its Al-Zulfikar connection. There is also no question that the twenty or thirty men who were then being trained in India under RAW's supervision would have been liquidated. Zia's murder on Indian soil would have made him the greatest martyr in Pakistan's history and wiped out the Pakistan People's Party. The general's place would have been taken by another general, but the political succession that Murtaza was later to claim would have remained a dream. The murder of the chief of the Pakistan army could also have led to a war between the two countries, and who knows how many lives that would have claimed? As it turned out, even the botched Delhi plan claimed the lives of two workers and the long imprisonment of three.

With Shinwari's death warrant practically made out, Tipu landed in Kabul on 12 March 1983. He had no Afghan visa, but such formalities were not for him. Everyone at the airport recognized the hero of the PIA hijacking. In fact, he was dropped at Murtaza's old house by a couple of airport intelligence officials themselves. Najibullah had no knowledge of his arrival and remained unaware of it till he had done his job. A shudder must have chilled Shinwari's spine when Tipu appeared at his house. He knew Murtaza's sentence for desertion. He knew that Tipu was the Tara Masih of Al-Zulfikar.[4] He must also have remembered that in Tripoli he had once had a fight with Tipu. At Murtaza's orders, Shinwari had accused Qayum Butt of disloyalty. When Tipu learned what had happened, he grabbed Shinwari by the collar and screamed at him. Butt was later expelled from Libya. Given this background, Shinwari had cause for apprehension at Tipu's arrival in Kabul.

Tipu was an old hand by now. He put Shinwari at ease by telling him that he was in the city to deal with 'old traitors' like Kausar Ali Shah and some others who had left the organization. In June 1983, Tipu told me that he wanted to kill Shinwari because it was people like him who had destroyed Al-Zulfikar. The fact is that he resented Shinwari and Sohail Sethi because they were close to Murtaza. Tipu wanted to dislodge and supplant them. He had come to Kabul to settle old scores. In order to further disarm Shinwari, he spent a couple of drinking evenings with him. He asked him in passing what had prevented his coming to Delhi, and found the explanation unconvincing. His mind was now made up. As commander of the botched operation, he would have to kill the man who had let him down. He said in his defence during the trial that he made a final check with Murtaza, who told him that the rules of the organization applied to everyone equally and he was free to follow his best judgement. Murtaza must have known what Tipu's 'best judgement' would be.

It would be an awkward job to murder Shinwari where he lived: there were too many people around, and problems getting rid of the body. Instead, Tipu chose a sparsely populated suburb of the city. On 15 March 1983, he invited the unsuspecting Shinwari to come for a drive in their jeep. 'Let's do a quick round before they clamp down the curfew', he suggested in a friendly tone. (Kabul used to be put under an all-night curfew at 10 pm.) They drove through Shehr-i-Nau and Tipu turned towards Khair Khana, the suburb he had picked out for the murder, about six kilometres from Kabul. The city had been without power for several days because of commando action by the Afghan resistance and the roads were dark.

Tipu told the court what happened next. Once they had left the populated area, he stopped the jeep and asked Shinwari to take the wheel. As soon as he was in the driver's seat, Tipu pulled out a gun, placed it against his victim's temple and fired two shots before he could react. Methodically, he emptied Shinwari's pockets, and even removed the new pair of shoes he was wearing. He drove the jeep into a field where he dumped the body, got home before the curfew hour, and washed the seats in his garage before the blood could congeal.

Shinwari had obtained his release from prison exactly two years earlier as a result of Tipu's hijacking. As he flew towards freedom and life, he was embarking on the journey that would lead him two years later to a rendezvous with death in a strange and desolate place.

The war-torn city of Kabul had neither the time nor the inclination to pick up unclaimed dead bodies. With so many corpses strewn about, the local administration had chosen the simplest way of getting rid of them. They were thrown into a pit and buried. There was every likelihood that the same thing would happen to Shinwari, leaving no evidence of his being alive or dead. Tipu's arrival in the city had not been officially recorded and no one had seen him leaving Shinwari's house that night with the victim.

However, it has been said that even the cleverest murderer leaves a clue behind. While Tipu robbed Shinwari of his money, he forgot to remove his identity card. All Al-Zulfikar members carried a card to keep them out of trouble with the police, who had pickets everywhere in Kabul, mainly to rope in recruits for the army. While these cards saved their bearers from forcible induction into the Afghan army, in Pakistan whoever was caught with an Al-Zulfikar card met a terrible fate at the hands of the security agencies.

It so happened that Shinwari's body was discovered and his identity card found by the police. Najibullah, then chief of the Afghan intelligence agency, was immediately informed. He deputed Nasrullah Mangal, one of his officers, to investigate. When he arrived at Shinwari's house, he found Tipu sleeping soundly. This was the first anyone senior enough had come to know about his presence in Kabul. Mangal also established without much difficulty that the tyre marks in the field where Shinwari's dead body was found were made by Shinwari's jeep. Although Tipu had done his best to wash the vehicle, Mangal was able to discover some congealed blood under one of the seats. It was clear that Shinwari had been murdered, most probably in the jeep, and the murderer was none other than Tipu. On 20 March, the eve of the Afghan new year, he was arrested. It was his fourth and last murder.

The infighting in Al-Zulfikar needs to be briefly analysed. Clearly the journey of revenge on which Murtaza had embarked in March 1981 with the sensational hijack of the Pakistani aircraft had declined into farce and disappointment by March 1983. That the operatives themselves were now at one another's throats was an outcome of this failure. The organization had been unable to attract new volunteers into its ranks and was left with no option but to recycle those it had. Normally, Tipu or Shinwari would not have been assigned to undertake fresh operations, but dwindling numbers left Murtaza no option but to use the same men. For example, Ayaz Sammu was sent to Pakistan four times on operational assignments between 1982 and 1984. In the end, he was caught and executed. Rehmatullah Anjum thrice went to Pakistan between 1981 and 1983, and died when a grenade exploded accidentally in his hand. Javed Malik was also in Pakistan three times in the same period as Anjum, and in 1984 he was arrested in Vienna and jailed for nine years. If any Al-Zulfikar worker or operative is left alive today, he should thank his own good luck, not Murtaza Bhutto's loving care.

The Afghans arrested not only Tipu but also Nasir Jamal for the murder of Shinwari, suspecting that it had been a two-man operation. However, right from the start Tipu bragged that the killing was an internal organizational matter and he alone was responsible for it. Nasir Jamal was freed on 28 March 1983. According to my information, while he knew about

Tipu's intentions, he had taken no part in the crime. He told me that he had actually advised Tipu to forget about the whole thing, a suggestion the Karachi hothead had rejected. Disclosing details of the Delhi plan to Afghan intelligence authorities for the first time, Tipu told them that Shinwari's visit to discuss the opening of an Al-Zulfikar office was a cover story. His real mission had been to pick up the arms required for the New Delhi operation. Since he had sabotaged the plan, he had been liquidated in line with Al-Zulfikar's rules and with the prior approval of its leader, Murtaza Bhutto.

Najibullah cared nothing for moral or legal niceties. He still wanted Murtaza back in Kabul so that he could use his presence as a propaganda ploy against Pakistan. The moment he heard of Murtaza's involvement in Shinwari's murder, he had Tipu taken out of his cell and put under comfortable house arrest. His three rooms included a living-room, a bedroom and a study, complete with volumes of Marx and Lenin, not to mention Babrak Karmal's inspiring collections of speeches. His food was brought in from the Hotel Intercontinental, since that had been Tipu's wish. It may be added that in Afghanistan there is no tradition of A or B class prisoners. The families of the former president and his cabinet ministers, for instance, were living in conditions of extreme hardship in jail. Tipu was the first inmate of a jail in Afghan history to be given 'VIP treatment'.

Afghan intelligence did not interrogate Tipu again. This was not his first murder, in any case: it was in Kabul that he had murdered Tariq Rahim and Mazdoor Yar Afridi. The only interest Najibullah took in Tipu's arrest was that it enabled him to re-establish his severed links with Murtaza. It mattered little to his tribal psychology if one Pakistani killed another. Lost on him was the tragic irony that the man who had been killed and the man who had killed him both belonged to Al-Zulfikar. Najibullah had buried one and he was quite willing to release the other if it could put Murtaza under an obligation. It was as if these men were Murtaza's bond-slaves whose life or death depended on the leader's pleasure. Najibullah laboured under the mistaken impression that Tipu was still important to the Bhutto family, and that to have him freed, Murtaza would contact him personally. When there was no move from Murtaza's side for several days, the Afghan intelligence chief summoned Tipu and asked him to phone Damascus. 'If Murtaza tells me on the phone that Shinwari's murder was carried out under his orders for organizational reasons, I will release you,' he promised.

The moment he heard about Shinwari's murder, Tipu's arrest and Najibullah's promise, instead of speaking to the Afghan and asking for his agent's release, Murtaza broke the connection. He was not so naive, after all, as to confess to sanctioning a murder over an open phone line. He had left Kabul because the former relationship of trust between himself and

Najibullah had ended. He may have feared that if he said, or even implied, that Shinwari had been killed on his orders, it might be used against him, even in an Afghan radio broadcast. Whatever his reasons, for several days afterwards he refused to come to the phone when Najibullah called.

In desperation, Najibullah decided to get in touch with Begum Bhutto, who was receiving medical treatment in France. He sent a message through the Afghan consulate requesting her to make contact with him. Her answer was short and straight: 'I do not talk to policemen.'[5] Najibullah must have found her attitude perplexing. Didn't she care about saving the life of Tipu, who had declared in Damascus that she was his mother? Was she not willing to talk to the Kabul government to which she had accorded public recognition after the hijack? What he could not grasp was that to Begum Bhutto the universe revolved around her children. With her true sons safe in Damascus, it was of no consequence to her who perished in a Kabul jail. Angry and insulted, Najibullah screamed at Tipu: 'You say that Begum Bhutto put a locket around your neck and called you her son. You went around claiming to be Murtaza's deputy. Are these the leaders you followed, who do not care whether you live or die? Can such people bring about a revolution?'[6]

Tipu was shattered by the indifference shown by Begum Bhutto and Murtaza. It did not take him long to conclude that those who abandoned him to die in an Afghan jail would not hesitate to liquidate him even if he survived. It was then that he decided he was through with Murtaza.

Tipu had learnt his lesson, but it came too late to bring him his freedom. He had to do something more. First, he had Nasir Jamal appeal for help to all those who resented Murtaza for his treatment of them. He even had an approach made to that implacable PPP enemy, Ajmal Khattak, the Pushtun leader who was living in exile in Kabul. He was hoping that these moves would somehow result in pressure on Najibullah to set him free.

Under the strange impression that I had influence with the Afghan authorities, on 2 April 1983, within a week of his release Nasir Jamal also came to see me. It was my first meeting with this young man. I took pains to explain to him that in the world in which we lived, famous families and names carried weight. In Najibullah's eyes, Murtaza's greatest asset was his family, so whatever I told him would not count. Second, I had known Shinwari and was sad that he had been murdered. How could I be expected to help his killer? Third, it was a matter between Tipu and Murtaza and they should resolve it amongst themselves. And, finally, on the night of 23 October 1980 when I had been arrested at Murtaza's behest, my relationship with him had ended for all time. I had no wish to revive that link in any form or manner. Nasir Jamal looked crestfallen and left.

Tipu then went on hunger strike in jail. On the seventh day, Najibullah felt worried enough to consult the more prominent Pakistanis in Kabul for advice. That evening he invited me to dinner and wanted to know my views. I told him that I had been released from jail only a few months earlier. I did not know the hijackers, my information about Al-Zulfikar was limited, and I was in no position to advise him. I received the strong impression that he wanted to get rid of Tipu by releasing him. He told me that he was going to send for him right away and talk to him.

His office was no more than a hundred yards from the house where Tipu was being kept, and it did not take him long to be brought in. There were fifteen to twenty Afghan officers at the dining table (Najibullah had dining facilities in his office). Tipu walked in giving the impression that his hunger strike had left him so weak that he would collapse at any moment. He was obviously putting on a show. Since he did not know my face, he paid no attention to me. What he said, though haltingly, sounded well-rehearsed.

I wish to spend the rest of my life in your service. Afghan rebels and leaders frequently travel to the Gulf states. I want to hijack a plane from Dubai in which these people are travelling.

My first impression of Tipu was that he was a man of extreme superficiality, performing like a circus animal, but I noticed that when he mentioned hijacking, Najibullah's eyes brightened. The bait that Tipu dangled, Najibullah happily bit, though only a short-sighted optimist could have been drawn to a scheme so full of holes. First of all, the chances of Tipu landing at Dubai without detection were slim, considering that his companions had been picked up there earlier. Second, he was not a professional hijacker who could just board an aircraft and hijack it. Third, even supposing he managed to bring a plane to Kabul, was Najibullah in a position to handle its political fallout? However, he was looking for an excuse to set Tipu free and would have done so anyway even if Tipu had not come up with his wild idea.

In May 1983, Najibullah released Tipu. The responsibility for his food, accommodation and other expenses was passed on to Afghan intelligence's Department No. 5, headed by a Dr Bahar, who took charge not only of Tipu but of the Dubai hijacking plan. He found Tipu a fine residential house in the city's expensive Wazir Akbar Khan quarter. He was also given a new car, which he had long wanted. He now had the privileged life that Murtaza had denied him in the past.

Tipu was on the loose again. The streets of Kabul daily heard and saw his racing turns. He liked to startle people – it made them take notice – and that became his special style. He would drive through the streets of Shehr-i-Nau, his right hand clutching a revolver, his left on the steering wheel. He believed that he had status because he had been a hijacker.

When he stopped to buy something from a roadside shop, he would summon the shopkeeper with his revolver and then introduce himself in pidgin Persian. 'Man Alamgir asti [sic]. Man taiyyara awurdi [sic].' (I am Alamgir who brought in the plane.)

Before long, Tipu became a figure of fun and a certain amount of fear in Kabul. Most people tended to avoid him. They would move away when they saw his car zooming in. He grew so wild that one day he fired at an Afghan named Ashraf who had had the nerve to overtake him. He saw his new privileges as the restoration of fair and well-earned rights, and convinced himself that he was now an acknowledged guest and honoured revolutionary, the sole claimant of the asset called Al-Zulfikar. He even snatched the keys of the Al-Zulfikar arsenal from Nasir Jamal and began to sell what arms it still contained to the Baluchi insurgents. When Nasir became afraid that Tipu's reckless conduct would lead to more trouble some day, and suggested that perhaps his friend should leave Kabul, Tipu was furious. 'Do you want to destroy the roots I have grown here?'

Tipu had a passport and around fourteen thousand dollars in cash. When circumstances now provided him with an opportunity to get out of Kabul via India, a man with any sense would have fled to India without breathing one more whiff of Afghan air. It would have been impossible to find him in the sea of humanity that was India. He could have buried his past and started a new life under a new name in a new city with the help of his family, half of which was living in India anyway. But safety and security had never been his goals. When he should have been running away from death, he was pursuing it with his eyes closed. He did not realize that he was fast approaching the point of no return.

As Tipu burned rubber on the streets of Kabul, a jirga of the Shinwari tribe arrived from Pakistan and asked the Afghan government for the head of the man who had killed their kinsman. This delegation called on Najibullah, and in accordance with Pushtun tradition, said to him: 'We have buried the dead body of Pervez Shinwari, but we have not said his funeral prayers, which must await the beheading of his murderer. We demand that his killer be handed over to us.' Although it was Kabul government policy to keep the tribes happy, Najibullah managed to put them off with a number of excuses.

When Murtaza learnt of Tipu's release and his high living in Kabul, he broke his silence and phoned Najibullah to request him to try Tipu for the murder of Shinwari. He was afraid that Tipu might set up a rival Al-Zulfikar by rallying its disgruntled cadres. Once again, Murtaza had got it wrong. If Tipu had that kind of sense, would he have murdered three men at Murtaza's bidding?

Dr Bahar, the man made responsible for Tipu, was a surgeon by profession, but his reputation in intelligence circles was that of a butcher. After fattening up Tipu for several months, some time in early August 1983 he ordered him to make preparations to leave for Dubai and bring back the aircraft he had promised to hijack. It was as if he had pulled out a butcher's knife and placed it across Tipu's throat. Tipu was stunned. He had dreamt up the Dubai thing just to get out of prison. He had even begun to believe that the Afghans had forgotten what he had offered to do. His answer to Dr Bahar was: 'Look, comrade, I am a communist and a revolutionary. I cannot restage such a terrorist act as a hijack.' The blunt Bahar rasped back: 'Look here, you are neither a revolutionary nor will you ever make a communist. You are a third-rate crook whose only objective in life is vice and extravagance.'

When Bahar informed Najibullah of the exchange, his chief took only a minute to decide that harbouring someone as dangerous as Tipu would bring nothing but disaster. Even then, he did not order Tipu's arrest but gave him an air ticket on a flight leaving for Delhi. KHAD made it clear to Tipu that he should try his luck in another country. This was a golden opportunity: Tipu saw it as a threat. Here in Kabul he had come to know a life of comfort and privilege for the first time, and he could not let it end. He tore up the air ticket Najibullah had sent, threw the pieces on the floor and screamed at the KHAD men who delivered it: 'We shall see who orders me out of here!'

Tipu believed that he had taken control, but he had signed his own death warrant. What he had come to regard as security was impending catastrophe. All of his signals were crossed. He had interpreted Najibullah's uncharacteristically polite attitude as a sign of Kabul's obligation, if not its bounden duty, to treat him like a VIP. One of the many things he failed to understand was that Najibullah was an Afghan version of Tipu himself. It was suicidally naive on Tipu's part to have convinced himself that the Kabul government could not afford to arrest him again. Instead, he persuaded himself that it was trying to get him to leave so as to escape its responsibility, indeed its duty. This at least is what I gathered from our later conversations.

Tipu's arrogant stupidity must have bemused Najibullah, who was reluctant to soil his hands with Tipu's blood, and wanted to give him one last chance to escape alive. Accordingly, on 28 August 1983 two tough Afghan security men arrived at Tipu's house with orders to physically remove him and put him on a flight leaving Kabul. They bundled Tipu and his belongings into a car and drove him to the airport, where an Air India flight was due to leave that day.

As soon as they entered the terminal, Tipu created a big scene. He climbed the Air India counter and began to shout at the top of his voice:

Listen everybody, I am Alamgir, the hijacker of the Pakistani aircraft. Under international law, no airline can knowingly carry a hijacker. I call on Air India to cancel my seat. If I am forced out of here, I will hold a press conference at the New Delhi airport and tell the world about the role of Najibullah and Murtaza Bhutto in the hijacking.

Since there were no Western press representatives in Kabul at the time, having been declared undesirable and thrown out, the story did not get filed, otherwise by the evening it would have been all over the world.

The intelligence men tried to restrain Tipu, but he charged them like a bull in mating season, kicking and hitting them. These were junior employees, not authorized to hit him back. Tipu then walked out of the terminal, climbed into a taxi and went home. His car was in the porch. He got behind the wheel and was seen driving imperiously on the roads of Shehr-i-Nau, happy as a lark, and foolish enough to believe that he had checkmated those who were trying to oust him from Kabul.

Tipu was incapable of thinking straight or interpreting anything logically. He now wanted Najibullah to reverse his decision to deport him from Kabul. While it is true that without the Tipu–Murtaza–Najibullah troika the hijack could not have taken place, by threatening to blow the whistle on Najibullah if forcibly flown to Delhi, Tipu was trying to blackmail the Afghan official into looking after him and his needs for the rest of his life, and in Kabul. He had realized that if he fell into Murtaza's hands, he would be forced to swallow the PLO-supplied poison which Al-Zulfikar's chief always carried.

The living conditions of former Al-Zulfikar men in Kabul were unspeakable. They had been dumped by their leader, who had also denounced them as traitors. Tipu had decided that this was his 'team' and he would try to look after them. These leftovers and misfits had nothing better to do, and were glad to have been even noticed. By now, the rift between Murtaza and Tipu had come into the open. Some of the men around Tipu who were keen to get back into Murtaza's good books started reporting everything they heard and saw to him in Delhi. When he received news of Tipu's big scene at Kabul airport, he phoned Najibullah. 'We are prepared to open an office in Kabul, but we have two conditions. First, Tipu's continued existence is a serious threat to us. Second, some of our opponents whom you have given asylum in Kabul must be expelled.'[7]

Murtaza's phone call was Tipu's end. For Najibullah, it was a perfectly profitable deal. By getting rid of Tipu, his involvement in the hijack would remain unpublicized, and the Shinwari tribe could be put under an obligation as well. He would also be able to re-establish his links with Al-Zulfikar. Additionally, the liquidation of Tipu would help lift UN sanctions and the boycott of Afghanistan by international airlines. In short, there was only advantage in the course he was being asked to take.

Nearly a week had passed since the Kabul airport incident when on the night of 6 September, five Afghan commandos entered Tipu's bedroom very quietly. By the time he woke up, his mouth had been taped. He was thrown like a parcel into the truck they had brought and taken straight to the Pul-i-Charkhi prison. In March he had been housed in special facilities. Now he was in that notorious place, and he quickly found out what a real Afghan jail was like. At first he tried to stage a hunger strike, but as they say in Kabul, the camel now lay under the mountain, and no amount of screaming could penetrate the rock. After a couple of days, he realized the situation and called off the hunger strike.

Pul-i-Charkhi was not a jail in the sense in which this word is used elsewhere. It could best be compared to a cave at whose entrance the footprints of those who have gone in are discernible, but where there is no sign that any have ever walked out towards life and freedom. The days and nights of its inmates swung like a pendulum between life and death. While I was there, the overall supervision of the prison was in the hands of workers of the ruling party, the PDPA. Like me, these men too were under the spell of socialism, so I was their ideological compatriot. I was also innocent, basically sympathetic to the revolution and above all a man without a country. Perhaps it was because of these factors that they always treated me with kindness. Even after I was released, I maintained good relations with them. There was hardly a week when the commander of the jail, Khwaja Ata, the jail doctor, Ghairat Mal, the deputy jail commander, Shamsuddin, or comrades Ashraf and Issa did not visit me. That was how I continued to remain well informed about Tipu, his state of mind and other developments. Only two or three weeks after landing in Pul-i-Charkhi, his feet had come to rest on solid ground. He would bang his head against the walls and wail: 'Comrade Najibullah, give me one more opportunity to go to the Kabul airport and I will leave this great land of revolution forever.'

An Afghan saying states that what comes last is often the best, but it is not always so in real life. Sometimes what comes last is the worst, if you have spurned the opportunity that came earlier. This was the case with Tipu, who now lay helpless behind the impregnable stone walls of the Kabul prison, desperately trying to turn back the clock.

Two months after he came to Pul-i-Charkhi, Tipu began to be haunted by his innocent victims, men he had cruelly killed. Shamsuddin told me:

I was in a chair outside my office, taking the sun, when the guards brought Tipu out for his daily walk. I called him over and asked him how he was. While we were talking, a fresh batch of wooden coffins made here by the inmates was being taken out. Tipu was taken aback, and he asked me: 'Do you make coffins here too?' I told him that these were specially made for the 'martyrs' of the 'friends' army' [which was how the Soviet troops were referred to]. I added that the coffin in which Tariq Rahim, the man he had murdered during the hijack, was sent home had also been made in our jail. The moment he heard Tariq Rahim's name, he began to weep. That entire night he spent wailing and talking to himself.

Shamsuddin was an Afghan and, as such, unable to understand why Tipu was making such a scene, because Afghans do not wail either when they are about to die, or after they have killed someone.

In October 1983, Tipu's case went to court. According to his statement under oath, he had killed Shinwari with the approval of Murtaza, with Nasir Jamal as an accomplice. He told the court that when he informed Murtaza of Shinwari's murder, he ordered him to kill two other 'traitors' too, and then get out of Kabul. Had Murtaza not asked him to do that, he would have taken the flight to Delhi the next morning, he added. Nasir Jamal was summoned. As was to be expected, he testified against Tipu. To save himself, he tried his best to prove that Tipu alone was the murderer. But even had Nasir not given his testimony, the court would still have reached the same conclusion. The judgement against Tipu had already been made, in line with the revolutionary justice of Najibullah. The hearing was no more than a legal formality.

As for myself, all I wanted was to get out of Kabul. Various problems had kept me there following my release in March 1983. I had no travel documents, nor had the authorities formally permitted me to leave the country. At the end of December, the Afghan authorities told me that I was free to travel. My flight was to take off on the morning of 1 January 1984. On the night of 28 December, the jail commander, Khwaja Ata, invited me for a farewell dinner. Tipu's name came up during the conversation, and the Afghan told me that when he informed Tipu that I was leaving, he had begged him to arrange for him to see me. He made him swear on his children that he would do so. Khwaja Ata was not a professional jail official but a party functionary. In his book, only those who were fighting against the regime were criminals. Since Tipu did not fall into that category, in Khwaja Ata's eyes any help rendered to him amounted to a gesture of 'socialist humanism'.

In the Pul-i-Charkhi prison, such 'imperialist facilities' as visits from friends or family did not exist. The comrades had caged their enemies and opponents like animals, and Khwaja Ata was the man in charge of this human menagerie. Ata told me to come the next day as if I was there to say farewell. 'Leave the rest to me', he added.

Next day I turned up and was taken to Khwaja Ata's office. He ordered Tipu to be brought in. Tipu had changed so much that at first I had difficulty recognizing him. Instead of the military-style haircut he used to wear, his head was shaven. He did not have the old 'officer's moustache' any longer, but an orthodox Muslim's beard. The fingers which used to play with the trigger of a gun were busy telling a rosary. He did not look like Tipu so much as Maulana Salamullah Khan.

My first reaction on seeing him was to wonder: Is this terrified man who resembles a trapped rat the same Tipu who shot dead the young Hafiz Aslam in Karachi in front of hundreds of people? Is he the same Tipu who killed Tariq Rahim so cruelly in the hijack? Is he the same person who emptied an entire magazine into Mazdoor Yar Afridi in the presence of scores of party men? Is he the same desperado who shot at Ashraf, the young Afghan, because he had committed the crime of overtaking him, and is he really the same gunman who shot Shinwari twice through the head? Can I recognize in this man the trigger-happy fellow who used to summon roadside shopkeepers with his revolver? I felt that Tipu knew his end was near and there could be no going back. Death was in wait around the corner.

'Please tell Dr Sahib [Najibullah] before you leave that he should give me one more opportunity to leave Kabul,' was the first thing he said to me. I realized that he had reached a point where a mere straw like me appeared to him to have the strength of a tree. Had no one told him that I had spent two and a half years in this very prison, my entire wardrobe a single change of clothes? Had I had any influence with Najibullah, would he have kept me imprisoned at Murtaza's whim? But Tipu continued:

You are about to leave. If circumstances ever change and you get the opportunity to return to Pakistan, please tell my parents that I regret the past and I seek their forgiveness. It was an evil day and the worst moment of my life when I spurned my father at Damascus airport to gain favour with the Bhutto family. Had I listened to my father, today I would have been standing on the blessed soil of my own country. If God ever allows me an opportunity to make up for my sins, I will scream to the world that Bhutto is not my father any more than Nusrat is my mother. Those sycophants and fools who disown their real parents for false ones should learn from my end.

The revolutionary fever had left him by now.
I said to him:

Bhutto is not among us today. Whether somebody shouts slogans for him or screams obscenities, it will make no difference to him. People like us are guilty, not Bhutto, because we are given to worshipping the past and running after the shades of the dead. Our masses are no different, who rain stones on the living and worship those who lie in their graves.

But Tipu cut me short:

You are alive, and that is why you are looking for your future by searching through your past. As for me, I stand at death's door. I cannot lie to myself. Neither my greed nor my opportunism, nor flattery nor sacrifice can be of any use to me. I alone destroyed twelve families for the sake of that one 'persecuted family'. Our three families, the families of the hijackers, were destroyed. Five friends who assisted us in Karachi now await death or a life in prison. I was made to murder four people. Come to think of it, General Zia had not hanged my father. I had no personal quarrel with him. Was I his rival for the seat of power? By using words like brother and son, this Bhutto family placed the burden that was theirs to carry on our backs. Today, the sons of the late Bhutto are in Delhi, having a good time, and Nusrat is in France, but where is Tipu? He stands on the gallows. First they made us kill others; now they are getting us killed. What quarrel did I have with Tariq Rahim? I was told: 'This man is a traitor. He was responsible for papa's martyrdom. Beat him black and blue with your shoes and kill him. That's what the Martyr's spirit demands.' I didn't know that man. He wasn't my father's ADC. If I am meeting my end today, their day of reckoning will also come.

I felt as if he was speaking to himself more than to me. It was like a soliloquy. While the innocent men he had killed had crossed the dividing line between life and death in a matter of seconds, he, their killer, was painfully crawling towards his end. Each moment that was now left to him was like a new crucifixion. What greater punishment could Tipu suffer than to realize that only a couple of years earlier the same Najibullah who now was his executioner had stood under that plane at Kabul airport and cheered his action? Murtaza, once his mentor, was calling the tune that would take him to the gallows – the same man at whose bidding he had doled out death and destruction. Today, he was going to die at his hands. Nothing could save him, nor in the end explain what had happened.

I felt that Tipu knew there would be no mourners when the last breath left his body. There would be no funeral, and no grave. As he had dumped the dead body of Mazdoor Yar Afridi in a ditch, some ditch, somewhere, now lay in wait for his. He wanted to scream out his confession, but there were no listeners. The faces of those he had murdered in the name of

Bhutto's politics were haunting him, and he was feeling death come closer with each passing minute. He must also have wondered how he would be remembered or described by those to whom he had sworn lifelong allegiance. And what about the mother whom he had sacrificed at the feet of Begum Nusrat Bhutto, and the father he had snubbed at Damascus airport? I said nothing. I just listened to him. Perhaps that was what he expected.

He paused for a moment, then said:

Maybe they will keep my death a secret; but whenever it is possible, please let my parents know. Tell them to beg the families of Tariq Rahim, Hafiz Aslam, Afridi and Shinwari to forgive me. I have spent my life causing pain to others. I realize today the sins I have committed, but it seems life is not prepared to give me a chance to expiate. I often think how unlucky my father is. When he was a child, he lived through the trauma of his father's execution. Today, when he is an old man, he is going to witness his son's hanging. And then go on living.

At that point, he was overcome and began to weep. I felt my own eyes getting moist.

I left Kabul for East Germany on 1 January 1984. Although Tipu was tried for the murder of Shinwari, he was given the death sentence for the hijacking. It is interesting that the two other hijackers, Nasir Jamal and Arshad Ali Khan 'Tegi', were given fourteen years each in absentia. Nasir was in Kabul when the judgement was announced. Somewhere around the middle of June 1984, the Afghan government repatriated him and his entire family to Libya at state expense. Faithful to his promise to Murtaza, by the end of 1984 Najibullah had expelled all Al-Zulfikar dissidents from Kabul, including the two who had ratted on Tipu to Murtaza. Murtaza sent a representative to the Afghan capital to confirm the expulsion of his opponents and the death sentence to Tipu. If I recall, it was in July 1984 that Tipu was executed by firing squad. His dead body was shown to Murtaza's envoy, the elders of the Shinwari tribe and a UN representative. However, Najibullah's objective, namely normalization of relations with Al-Zulfikar, remained unfulfilled.

But what happened to Tipu's two co-hijackers? The course they had embarked on in March 1981 led them through great hardship. 'Tegi' practically opted out of Al-Zulfikar as soon as the drama was over and they were in Kabul. He was not much use to Murtaza, and so he was permitted to go to Libya. In fact, it was at Murtaza's recommendation that Libyan Airlines employed him at company headquarters in Tripoli. His thirteen-day 'experience' of air piracy turned out to be of some benefit in the end. He not only got a job but a good place to live and a car to drive. 'Tegi' was by nature an honest and hard-working young man who began to save money and send it to his family regularly every month, and until the middle of 1992 he was still working for the airline.

As for Nasir Jamal, after the hijack he began to take active part in internal Al-Zulfikar politics. In 1982, along with Tipu, he was sent to Libya, but was allowed to return to Kabul after a few months so that he could be with his family. The Kabul authorities gave him a house and a car and the Libyan embassy put him on a monthly stipend of $200 as 'pension' for serving Libyan Airlines in 1982 for a few months. In 1983, because of Shinwari's murder, his relations with Murtaza soured. A year later, he was expelled from Kabul and landed in Tripoli with his wife and children. Despite Murtaza's disapproval, Salem bin Aamir provided him with a job and a place to live. He was put on the staff of the Urdu magazine *Sultani Jamhoor*, brought out by the Libyan government. This publication was edited by Shaukat Ali and Zafar Yasin.

Had Salem bin Aamir not taken these two men under his wing, they too would have met the same end as Tipu. By accepting responsibility that should have been Murtaza's, the Libyan intelligence official saved these people from a tragic fate. He might have continued to support them but for the fact that after the destruction of the Soviet Union in 1990, Libya suddenly became friendless. The pendulum of history had swung against Colonel Gaddhafi, and the United States and Britain, to settle old scores, had demanded that Libya hand over men who were believed to be responsible for the 1986 bombing of the Pan Am passenger airliner over Lockerbie, Scotland. While Western sources themselves believed that the bombing was a Syrian operation, by getting under the American flag in 1991, Syria was forgiven its sins, which were transferred to Libya. Gaddhafi found himself in the galling situation of having to protest to the Americans that he was innocent of Lockerbie. It was a re-enactment in real life of the fable in which a thirsty lamb, drinking from a stream, is eaten by a lion for the crime of muddying the water, though he is drinking downstream and it is the lion actually who is muddying the water.

By 1992, the United States, the only superpower in the world, had tightened the noose around Libya, in the process reaching its real objective: the political and economic consolidation of its regional friend and ally, Husni Mubarak of Egypt. The American strategy was successful. Not only was Libya forced to use Egypt to stay economically alive, it even had to accept Mubarak as a friend and helper, the same Mubarak who used to be referred to as an imperialist agent. Taking advantage of the changed position, the United States conveyed to the colonel through Mubarak that if by a certain date Libya did not dismantle all the guerrilla training camps that it ran, they would be destroyed by the United States itself. Gaddhafi's desert instinct told him that under the circumstances the most prudent course lay in getting rid of all revolutionary remnants of the past. Can there be a greater irony than the bulldozing under Gaddhafi's personal orders of every 'revolutionary camp' in the country, including Ma'askar-i-Nasser?

The next American and British demand was that the terrorists believed to be responsible for the Lockerbie bombing should be handed over to them. But this was where the Libyan leader drew a line, while looking for an honourable face-saving device. Offering to try those charged in an international court, he kept the two men wanted by the West jailed in Tripoli.

Under the circumstances, it was no longer possible for Libya to carry Murtaza and take responsibility for his actions. In March 1992, both Nasir Jamal and Arshad Ali Khan 'Tegi' were taken into custody, but Libya did not hand them over to the anti-Bhutto government in power in Pakistan at the time. It is interesting that to date no Pakistani government has demanded the return of the two hijackers. While the Colonel's refusal to hand over a weapon to the enemies of the Bhutto family is commendable in its own way, even he would have been incapable of imagining that a reminder of that past would someday become a nightmare to the Bhuttos. If Gaddhafi believed that by returning the hijackers to Pakistan, with the Bhuttos in power, he would help save their lives, then all one can say is that the Libyan leader was unaware of the glorious political traditions of the family.

14

Forgotten Victims

The young men who followed the mirage of Al-Zulfikar had nowhere to go. What they underwent in their camps in Kabul, Delhi, Tripoli and Damascus remains an untold story because, for one thing, the Pakistani media failed to fulfil its duty. While journalists and writers on the right could not be expected to have sympathy for their plight, or any interest in their internal squabbles, those on the left were so taken with the Bhutto family between 1977 and 1989 that anyone deleted from the list of family loyalists was either played down or ignored. The hanging of Bhutto was a collective political tragedy. Sycophants reduced it to the tragedy of one family which had been singled out for persecution. It simply did not fit the bill to highlight or even mention the fate of those who had suffered at the hands of the 'persecuted' Murtaza Bhutto.

If the leadership of the PPP was in the hands of the Bhutto ladies, the sole proprietary rights for Al-Zulfikar belonged to the male side of the family. In other words, Bhutto's revolution and democracy coexisted under the same roof. Whereas it was customary for all party faithfuls to declare that there was no link between the PPP and Al-Zulfikar, the fact was that whenever an Al-Zulfikar member was hanged by the army junta, the Bhutto ladies lost no time in inscribing the word 'martyr' on his grave. Likewise the Al-Zulfikar guerrillas, workers and volunteers in Kabul, Delhi and Damascus whom Murtaza declared to be traitors invariably found the doors of the PPP closed to them by the Bhutto ladies. The strategic wall erected between the party and Al-Zulfikar during the Zia era later gave rise to a feud involving the control and overlordship of the PPP between Benazir and Murtaza.

It is not possible to make sense of Murtaza's statements and actions without understanding the complex personality of the man. As leader of Al-Zulfikar, his lack of equipment in a new and hostile setting developed in him a fear of death and a sense of insecurity. For years his mother had drilled just one message into his head: 'Beware of army commandos; they are out to get you.'[1] Begum Bhutto, however, could not foresee that her son's life was at risk when her own daughter was in power.

His mother's obsessive and constant warnings, coupled with his own sponsorship of armed actions against the military regime and other targets in Pakistan, soon turned Murtaza from a normal young man of a strong temperament to the child 'Mir Baba'. He began to see dangers that did not exist, conspiracies that had no basis in fact, and threats that never materialized because there never had been any in the first place. These factors combined to distort his pleasant and friendly nature and turn him into a split personality, his paranoia at times giving way to a vision of himself as some kind of a legendary hero of whom even death was fearful.

I have had to face death so many times that sometimes I begin to wonder why it stares me in the face and then always runs away, I am not afraid of death; it seems, death is afraid of me.[2]

Only four months after this statement, this man of whom even death was afraid was living in constant fear for his life. Among other things, he was terrified of rats.[3] In order to prove himself even more persecuted than Benazir had once been, he started to claim that he had been the target of many assassination attempts in Kabul and his body bore the marks of those attacks.[4] Here he was taking a leaf from his sister's book, who, after the death of her father and of her brother Shahnawaz had compared herself to Zainab, the apostle Ali's daughter and the most perfect ideal of Muslim womanhood.[5] She had seen sympathy for her sufferings turn into loyalty to her person. Murtaza, who in 1993 was politically off the rails, tried to resume his journey by emulating what his sister had done so successfully more than fifteen years earlier.

Bit by bit, Murtaza had shed all his old baggage by the time he returned to Pakistan in 1993 accompanied by no more than two of his old guards, both of whom had lived in Bangalore, India, since 1982 as guests of the Indian government, more particularly the intelligence agency RAW. What was the fate of the rest of Al-Zulfikar? Most of them died during the 'struggle', while some were declared traitors and expelled from both the PPP and Al-Zulfikar. Murtaza himself pronounced the death sentence against twenty-seven of them. Four of these were shot dead. Seven of his companions he got jailed in different countries, and until the end of 1996, two were still held in an Arab country. The same charge had been made against all these friends and companions, that they wanted to murder him. It was a classic case of paranoia.

I have described in chapter seven how Murtaza came to see me as an enemy and had me imprisoned in Kabul's Pul-i-Charkhi jail. Unfortunately being out of his sight did not put me out of his mind. The leader whose attention span did not allow him to brief his commandos more than superficially on the use of a SAM-7 missile could be far more thorough when it came to avenging a personal grudge or imagined betrayal, or to acting out the ruthless dynamism of an embattled leader compelled sometimes to sacrifice even his own people for the sake of security.

Five months after my arrest, the PIA hijack intoxicated Murtaza with what he saw as a great victory. Even then he could not forget me. Through Major Iftikhar, who was then based in London, he had a story released from Damascus that I had been executed. The story that he planted went something like this.

The KGB has unearthed a conspiracy to have Murtaza and Shahnawaz Bhutto kidnapped and handed over to General Zia-ul-Haq. It is said that Raja Anwar who was accompanying the two Bhutto brothers on a secret visit to Pakistan to meet their mother and sister behaved suspiciously when they were crossing over into Pakistan and the Soviet guards tried to intercept him. When he was challenged, he opened fire at the Bhutto brothers but they escaped. Raja Anwar was arrested, tried in a Kabul jail, condemned as a traitor and shot by Soviet soldiers.[6]

The story concocted by Murtaza not only provides an insight into his nightmares but also shows how proud he was in those days to have his name associated with the KGB and RAW. After he returned in triumph from Damascus to Kabul following the hijack, he addressed his men and told them that Raja Anwar had been arrested by the KGB for having betrayed the revolution. As he had been proved guilty, it had been decided to hand him over to Al-Zulfikar. He asked for volunteers to carry out the sentence of death by firing squad passed on the traitor Raja. He talked to about sixty Al-Zulfikar men in that meeting, and some of them were persuaded to kill me. He even had a grave dug for me in the courtyard of a house in Kabul's Karta Chahar residential area.[7]

On 26 April 1981, Murtaza met Najibullah and asked to have me handed over to him. He was confident that the moment the wish was spoken, the Afghan intelligence chief would grant it – after all, I was in jail by his request to Najibullah. So it is all the more surprising that Najibullah refused. Had he agreed, I would not have lived to write this book. Why did Najibullah refuse? Did he not know that Murtaza had had a grave dug for me in Karta Chahar? The truth is that to this day I have not been able to understand why Najibullah did not grant Murtaza's wish.

Not only was the story of my execution published prominently in newspapers such as the London *Guardian* and *Sunday Times*, but it was also broadcast by Radio Pakistan, All India Radio and the BBC. The only inference that could be drawn from this report was that Murtaza was under the protection of the KGB, which had not hesitated to execute those who had 'betrayed' him. The KGB was thus directly involved in terrorism:

Murtaza had soiled its hands with my blood. After the story's publication, it can be assumed that the Russians looked into the entire affair, and in all probability had a word with Najibullah. Perhaps that explains why I was not handed over to Murtaza. The truth is that the two and a half years I spent in the Pul-i-Charkhi prison were like standing in the shadow of the hangman's noose. I used to wonder every evening if I would be alive next day to see the sun rise. Anything was possible in the Kabul of those days. Every night people were executed in the jail. Why should I not become one of them, having already been declared dead by Murtaza? I was quite sure I would not walk out of Pul-i-Charkhi alive.

By September 1982, Murtaza was living in New Delhi under the benevolent protection of Mrs Indira Gandhi. In Delhi, he told the BBC that Raja Anwar was being kept in jail by the Russians because he was a pro-China communist. By now, he had completely forgotten planting the story that reported my death. At the same time a delegation of European socialist parties led by British MP Ron Brown arrived in Kabul and raised the question of my imprisonment with the Afghans. The Red Cross had also been pursuing my case with deep concern. Besides, Murtaza had by now left his base in Kabul. Under the circumstances, the Kabul government was forced to release me. No case was ever registered against me, nor had I been tried on any charge at all. Even under Afghan law, my imprisonment was illegal, since it was illegal to keep anyone in detention for more than nine months without a court order.

For ten years after my release, I did not issue a single statement. What did my personal tragedy matter, once I was pitted against Pakistan's most famous, influential, and perhaps most powerful family? In 1992, when I spoke for the first time about Tipu's murder in Kabul by Murtaza,[8] Begum Bhutto came out with a brand-new story. This one said that the hijacker Tipu had fired a 'whole burst' from his Kalashnikov at Murtaza and Shahnawaz. It was a 'miracle' that they had survived the attack.[9] Begum Bhutto may not have known till then that a Kalashnikov fires thirty bullets in a single burst, and no one can survive this lethal onslaught. And she may have forgotten that she had once called Tipu her son. Tipu had been used by the Bhuttos and then sent to his death in Afghanistan. How could a dead man fire 'a whole burst' at Murtaza? Such logic cuts no ice with Begum Bhutto. One year later, she replaced this story with another.[10]

The myth that began with my arrest by Russian soldiers and my subsequent death was still being peddled in rehashed versions, fifteen years later. It will not grieve the Bhutto family to learn that on the day Radio Pakistan broadcast the news of my execution, my mother suffered a heart attack which she did not survive. After my release, the Afghan authorities did not let me leave Afghanistan. Perhaps they were afraid that I would become a source of propaganda against them. My case was much publicized by the media and they wanted it to die down before I left. However, they treated me well once I was released. I was given a house and guards. Transport was available whenever I wished. Here Tipu and Nasir Jamal would visit me frequently. Another visitor was Mir Ghaizan Murree, a son of a famous Baluch leader, Nawab Khair Bux Murree. Mir Ghaizan became a minister in Baluchistan from 1993 to 1997.

The nemesis of Kausar Ali Shah, the man who had informed against me to Murtaza, lay in the future. After I was jailed, he said that the vital tape had been sent to Pakistan for safe-keeping. Murtaza ordered him to go to Pakistan and procure the tape. Once he had that evidence, he was confident that Najibullah would hang me. Shah returned after about six weeks from Pakistan, without the tape, but bearing a letter written by his aged mother-in-law which accused me of all kinds of things. Murtaza was more than disappointed. In May 1981, seven months after my imprisonment, Shah went to Delhi to meet his parents, who had come to India on the excuse of visiting holy Muslim shrines. While he was still in India, Murtaza declared him a traitor and sentenced him to death.

Murtaza had tasted blood during the hijack, and found a ready killer who longed to shed some more. At Murtaza's orders, Salamullah Tipu stole Shah's Toyota car, drove it to Jalalabad and sold it for Rs 10,000 to a junk-dealer.[11] When Shah returned from India with his family, Tipu was waiting for him outside his house and opened fire, though not aiming at the family. It was a miracle, that due to the presence of children, this cold-blooded man decided not to kill anyone.[12] Shah ran to Ajmal Khattak's house and sought refuge there. Murtaza tried very hard to have him jailed, but the influential Khattak kept him safe.

The first lesson taught in Pakistan's politics has always been the vilification of rivals, and Murtaza must have paid close attention to this ugly art. In July 1981, he issued a pamphlet entitled *The Conspiracy against Al-Zulfikar*, of which I still possess a copy. It was meant to be a demolition job on me, but the man who had reported falsely against me had not been spared either. His wife and mother-in-law had been made targets of the most scurrilous attack. Shah deserved more pity than wrath. Thanks to the Bhutto brothers, the atmosphere prevailing in Kabul was so thick with suspicion that it inspired people to indulge in the most despicable acts of intrigue against their friends and comrades. Had Shah not borne false witness against me, he would have done so against someone equally innocent.

Let me now return to Damascus, where as a result of the PIA hijack, fifty-four prisoners from Pakistan's various jails had been flown on 14 March 1981 in exchange for the aircraft, its crew and passengers. A few days after his arrival, Murtaza addressed them in the Hotel Damascus as if he were an absolute monarch and they his courtiers. Two of the men released were Zia's agents, he declared, and they were to be jailed. A third was to be hanged. This man was Sami Munir, a former PPP member of the Sind Assembly and son of K.M. Munir, one of the country's major industrialists. Father and sons had been lifelong friends and supporters of the Bhutto family. Few people were closer to Zulfikar Ali Bhutto than Sami's elder brother Rafi. It was also well known that when Bhutto formed the PPP, one main source of its funds had been the Munir family.

Sami was a nice, affable, plain-speaking but charming young man who had not been given a cabinet post in Sind in 1977 because he had criticized certain government and party policies in the presence of Bhutto.[13] It has been the continuing tragedy of Pakistani rulers that they have recognized only sycophants to be loyal, thereby failing to grasp the simple truth that someone who dares not speak his mind even before his own leader will never defend him against his enemies. In July 1977, when Zia removed the Bhutto government, Sami took a brave and principled public position against the martial law regime. Several cases were registered against him and he fled to London, where he played a vigorous role in the efforts to save Bhutto's life that went on for most of 1978 and early 1979. But Murtaza was not happy with Sami, ostensibly because he had not liked the speech he delivered at a convention called in London as part of the save-Bhutto campaign, but actually because Sami had given less by way of money to the cause than he expected him to.

After Bhutto's hanging in April 1979, Sami returned to Pakistan, where he was sentenced to a year's imprisonment by a military court. It was grotesque that he should have been flown all the way to Damascus as a result of the PIA hijack only to be declared a traitor by Murtaza and sentenced to death in a judgement passed, as its author preferred, without a hearing. After the cold-blooded murder of Tariq Rahim, Tipu had come to assume the position of official executioner. He was assigned the task of killing Sami Munir,[14] in Murtaza's new tradition of turning on those to whom his family had most reason to be grateful. The son of the man for whose sake Sami had undergone so much personal suffering and hardship was now out to have him killed. It is said that when finally Murtaza relented and lifted the death sentence, it was only after Sami had been made to beg for his forgiveness in a most humiliating manner. It was thus Murtaza who was responsible for destroying the political career of an upright and intelligent young man. By some tacit family agreement, Sami found the doors of the PPP closed to him thereafter.

The two workers, Moeenullah Zahid and Fazal-ur-Rehman Kayani, whom Murtaza had jailed in Damascus, came from Peshawar. They had been in jail in Abbottabad, Pakistan, since August 1979 for having gone to Kabul. Another man who was locked up with them in Pakistan was

Misbahuddin, a worker who – in keeping with *jiyala* tradition – told Murtaza in Damascus that after their arrest, these two sincere and committed workers had collaborated and got many other comrades picked up.[15] Murtaza promptly phoned General Kholi, head of Syrian intelligence, and told him that according to the Al-Zulfikar intelligence department there were two army 'agents' among the prisoners repatriated from Pakistan who had been sent to murder him, Murtaza. He then offered to hand the two men to the Syrians so that they could look into the matter.[16] Here was the old murder fantasy again. What did Murtaza know of Pakistani police brutality? Those who were caught in the vice of martial law were tortured and made to confess to even things they had not done.

These two young men who had just found release from Zia's jails found themselves thrown into the notorious torture centre where thousands of opponents of Hafiz al-Asad had been sent over the years as 'Mossad agents'. They were kept in a cell which had no window and was always pitch-dark. They could neither shave, nor wash, nor bathe, nor trim their nails, nor change their clothes. Day and night were alike and they had no concept of time. They were subjected to such inhuman torture that if what happened to them was described in detail to a normal person, he would experience fear bordering on terror. Four months after their arrest, Kayani had a heart attack, but the Syrian secret police did not believe in such comforts as medical attention. Moeenullah looked after his friend, and it was a miracle that he recovered, considering that his only treatment was the constant massage he was given by Moeenullah. After the heart attack, Syrian security stopped the use of third degree torture on the two men. In the end they were saved by the Red Cross, which helped them find political asylum in Sweden. When they were released after six months in Damascus, they were unable to recognize themselves in a mirror. They had long, animal-like nails, unkempt hair and flowing beards which had not touched water or soap for six months. Fourteen years later, when Murtaza was the inmate of a jail in Pakistan, he blackened the pages of Pakistani newspapers with protest statements because just once, for some reason, he was unable to have a bath in the morning. This example of 'ill treatment' was reported by the press of a country where millions have no clean drinking water. Because so many are forced to drink contaminated water, the highest incidence of diseases of the stomach and intestines is probably to be found in Pakistan. For the Pakistani press, so commonplace a fact is not a story. Murtaza's going without his bath – that was a story. In a country where thousands of women and babies die every year because they cannot receive even the most rudimentary care, the story that makes the newspapers deals with the colour of the silk sari some famous woman wore the night before. To Pakistan's media, only the lives of the privileged make news: the poor do not exist. They are invisible to our journalists.

Moeenullah and Kayani consider themselves to this day to be *jiyalas*, though to Murtaza they were traitors, and to Zia they were 'bad eggs' which had been thrown out. To Benazir Bhutto, they are the terrorists of Al-Zulfikar, and to the intellectuals, just vermin. Consequently, no one has bothered about them or cared what fate they met.

Another tragic story concerns the firebrand revolutionary poet from Gujranwala, Rashid Nagi. Out of Pakistan's population of seventy-five million, in 1978 there were only eight who underwent self-immolation to save Bhutto's life, and of these brave men there was only one who survived. A military court ordered twenty-four lashes to be administered to his scorched body. In 1980, when he came out of jail, he ran in the local elections and won by a landslide. However, the military government declared him ineligible to hold public office. In January 1981, he arrived in Afghanistan from Gujranwala with a woman named Tanvir Begum. He had brought various copies of the PPP newspaper *Musawaat* to the Afghan authorities, which carried stories about his self-immolation attempt. They gave him political asylum, a place to stay and food.

Nagi now went to see Murtaza, carrying the same newspapers and fully expecting to be received with honour because of his sacrifices. What Nagi had not realized was that his seeking political asylum in Kabul off his own bat and making his own living arrangements would be seen by Murtaza as a challenge to his leadership. Murtaza alone must have the authority to speak on behalf of the PPP, be it to the Afghans or the Indians. He wanted everyone to be at his mercy, even for the smallest favour or privilege. In their very first meeting, Murtaza screamed at him: 'By setting yourself on fire, you haven't done anything extraordinary.' This wounded Nagi who had the sensitivity of a poet.

Nagi had worked with me in the People's Action Committee, and must have spoken well of me, not knowing where I was. It was three months since Murtaza had had me imprisoned, but none of the workers had yet been informed of it. Although Nagi had risked his life for Murtaza's father, the mention of my name was enough to place him on the enemy list. Under pressure from Murtaza, Najibullah's close aide Farooq Yaqubi told Nagi and Tanvir to get out of Kabul as soon as possible, since the country was in a state of war and the government could not guarantee their safety.[17] The two had neither passports nor money, and Tanvir had her children from her earlier marriage with her. Even so, they were too proud to plead for favours – an attitude that further inflamed Murtaza's swollen ego.

The three PIA hijackers and twenty-five of the prisoners released by Pakistan had landed in Kabul from Damascus on 24 April 1981. With a new force of men at his command, Murtaza decided to teach Nagi a lesson. He wanted Chaudhary Azam to 'sort him out' but Azam refused. He knew, and others who had come from Punjab knew and respected, the supreme sacrifice Nagi had offered. Murtaza had to hand over the operation to kill Nagi to the boys from Karachi. Latif Hasan Dalmia was put in charge of the exercise, under the supervision of Tipu and Shahnawaz.

Nagi and Tanvir were living in the city's Shehr-i-Nau area. On 23 May, when Nagi left the house to change some money, Dalmia's squad caught up with him in the bazaar and began to beat him. They tore off his clothes, pinned him to the ground, and forced him to rub his nose repeatedly in the shoes of Shahnawaz, who was personally guiding this operation. All the while they kept shouting: 'Quaid-i-Inqilab Murtaza Bhutto zindabad' – Long live leader of the revolution Murtaza Bhutto. Then Dalmia pulled out a knife and stabbed Nagi in the back several times, screaming: 'These are our signs.' This attack took place in the heart of the city, and so terrified and disgusted were the shopkeepers round about that they began to pull down the shutters. Some people started to scream and run down the street in horror. Although the Afghans had plenty of stomach for violence, they had never seen the Karachi style of violence where a whole gang victimized a single unarmed man. The half-dead Nagi was removed to a hospital. Tanvir Begum was a very brave woman. She at once got in touch with the local UN office and asked them to send one of their officers to the hospital where Nagi was. By that time, Farooq Yaqubi and Engineer Kifayatullah Afridi had also arrived there. Tanvir Begum was shouting loudly, telling everyone what had happened. So embarrassed were the two Afghan officers that they thought it best to slip quietly away from the scene.

In February 1979, Zulfikar Ali Bhutto had proudly told the Supreme Court of Pakistan that eight of his workers had set themselves on fire for his sake. Could any of them have imagined that only two years later, Bhutto's sons would humiliate one of them on a Kabul street and almost have him killed? Nagi had walked through fire, only to be beaten up and knifed by their henchmen. True justice would not consider that even the entire landed property and assets of the Bhutto family could recompense this brave idealist for his sacrifices. Had the black night of 4 April 1979 not extinguished the flame of Bhutto's life, men like Nagi would have been declared the PPP's great heroes. However, Bhutto was dead and those who claimed his mantle were inventing their own heroes. The former deputy commissioner of Larkana, Khalid Kharal, was one such new hero who was celebrated at length in Benazir Bhutto's autobiography, *Daughter of the East*. Tanvir Begum was the only woman member of the PPP against whom a case of sedition was registered and decided ex-parte, with a sentence of fourteen years' hard labour. She did not figure in Benazir's book.

In Kabul, Tanvir Begum looked after Nagi day and night for three months. When he grew well enough to walk, the two travelled eight hundred kilometres through Afghanistan through the fires of war to get to Iran, where the Iranian government duly jailed them. It took them months of suffering to obtain asylum in Canada. The two of them had never faltered, and fought their misfortunes with exemplary courage. Today, they are living happy and honourable, though separate, lives in a free and democratic country.

In 1981, Libya decided to recruit Pakistanis to fight in Chad, and the contract to procure this cannon fodder went to a firm called Murtaza Associates. The story got out, and the Pakistani media played it up for weeks. As it happened, this company had nothing to do with Murtaza, but it gave him an idea. In February 1981, he turned up in Tripoli with an offer to recruit as many mercenaries as were required from Pakistan's Frontier province and tribal areas. The Libyans accepted. On returning to Kabul later that month, with the help of the Mazdoor Kisan Party (Bhangash group) Murtaza embarked on a drive to recruit unemployed young men from the tribal areas. A transit camp of sorts was set up in Kabul's Karta Chahar under the charge of Zahid Hussain Shah and 'Chacha' Safdar Hamdani. According to the plan, these men were to be flown to Tripoli. Murtaza wanted them to be seen as Al-Zulfikar volunteers, so that the Afghan government should not catch on. He was like a pregnant woman who wants to deliver the baby she is carrying without the midwife knowing. The midwife in this case was the KGB, which told the Afghans not to permit these men to fly out.

The Afghans later said that a mercenary army was an imperialist concept and Afghan soil was not to be used for this purpose. Seventy or eighty of these poor men languished in the transit camp, cursing their fate. In desperation, some members of the Mazdoor Kisan Party who were also part of this 'army' seized control of the camp from the two Al-Zulfikar operatives and only let go when the Afghan authorities intervened. To Murtaza, this was nothing short of mutiny. In order to impress upon everyone what a stern disciplinarian he was, he decided that seventeen of the rebels were to be shot, and appointed Pervez Shinwari a one-man firing squad. Shinwari, of course, was going to do no such thing. He threw down his Kalashnikov and refused to perform Murtaza's massacre. This was the end of the 'Libyan army'. The camp was eventually disbanded. Some people went home, others found employment in Kabul, while some joined the ranks of Al-Zulfikar, having nothing better to do.

In September 1981, Shahnawaz's intelligence agents came up with the disclosure that one of the recruits to the 'Libyan army', a man named Buneri, was a Pakistan commando. Murtaza, convinced at once that this was part of another 'attempt' on his life, ordered him to be locked up in Al-Zulfikar headquarters. When interrogated, Buneri turned out to be a retired subedar of the Militia, an irregular force. It was the misfortune of this poor tribal Pushtun that he had fallen into the hands of a man so

187

obsessed with plots to kill him that he would go to any length to assuage his nagging fears. Their verdict, of course, was to liquidate Buneri. This time the method chosen was poisoning. Buneri was administered cyanide which the Syrians had supplied to Murtaza in 1979. It was the first time this lethal poison was used. The poison was kept by Al-Zulfikar's director of intelligence, Shahnawaz. The man who committed the murder was a tribal agent known by the code-names 'Chitrali' and 'Haji Bay-Iman', but his real name was probably Said Muhammad. Al-Zulfikar men later told the story of how 'Chitrali' had murdered Buneri. He took him out of Kabul on a pretext, and put cyanide in something he gave him to eat. Buneri died in minutes in great agony. The murderer then took photographs of his dead body and handed them over to the Bhutto brothers. Murtaza mailed pictures to General Zia-ul-Haq and General Fazle Haq, Governor of the Frontier province, with the message: 'See the fate of your agent.' Later 'Chitrali' was arrested in Pakistan as a 'terrorist' for carrying a bomb concealed in a copy of the Koran, and sent to prison for fourteen years. His real character and what he did never quite came through to the Pakistani intelligence agencies. He was released in 1988 as part of a general amnesty declared for pro-Bhutto men in different jails.

I have already described the sadistic public murder of Mazdoor Yar Afridi, whose 'crime' was to have been informed upon to a man who could not ignore an informer (see chapter 13). Who had given Murtaza the power of life and death over others, one should ask? Had Buneri and Afridi really been working for an intelligence agency, there can be no question that those agencies would have left no stone unturned to find out what had happened to their men. However, as far as I have been able to gather, not even one Al-Zulfikar man was ever questioned by any Pakistani intelligence agency about these two murders. Two innocent men were simply wiped out of existence because of Murtaza's paranoia. I am not sure whether their families know what has happened to them, or if they are still hoping against hope that one day their sons will return.

Murtaza drew upon a store of hard-working idealism and resolution that he exploited but did not repay. He and his sister between them dashed the hopes of a generation that believed in democracy and social justice. They did not expect it from General Zia-ul-Haq, but they thought that a Bhutto might begin to restore it. The men that Murtaza damaged or destroyed were the kind that his country most needed. I name a few here, in the hope that their memory will survive.

'Baba' Mohsin of Krishen Nagar, Lahore, was a popular PPP worker whose ill luck brought him to Kabul. At the time he was between fifty-five and sixty years old. He belonged to that cadre of the PPP which had devotedly believed that Bhutto was a great revolutionary who would change

Pakistan's unjust social and political order. Murtaza had him jump about like a frog in front of the entire camp of Al-Zulfikar men because of 'indiscipline'. In August 1982, before leaving for New Delhi, he condemned 'Baba' Mohsin as a traitor. Friendless in Kabul, and without any means of support, after much hardship he returned to Pakistan but as soon as news of his return spread, the police began looking for him. To escape arrest, he fled from Lahore and found refuge in the Kurrum Agency in Pakistan's tribal belt at the house of Muhammad Hussain Nashha, who took him back to Kabul. I saw him for the first time in July 1983 in Kabul. He looked old, helpless and ill. In November, he died of a heart attack. He was alone and friendless, and had it not been for some old PPP workers who heard the news and buried him, his body would just have been thrown away. So many people were dying in Afghanistan in those days that often they were not buried.[18]

As mentioned earlier, Muhammad Ashraf had been arrested for attempted sabotage of the railway track near the town of Wah and sentenced to twenty-four years in prison and twenty-five lashes by a military court. In March 1981, he was flown to Damascus as part of the hijack settlement. He was later granted asylum by Libya. In 1983 Murtaza declared him a traitor and threw him out of the organization. He died suddenly in Libya in June 1989, aged only twenty-nine. Four years later, the journalist Khalid Hasan (this book's translator) wrote about him in a Lahore newspaper and asked that his body should be brought back to Pakistan for reburial. This was done during Benazir Bhutto's first government, so if not in life, then at least after his death his existence was acknowledged by the party for which he had offered such sacrifice.

Azam Chaudhari of Faisalabad, mentioned earlier, was one of the two men who fired a missile at Zia's aircraft in Rawalpindi, though unsuccessfully. In 1986, he was shot dead by a Dutch fascist gang in Amsterdam. His family made arrangements for his body to be brought to Pakistan for burial.

Qayyum Butt was another worker of such sterling honesty and uprightness that one doubts if the PPP will ever find another like him. When he joined the party in 1968, Murtaza was in primary school. He was the only PPP member of the National Assembly who was lashed by the army, in 1978. When Bhutto saw him in the Supreme Court during his final appeal, he said to him: 'Qayyum Butt, I am proud of you.' Murtaza, however, felt no hesitation in declaring him a traitor – Murtaza who claimed leadership of the party not on the basis of his knowledge, wisdom or political struggle but because he was who he was. It was always the PPP's tragedy that it failed to outgrow its feudal character. In 1982, Murtaza made sure that Butt was thrown out of Libya, where he had earlier been given asylum. When he landed in London, he was arrested at Heathrow airport and was not released for several months. Since he was Murtaza's traitor, it follows that he became Benazir's, who officially cancelled his party membership. He has continued to live in London in exile.

'Chacha' Safdar Hamdani also joined the PPP in 1968, and was perhaps its most active member in organizing support for its programme among students. From 1977 until 1978, he was with Benazir Bhutto; it was only his misfortune that in 1979 he found himself with Murtaza in Kabul. Two years after that, Murtaza declared him a traitor and ordered him to be shot. Later he changed his mind but ordered him to be banished to Libya. His future in the PPP was thus sealed by the Bhutto family.

Two other workers who became victims of Murtaza's dictatorial moods were Sheikh Gul and Zubair Shad, both from Gujranwala, who suffered jail and lashes in Pakistan for the sake of the PPP in 1979. In August that year they managed to escape to Kabul, but after my arrest in 1980, Murtaza denounced them as traitors. They returned to Pakistan and were immediately jailed for their association with Murtaza. They spent the years between 1981 and 1988 mostly in the torture chambers of the Lahore Fort. I remember only too distinctly that when Zubair Shad came forward to volunteer arrest in 1978, he was only eighteen. The next eighteen years of his life were spent chasing the mirage of revolution. Sheikh Gul was one of that handful of PPP supporters who spent the entire eleven years of martial law in Pakistan doing hard labour in different jails. He was lashed twice in jail, and for months he was tortured in the Lahore Fort. His elderly mother had only one wish – she wanted to see him married while she was still alive – but he sacrificed his mother's happiness and peace for the sake of the Bhutto family. I am sure that he is somewhere in Pakistan, trying to eke out a living, because the party he wrecked his life for does not remember either his face or his name or what he did.

Another comrade was Manzar Alam from Karachi, who had been sprung from jail as a result of the PIA hijack but whom an ill wind brought to Kabul. In 1981 he was sent back to Pakistan with a group of seven others, but they were either killed on the way or met some fatal accident. Nobody ever heard of or from them again.

But let me tell the story of Tajbar Khan. He came to Kabul for the first time in July 1979 to see Murtaza. When I was arrested in October 1980 at Murtaza's orders, he protested strongly and thus got himself placed on Murtaza's enemy list. Murtaza never could tolerate any dissent or permit his authority to be questioned, even by his well-wishers, friends and followers. Accordingly, he sentenced Tajbar Khan to death. This fiery young man who had served the PPP so sincerely was now on the hit-list in both Pakistan and Afghanistan. To save himself, he went underground in Kabul. For some time, he disguised himself as a dervish and lived in a shrine. When a band of renegade Afghan soldiers who had deserted the communist regime passed his way, he told them who he was and joined them. In 1983 when he learnt of my release, he sent me a message of congratulation through Qadir Shah. At the time, he was commanding three hundred Mujahideen somewhere in Afghanistan. I do not know what happened to him. He did not return to Pakistan, and during 1989 and 1990, when Benazir Bhutto was Prime Minister, his old father was often seen sitting outside her grand secretariat in Islamabad, an application clutched in his hand begging her to find his son for him. I have no idea if Tajbar Khan is alive or dead.

The suicide of Shahnawaz Bhutto is also part of the collective tragedy of Al-Zulfikar. Unlike Benazir or Murtaza, this young man did not desire any leadership role, nor was he committed ideologically to any special viewpoint. He used to say that whenever the Bhuttos came back to power, he would be a candidate for the ministry of tourism. In 1975, he was admitted as a student at the Cadet College, Hasan Abadal, not far from Rawalpindi on the Grand Trunk Road to Peshawar. Because of the semi-military nature of the establishment, he was not permitted to keep his long Che Guevara-style hair that he loved, but he would not let them give him a regulation cut. When his father came to know of it, he was furious.

Bhutto's hanging came as a tremendous shock to this sensitive youngster, and twice he suffered nervous breakdowns. He had another shock when Nasrulli, his Turkish fiancee, returned his engagement ring – actually gold bangles – to him in September 1980. We were both on a European tour at the time, and I often saw him wiping tears from his eyes. He was shattered. Nasrulli, the girl, wanted him to get out of Kabul before she would marry him. Had he done so, he would perhaps have been alive today, because he needed someone to calm his nerves and comfort his troubled spirit.

From the bloody extremism of the Al-Zulfikar environment in Kabul and Delhi he found himself living in Cannes, which was the other extreme in a sense. This sudden transition proved fatal. He had married an Afghan girl in Kabul – Murtaza had married the other sister – but the marriage fell apart in the Riviera resort. Husband and wife would fight frequently. Everyone knew that he still kept Syrian cyanide, and it should have been removed. He was in a highly unstable state and could explode like a volcano if provoked. A few days before his death he had said: 'We carry vials of poison with us wherever we go. I will drink mine if Zia catches me. It works in seconds.'[19] In August 1985, the couple had a bitter quarrel, and he either took the cyanide by mistake or out of disgust. The empty vial was later found in the kitchen.[20] General Zia-ul-Haq sent Begum Bhutto a message of condolence. Why he expressed sorrow at the death of someone who in his book belonged to a family of traitors, only he could tell. Whether Shahnawaz's death was accidental or whether he killed himself, the PPP held General Zia responsible for it. When Benazir arrived in

Larkana with the dead body of her younger brother, it was a heart-rending scene.

> As I stood in the doorway of Al-Murtaza, a woman's voice rose above the men's in the courtyard, re-enacting the tragedy at Karbela. 'See, see Benazir,' the woman keened in the cadence of the Subcontinent. She has come with the body of her brother. How young he was, how handsome, how innocent! He has been slain by a tyrant's hand. Feel the grief of the sister. Remember Zainab going to the court of Yazid. Remember as she sees Yazid playing with her brother's head.[21]

It is not possible to comment on this moving scene, but at the same time, one cannot help saying that every family has its own Karbelas and its individual Yazids. There are some Karbelas which are mourned, but there are others whose Zainabs remain unknown and nameless. All those young and handsome men like Tariq Rahim who were killed on her brothers' instructions must also have been mourned and cried over by their families in the same way, with the difference that the poor suffer their sorrow in silence. I wonder if the woman standing in the courtyard of Al-Murtaza had seen Shahnawaz with his Kalashnikov mercilessly blowing out the brains of innocent Mazdoor Yar Afridi in Kabul, how she would have re-enacted this tragedy of Karbela? One can just imagine Tariq Rahim's young wife and sisters wailing over his dead body when it came from Kabul, hitting their heads against the wall and crying hysterically when they saw the bullet hole in his forehead. 'See how young he was, how handsome, how innocent. He has been slain by tyrants, by Yazids!' If Benazir had imagined this equally heart-rending scene, perhaps she would not have written the words above.

15

Sindhi Ambitions and Laundered Reputations

In 1977, when General Zia-ul-Haq grabbed power, it so happened that in neighbouring India a non-Congress government was voted into office for the first time in its history since independence. The new Prime Minister of India, Morarji Desai, and the Pakistani dictator had one thing in common: their dislike of Mrs Gandhi and Bhutto. Naturally, this brought them close, which was why the period from 1977 to 1979 brought the warmest ever interlude between the two countries. In comparison Mrs Gandhi's relations with Pakistan always remained cool. Her first eleven years in power (1966 to 1977) had seen Pakistan's dismemberment in 1971, war and continuing tension. When she returned in 1980, General Zia viewed her restoration as a danger signal both for Pakistan and himself. He was convinced, among other things, that she would want to bring the Bhutto family back to power.

The 1971 military defeat and the separation of East Pakistan had enlarged the military imbalance between the two countries, and it now stood at a ratio of ten to one. Zia was realistic enough to know that in the event of another war, the military defeat of what was left of Pakistan and its occupation by India had become a nightmare possibility. In order to avoid it, he decided that it would be necessary to keep Mrs Gandhi embroiled in internal troubles. Until then, no Pakistani government had paid serious attention to the Sikhs of East Punjab, even though they were plainly at odds over the issue of Khalistan, a pure Sikh state, with the government in New Delhi. Zia's was the first to depart from that course. He extended support to the Sikhs with the same readiness with which Mrs Gandhi had helped East Pakistani nationalists in 1971.

Zia was born in Jullandur, East Punjab, and had grown up there. He found not the least difficulty in winning the confidence of the Sikhs. He was on familiar ground with people whose ways he knew. With his encouragement, the Sikhs raised the banner of Free Khalistan and launched an armed revolt against the Indian government. This policy was later to have far-reaching consequences for Kashmir. Zia was the first Pakistani ruler who, instead of noising cheap slogans against India, took practical

193

steps to create grave internal problems for this feared and contentious neighbour. His admirers like to give him credit for the fact that as long as he was alive, he did not betray the confidence that the Sikhs and Kashmiris reposed in him. Unlike those who followed, he did not bend under pressure or for other considerations, not excluding personal advancement, to provide the Indians with the names and locations of those who had risen against them.

In June 1984 a band of Sikh hotheads under their maverick leader Sant Jarnail Singh Bhindranwale ensconced themselves inside the Golden Temple in Amritsar. Paying no heed to the consequences, Mrs Gandhi launched a military attack on this holiest of Sikh holies. Although she was successful in liquidating Bhindranwale and over four hundred companions, she inspired such blind hatred and feelings of revenge among their co-religionists that in October of the same year, two of her own Sikh body-guards riddled her body with bullets on the lawns of her residence in New Delhi. It is said that her precipitate action against the Sikhs was taken on the advice of her son and political heir, Rajiv Gandhi. Riding on the huge wave of sympathy that her death created in India, Rajiv won the elections held to choose a successor. Mrs Gandhi's wish was thus half-granted: her son, though not the one she had in mind, became her heir in office.

Power is blind and so often is the logic behind it. After his mother's murder, instead of trying to begin the process of reconciliation with the seething Sikh community, Rajiv chose to crush them. He also decided to pay Pakistan back in its own coin. He ordered an exercise aimed at identifying persons and elements in Pakistani Sind who, like the Sikhs, would be willing to begin a separatist movement in that province. He also decided to approach Murtaza, who was living in France licking his wounds. Having surrendered his remaining guerrillas to the Austrian authorities in Vienna following the botched operation there, he now found himself with nothing in particular to do. Although three old Al-Zulfikar loyalists[1] still maintained an office in New Delhi under RAW's watchful care, it did nothing more heroic than hang the pictures of its 'martyrs' on the walls.

As soon as the summons from New Delhi promised him Indian backing if he was prepared to run a movement for the liberation of Sind from Pakistan, Murtaza made ready to move to Delhi. It seemed to him that his dream was not yet dead. Benazir Bhutto had by now returned to Pakistan, having brought her self-imposed exile in London to an end. Murtaza was confident that he had all bases covered. If he succeeded in separating Sind from Pakistan, he would have won, and if his sister managed to reclaim power in Pakistan, he would still have won. It should be remembered that in those days he considered himself the one and only political heir of Zulfikar Ali Bhutto and the undisputed leader of his party, the PPP.

So, for all practical purposes, Al-Zulfikar was reborn in January 1986. In its new incarnation it had only one objective: the independence of Sind which required expelling all non-Sindhis from the province, including Punjabis, Pathans and Mohajirs. That is why no one from these three groups was permitted to enrol in Al-Zulfikar. Between 1986 and 1993, only Sindhi nationalist youths could join its ranks. Their optimal number can be said to have varied between three hundred and four hundred men. Every single Al-Zulfikar operation in the second phase was undertaken in Sind.

The new Al-Zulfikar had the following command and operational structure in India and Sind:[2]

Mir Murtaza Bhutto	Secretary General
Sohail Sethi	(India-based)
Sardar Mohammad Salim	(India-based)
Ehsan Bhatti	(India-based)
Ali Mohammad Sonara	Commander Karachi (South)
Ibrahim Bholu	Commander Karachi (East)
Ayub Atiq	Deputy Commander (area unclear)
Shahnawaz Shani	Deputy Commander (area unclear)
Wasi Haider	Deputy Commander (area unclear)
Saifullah Khalid	In-charge Liaison (Sind)
Younus Bond	Commander (Thattha, Sind)
Ghulam Mustafa	Commander (Badin, Sind)
Dodo Jatoi	Commander (Hyderabad, Sind)
Hazoor Bakhsh	Commander (Khairpur, Sind)
Rafiq Dahri	Commander (Hyderabad II, Sind)
Rasul Bakhsh Mangrio	Commander (Nawabshah & Nowshehra, Sind)
Ali Mohammad Jamali	Commander (Dadu City)

What were the factors that led to public disaffection in Sind? Social and political tensions in the province dated back to independence in 1947, but they reached their apogee between 1949 and 1952 when a flood of refugees from India's Central and United Provinces descended on Sind. It is said that Nawabzada Liaquat Ali Khan, the Prime Minister, encouraged these Mohajirs to settle there because he saw them providing him with the constituency which he had left behind in India. Instead of spreading this influx all over Pakistan, the government settled them in the urban areas of Sind in large clusters. Many of these refugees continued to have half their family living in India while they used the opportunities available in the new state of Pakistan to improve their lot. The migration of these refugees from India was not linked to the formula under which India was partitioned or Pakistan created, which was why the principal Sindhi nationalist leader, G.M. Syed, denounced this influx from India.

During his years in power (1971 to 1977), Zulfikar Ali Bhutto provided some protection to the disadvantaged native Sindhis by fixing a quota for them in the civil services. In Sind, the ratio between locals and non-locals was 55:45 and it was clear that no Pakistani ruler could possibly meet even the basic economic needs of the two communities simultaneously. While the Sindhis felt pleased by the quota system, the Mohajirs, especially those among them who held government jobs, considered it a direct threat to their survival. It was the same political and economic divide or rivalry which some years later gave birth to the urban-based Mohajir political party, the Mohajir Qaumi Movement (MQM).

When in 1986 Murtaza raised the slogan of Independent Sindhu Desh, many young members of the Sind People's Students Federation (SPSF) stepped forward to join him. In January 1987, the first group of twenty of these idealistic young Sindhi nationalists, all dreaming of freedom, set out for India on Murtaza's orders to receive guerrilla training. Trudging through the desert, these determined youngsters crossed into India in the Bahawalpur region, arriving in Sri Ganga Nagar. This group was given military training by the Indians at Bhuj and sent back to Pakistan. In June the same year, another group of young Sindhis entered India taking the same route. The credit for recruiting these men into Al-Zulfikar goes to Ali Muhammad Sonara, Munir Soomro, Sajjad Ghakro and Hasan Rajar, all firebrand Sindhi nationalists. Rajar alone supplied Murtaza with more than three hundred volunteers. Hailing from Jamshoro, Rajar was the general secretary of the SPSF and had also had the 'honour' of being Benazir Bhutto's security guard. His name can be added to the long list of those who offered blind and unquestioning sacrifices for the Bhutto family.

The fateful step taken by General Zia on the night of 5 July 1977 finally led him to his death in the skies over Bahawalpur on 17 August 1988, when his C-130 aircraft turned into a fireball and destroyed both its occupant and his power. His death opened the way for the return of the PPP to power. This double dose of happiness was too much for Murtaza to contain, and the very next day, on 18 August he ordered an RPG rocket attack on the oil storage tanks of the National Refinery in Karachi. If he wanted fireworks to celebrate the occasion, he was successful. For days afterwards, the oil kept burning, emitting huge clouds of black smoke that could be seen for miles. How unlucky are the poor people of Pakistan who have to pay for the mishaps no less than for the celebrations of the ruling classes.

The attack on the National Refinery was carried out by Rafiq Memon,[3] one of the *jiyalas* of the People's Party, who took part in every march, demonstration and protest to save Bhutto's life. In February 1979, PPP workers held a protest demonstration in Karachi and set a government-owned bus on fire in the Jamia Cloth Market area. Four passengers died. A martial law court held Rafiq Memon responsible for the incident, and sentenced him to life. He was released in 1987 on a mercy appeal by the Governor of Sind, having spent eight years in prison. In 1988, as soon as Benazir came into power, she put him in charge of security at Bilawal House, her husband's residence, where she now lives when in Karachi. When her government was dismissed in 1990, Memon quietly slipped away to Colombo.

During Benazir's first stint in office (1988 to 1990), Al-Zulfikar carried out no operation against any government agency or institution. Assuming the name of 'working committee', Al-Zulfikar men staged a number of hunger strikes with the object of creating a congenial atmosphere for Murtaza's return to Pakistan from his long exile. However, the group did not entirely give up its 'revolutionary' work of liquidating its opponents. In 1989, it murdered Aftab Alam Shoro and Dr Niaz Marai in Hyderabad, Sind, and in 1990 when Benazir lost power, Murtaza found an excuse to resume his anti-government activities. In 1991, Al-Zulfikar undertook the liquidation of Khalid bin Walid of the MQM and Judge Nabi Sher Junejo, who was hearing a number of cases involving the group. The message intended to be conveyed was that any judge who proceeded against Al-Zulfikar would not be allowed to live. For the murder of Junejo, the Jam Sadiq Ali government in Sind arrested the following Al-Zulfikar operatives on 16 June 1991: Rajab Ali Brohi, son of Abdul Rehman Brohi, Kamil Gali, Karachi; Bashir Ahmed Baloch, son of Daud Baloch, Purana Golimar, Karachi; and Akram Memon, son of Muhammad Ismail, Purana Golimar, Karachi.

One should add that Jam Sadiq Ali's sympathies were with Murtaza. Jam Sadiq Ali told me in 1991 in London that the murder of Junejo and the destruction of the storage tanks of the National Refinery were the work of Al-Zulfikar. He said: 'What Al-Zulfikar men I arrested, I did on frivolous charges. I did not want them to fall into the hands of the army during its operations in Sind, because they would not have been arrested: they would have been shot.'[4] When this conversation took place, the army's cleanup operation was in full swing in Sind.

Al-Zulfikar also used the sea route to India to conduct its operations. In 1992, its men blew up a gas pipeline near Hyderabad, and firing on passenger trains was quite common. It did not hesitate to accept responsibility for these acts of terror. On the night of 8 May that year, an Al-Zulfikar detachment led by Hasan Rajar set sail from Thatta for Ketty Bunder. Along the way, it encountered a Pakistani naval patrolling party and was taken captive. Rajar was escorting this group to Delhi to meet Murtaza. The navy not only captured ammunition but Rs 1.2 million in cash. Investigation showed that Hasan Rajar had held up the National Bank of Pakistan in Pad Idhan, Sind, in January 1992 and had got away with Rs 38,000 in cash and sixteen kilograms of gold. He had obviously sold the gold for cash which he was taking to Delhi to give to Murtaza. Although the administration had declared Rajar a wanted dacoit, as it had Barnani Khoso and Laiq Chandio, it turned out that next he was planning to abduct foreigners and diplomats. Rajar was not a dacoit in the customary meaning of the word but an aggressive Sindhi nationalist. How long till Murtaza might have relived his hijack triumph?

Certain parallels between the two political dynasties of Pakistan and India, the Bhuttos and the Gandhis, bear out the judgement that republican democracy in the whole subcontinent is still at war with an older, feudal, tradition that requires latter-day kings and queens, princes and princesses, who sometimes pay with their lives for the scale and dominance of their political ambitions. On 21 May 1991, a Tamil woman nationalist with a bomb tied to her body killed Rajiv Gandhi and herself while pretending to garland him – a tragic consequence of the disastrous Indian policy of suppressing smaller nationalities. The Indian National Congress which had pioneered the freedom movement and which could rightly claim to have mothered Indian democracy was reduced to a hollow mockery of its past glory by Nehru's daughter and his grandsons. The party, the oldest in the subcontinent, became subservient to the whims of 'The Family', and a protector of their personal interests and status. The degradation of the Congress could not have fallen lower than after Rajiv's murder, when it offered the presidency of the party to his Italian-born wife, Sonia. Had she not refused the offer, the seat of power in New Delhi would have been hers. But 'Never say never' is one of the oldest maxims in politics: Sonia or her progeny could well reappear one day in the power equation of India.

The subcontinent's ruling classes have always taken full advantage of the belief among the poor, starving masses of their countries, still slumbering in the caves of the past, that they are poor and the rich are rich because such is the way the world has been fashioned by the creator. Their acceptance of this inequity is unquestioning and total. The psyche of the common man is reconciled to the idea that every person, every family, is fated to plod on along the groove that it was born into. Change is not to be contemplated. For the people of the subcontinent, therefore, it is most natural to accept the son or daughter of a ruler as their next ruler. They take it as a settled social and natural reality that must not be resisted. This dynastic concept is so widely accepted that there are families in the subcontinent whose members have sat in every elected or nominated chamber since British times by matter of unwritten right. They consider their constituency as their family seat, and the votes of its people as purchased in perpetuity by their ancestors.

Powers like these cannot be taken for granted. They have to be maintained. It needs to be recorded that under an ingenious plan, the

Benazir Bhutto government acquitted Murtaza from all important and life-threatening cases. In none of the proceedings did a single witness appear against him, nor were any of the official agencies represented. He was not even tried for the PIA hijack: the case was simply filed. However, to make it appear that the requirements of the law were being fulfilled, a tame and innocuous case was quietly brought before a special court in Lahore, and is still under way. The case involves the attempted overthrow of the Zia regime rather than blood-letting within opposition ranks. It has as many as ninety-six accused, some of them occupying important positions in Benazir Bhutto's party, others aligned with Murtaza's Bhutto Shaheed group. Not one of these ninety-six people has even once been forced to make an appearance in court. Had Murtaza survived to be acquitted of this charge too, his judicial laundering would have been complete. However, Benazir refused to accommodate Murtaza in her party or her government.

16

One More Assassination

Jam Sadiq Ali who became Chief Minister of Sind in 1990 and remained firmly in power until his death in 1992, suffered eleven long years of exile for the sake of the Bhutto family. Even through those hard and difficult times, he remained utterly devoted to both Benazir and Murtaza. He even helped the nine Al-Zulfikar men imprisoned after the bungled Vienna operation (described in chapter 12). Benazir had married the Sindhi feudal Arif Zardari in 1987. When she came to power in 1988, Benazir appointed Jam Sadiq Ali her adviser, but in deference to the wishes of her new in-laws, the Zardaris, she saw to it that he was not allowed to exercise any authority. She tried to justify it to him by hinting that the Pakistan army, uneasy with his former links to India, had opposed his being given any important position in her government.

It was naive of Benazir to think that she had successfully fooled the old fox that Jam Sadiq Ali was. He had a long-standing relationship with President Ghulam Ishaq Khan, and he knew exactly where the truth lay. Of course he felt embarrassed and offended, but before he could respond, Ishaq dismissed Benazir's government for corruption and inefficiency in 1990. The President was more than aware of the Jam's special talents, and decided to use him to teach Benazir a lesson. He appointed him Chief Minister of Sind. With the central government backing him, the new Chief Minister wasted no time in locking up Asif Ali Zardari, the deposed Prime Minister's husband, on charges of corruption.

As for Murtaza, he was convinced that Benazir's negative attitude towards him was the result of Asif's influence. Murtaza had nothing but contempt for his brother-in-law, whom he considered unworthy of his sister. And what did the man in the street think about Benazir's in-laws? He was convinced that in her the Zardaris had found the hen that laid the golden egg. It was commonly agreed that the last thing the Zardari family would want was the return of Murtaza to Pakistan. The Zardari factor also brought Jam Sadiq Ali and Murtaza Bhutto together. It was through the Jam that Murtaza established contact with the government of Nawaz Sharif, which had succeeded Benazir's. In September 1991, reportedly with the help of the Pakistani intelligence establishment, Kamran Khan, a

Karachi-based Pakistani journalist, arrived in Damascus to interview Murtaza. His 'scoop' made headlines in Pakistan. It was the view in the Nawaz Sharif camp that Murtaza should be pitted against his sister in Sind. Reportedly, the plan was to keep him in jail after arrival for four to six months, bail him out thereafter, and let him loose on Benazir. This move, it was argued, would break the PPP vote bank. However, before this scenario could be implemented, two things happened. Jam Sadiq Ali died in 1992, and Ishaq Khan sacked Nawaz Sharif and his government a year later.

In the elections which followed in 1993, Murtaza, who was still abroad, decided to run for twenty Sindhi constituencies, confident that the people of Sind would vote for him rather than Benazir. He was mistaken: the election was a disaster, and he could barely manage to win from Larkana, his home town, and that too for the relatively unimportant Sind provincial assembly. Even this minor victory would not have been possible had his mother Begum Nusrat Bhutto not gone around canvassing from door to door, and if the traditional Bhutto family rivals, the Khurros, had not agreed not to field a candidate against him. Later, explaining his poor performance, Murtaza argued, first, that he had been absent from the country and, second, that corrupt PPP candidates had spent millions on their campaigns to keep him out. While there was truth in both these arguments, the fact was that merely to trade upon the Bhutto name without access to the Bhutto political machine was bound to be a losing strategy for a man so unfamiliar with the people whose votes he required.

Murtaza finally returned in November 1993, having lived abroad for seventeen years. Because of the many charges on which he was wanted by the Zia regime, he was arrested on arrival by the government, now ironically headed by his sister. To justify her action, Benazir cited the old cliché and notorious fiction that everyone was equal in the eyes of the law. When she used the arrest to assert that she was so just and fair a ruler that even her own brother had been treated like an ordinary citizen, many saw it as yet another farcical episode in the comic opera of Pakistani politics.

Begum Bhutto on her part found the situation both as a mother and a politician embarrassing. Although she was the official head of the PPP, the ruling party, it was evident that her sympathies lay more with her son than her daughter. To avoid the power struggle that threatened to rip apart the family following Murtaza's return, after some dithering she came up with a peace solution, namely that while the sister should continue as Prime Minister, the brother should be appointed Chief Minister of Sind. This proved to be a non-starter, and the family dispute remained unresolved. In the end, Benazir called her party's rubber-stamping central committee to session and it duly removed her mother from the PPP chairmanship and 'elected' Benazir in her place.

Metaphorically, it was the grave of Zulfikar Ali Bhutto over which the two contenders, one his daughter, the other his son, were now fighting, each claiming to be the sole inheritor of the father's mantle and political legacy. On 5 January 1994, which was Bhutto's birthday, the brother and sister announced separate programmes to celebrate the occasion, and although Murtaza was still in custody, his armed followers decided to gather on the lawns of Al-Murtaza, the dead leader's ancestral home in Larkana. The plan was that Begum Bhutto would lead these emotionally charged young men to place a wreath on Bhutto's grave at Naudero, not far from Larkana. Benazir had other ideas. On the same day, she had had a poetry-reading ceremony – a *mushaira* – organized close to the grave site. As was to be expected, the police turned up in large numbers and prevented Murtaza's supporters from coming out. There was an angry confrontation, and according to the police, they were fired upon and had no option but to fire back in self-defence. Two young men who were inside the house and had come to join the march were killed. One of them had been standing next to Begum Bhutto, so it was only by accident that the bullet went through him and not her. Later that day, Begum Bhutto said in a heart-broken voice that even during the dark days of General Zia-ul-Haq, the sanctity of Zulfikar Ali Bhutto's home had not been so brutally violated. However, the federal minister for the interior, General Naseerullah Babar, and the Sind information minister, Pervez Ali Shah, justified the police action and alleged that there were RAW-trained commandos hiding inside Al-Murtaza.[1]

The reference to RAW, the premier Indian intelligence agency, was meant to point the finger at those Al-Zulfikar men who had been trained in India and who were on Murtaza's side, fair and square, in this family dispute. However Murtaza, who got them trained in India, was not considered a RAW agent by his sister. When Murtaza was finally released from prison in May 1994, the rivalry intensified between him and his sister. In 1995, Murtaza set up his own party, which he named the Pakistan People's Party (Bhutto Shaheed). While the new grouping managed to create some sort of a skeleton presence in Sind, it failed to generate excitement in other provinces of the country.

Benazir, while leaving her brother more or less alone, took steps to make life hard for his supporters, which was in keeping with the old court tradition whereby rebel princes are not interfered with while their followers are given the rough end of the stick. Hundreds of Murtaza's supporters or those suspected of being sympathetic to him were thrown into prison. One of them, Ali Mohammad Hangroo, fell ill while in jail, and although doctors pleaded that he should be sent abroad for treatment, the government did not relent, with the result that he died while still handcuffed. Major Aftale, who suffered six years imprisonment during Zia's rule, was arrested on 5 January in Larkana and remained in prison until Benazir's dismissal. The intelligence agencies made it clear to Murtaza's jailed friends and supporters that if they changed sides, they would be freed. In 1995, one of them, Saifullah Khalid, denounced Murtaza at a press conference in Rawalpindi. The dissident had been wined, dined and taken good care of by Mohammad Nawaz Khokhar, a local member of the National Assembly, on the instructions of Asif Ali Zardari.

Both Benazir and Asif did whatever they could to liquidate Murtaza politically. It is said that such was the contempt in which Murtaza held his brother-in-law, that he had hung a picture of him in one of the lavatories of 70 Clifton, his home in Karachi. Guests were encouraged to use that particular facility. In May 1996, Murtaza and Benazir met for the first time since his return to Pakistan. The meeting was not a success; the two failed to arrive at a mutually acceptable formula for sharing power.

Let us reconstruct the events preceding the tragedy of 20 September 1996 involving the gangland style execution of Murtaza and his companions by the Karachi police. It is said that something happened four days earlier on 16 September which triggered off the bloody climax that shook Pakistan and may have even led to Benazir's removal from office six weeks later. On that day, Murtaza, accompanied by his security guards, left Islamabad for Karachi. Also on the flight was a 'VVIP' – standard Pakistani newspaper shorthand for Asif Ali Zardari. Murtaza's guards kept glaring at Zardari with murderous eyes throughout the flight. Murtaza wanted Zardari to get the message loud and clear that not only did he detest him but he was ready to face him. Zardari was received at the airport and whisked away in a car. Murtaza followed in one of his big four-wheel-drive monsters with his guards. On Shahrah-i-Faisal, which runs from the airport all the way to the city, Murtaza's vehicle overtook Zardari's, and as it did so, his guards aimed their automatic weapons at the Prime Minister's husband.[2] Zardari was so terrified that instead of going to his own house, he turned towards his father Hakim Ali Zardari's unoccupied residence. Murtaza's men did not drive on but turned and followed him. Once inside, Zardari phoned Syed Abdullah Shah, the Chief Minister of Sind, and gave him hell. Two days later, Zardari chaired a meeting which was attended by the Chief Minister, some members of his cabinet and certain senior officials. The only topic of discussion is said to have been the incident of 16 September.[3]

Meanwhile, the police had been looking for one of Murtaza's top lieutenants, a man called Ali Mohammad Sonara. It so happened that only five hours after the airport incident, uniformed men surrounded the place where Sonara was hiding. As soon as he realized what was taking place, he phoned Murtaza, who immediately called his friend and trusted companion, Ashiq Jatoi, telling him that he was afraid the police were going to kill

Sonara in the kind of fake 'encounter' which had become their custom and style in Karachi. There was no time to lose, he insisted. This call is believed to have been made at 2.30 am on 17 September. Murtaza and Ashiq Jatoi took a handful of armed followers to raid the police station where they were sure Sonara would by now have been taken. Once inside, they ordered the officers and men to raise their hands. One by one, they searched each room and cell in Karachi's most dreaded police station. It was probably the first time in Pakistan's history that a police station had been raided by a politician with his armed men in order to spring a companion. However, Sonara could not be found. While leaving, Murtaza warned the policemen in his characteristic style that if something happened to Sonara, none of them would be left alive.

Had Murtaza not been the Prime Minister's brother, the police would have gunned him down. Murtaza had become a terror. It was well known that Sind cabinet ministers were so terrified of him that before leaving their residences they would find out where in the city Murtaza was at the time, so that they could avoid the area. Murtaza was headstrong and everyone knew it, including the police. In 1996, he had slapped a member of the National Assembly publicly during a by-election campaign in Sanghar, Sind.

The law and order situation in Karachi was already catastrophic. In 1995 alone, three hundred policemen plus two thousand members of the public had died violent deaths.[4] The movement launched by the Mohajir Qaumi Movement to assert the rights of the Mohajirs was crushed through fake police 'encounters'. Those on the wanted list were picked up by the police and other security agencies, tortured, killed in cold blood and left on the streets, often with their hands tied behind their backs. They were officially said to have died in armed clashes with the 'law-enforcing agencies'. You could be shot on the street in Karachi if it was suspected that you were armed. However, Murtaza's guards drove around the city openly brandishing their weapons and daring anyone to challenge them. The police naturally saw them as dangerous adversaries who thumbed their noses at the law and defied state authority. All reports sent from Karachi by various agencies invariably identified Murtaza as a menace to public order.

It is said that in the second week of September 1996 Benazir sent a letter to Murtaza through Sanam, their younger sister, advising him not to go around Karachi defiantly displaying his weapons accompanied by his security men. Murtaza did not take the advice, so it was only natural that his attack on the police station came as the last straw. On the morning of 18 September, there were three bomb blasts in Karachi for which the police and intelligence agencies blamed Murtaza. The Prime Minister, the interior ministry and the Sind Chief Minister authorized the police to arrest Murtaza's guards, who were described as RAW agents. On 20

September, Murtaza addressed the last news conference of his life at 70 Clifton, at which he severely criticized the Benazir government for corruption and inefficiency and called upon his sister to resign. He also showed journalists pictures to prove that Ali Mohammad Sonara had once been Benazir's personal security guard. Murtaza said that any worker who took his side was denounced as a RAW agent.[5]

In a way, it was misleading of the government to accuse these men of being RAW agents, because although some of them had been trained in India, their allegiance did not lie there. These volunteers had gone to India at Murtaza's instance, and it was he who had arranged for their training. They were blindly loyal to Murtaza and the Bhutto cult. Anyone who died for the cause was a martyr, anyone who expressed dissent a traitor – words that Murtaza used often and indiscriminately.

At 5.40 pm on 20 September when Murtaza left home to speak at a protest meeting in a Karachi suburb, the police were waiting outside his 70 Clifton residence to arrest his guards. Murtaza had expected this and was not surprised; his motorcade drove right past the police picket without permitting a search. At 8.45 he returned after the meeting to find a police road-block in place about a hundred yards from the front gate of his residence. The road had been blocked at both ends, and a posse of armed policemen deployed, in an operation mounted by Superintendent Wajid Durrani. Minutes before the motorcade arrived, all the street lights had been switched off. According to a statement made before the Sind High Court by the Karachi police, Haq Nawaz Sial, station house officer of the Clifton police, ordered the red Pajero jeep in which Murtaza's guards were riding to stop. They responded by pointing their guns at the police and some shots were fired which injured Sial and an assistant superintendent of police, Shahid Hayat. According to the police account, they now opened fire in 'self-defence', and in the fire-fight that ensued seven men were killed or fatally wounded, including Murtaza and Jatoi. One of the officers, an assistant superintendent, took Murtaza to the nearby Mid East Medical Center, where he died two hours later. Murtaza had always been terrified of death throughout the years of struggle, despite callously killing others. I wonder what his thoughts would have been in those last moments when death confronted him?

According to the police version, Murtaza's death did not result from a conspiracy, but was accidental.[6] In the circumstances, few people believe this account of Murtaza having been killed in cross-fire. Other reports said that the firing had continued for twenty minutes and Murtaza was shot in the last two minutes. It also took the police a full fifty-five minutes before he was taken to hospital, bleeding heavily from bullets to the chest, arm, neck and face. Benazir did not get to see her brother until five hours later. She was wailing and calling on Murtaza – in English – to come back to life.

205

Benazir is an ill-fated woman, for it was while she was in power that the police fired at her father's house, narrowly missing her mother and killing two of her young supporters, and subsequently shot dead her brother. So enraged were Murtaza's supporters after his death that they blocked Benazir's and her husband's entry into 70 Clifton. She could not even take a last look at her brother before he was buried. As insurance against the enraged and emotionally charged followers of Murtaza, Asif even shaved off his moustache so that he should not be easily recognizable. (According to another story, his moustache was shaved off by Murtaza's guards on 16 September.) However, when Murtaza's supporters and the heaving crowd of mourners spotted him at Larkana, they threw stones at him and cursed him ferociously.

Murtaza's murder while his sister was Prime Minister can be seen as reflecting the kind of administration Benazir ran. Those who say that she is autocratic by temperament, unwilling to share power, dependent on what her sycophantic bureaucrats tell her and extremely obstinate may, after all, be right. Perhaps these aspects of her personality kept her from making up with her brother. As astute political observers expected, she appealed to public sympathy by blaming the murder of Murtaza on a 'deep conspiracy' against the Bhutto family and holding a third unseen force responsible for the tragedy. A day after the murder, when a reference was filed in the Supreme Court of Pakistan on behalf of the President of Pakistan, Farooq Leghari, she said that forces opposed to her were working according to a set 'timetable'. The President's reaction was strong and immediate. A month after the killing of Murtaza, Benazir said: 'I don't know whether they are going to hit me next, my husband next, my children next or other members of my family. I do not feel safe any more . . . I do not believe the story of cross-fire. Why did they let my brother bleed on the street, in the hospital, and bleed and bleed . . .?'[7]

What did Benazir mean by 'they'? It could not have been the police who took their orders from her. She has hinted that she meant the Pakistan army, and behind it the influence of the intelligence agencies. If her argument is to be believed, they wanted to end both democracy and Benazir Bhutto's political career. Whatever the merits of her indirect accusation, it did not gain much public support. The wave of popular sympathy witnessed after the hanging of Bhutto and the death of Shahnawaz, his son, was nowhere in evidence this time. It was not lost on the people that Murtaza had been mercilessly killed while his own sister was in power. If Benazir wanted the people to see her as a 'victim-ruler', she was disappointed by the popular response.

Her opponents argued that if Murtaza's killing was a conspiracy, then there must be someone who stood to benefit by it. According to this line of reasoning, the obvious beneficiary was Asif Ali Zardari. The leader of the opposition in the Senate, Pakistan's upper legislature, refused to permit the session to begin unless the Karachi police stopped stalling and registered a first information report (FIR) concerning Murtaza's 'real' murderers. It was quite clear that he had in mind Asif and those who had acted on his behalf. It demonstrates the shoddy state of Pakistani politics that this leader of the Senate opposition was Raja Zafar-ul-Haq – described by General Zia-ul-Haq as the 'opening batsman of my team' when he served in Zia's government. As a minister from 1980 to 1985, the period when Al-Zulfikar was active, he was loud among those who demanded exemplary punishment for the 'terrorist and anti-Pakistan traitor' Murtaza Bhutto. Now this same Raja Zafar-ul-Haq was wailing that Murtaza's real murderers were not being brought to book.

Why did Murtaza decide to attack police stations in Karachi and take on the police? Why turn the most powerful and coercive organ of the state into his personal enemy? The answer lies in Murtaza's peculiar psychological make-up. As leader of Al-Zulfikar he had led a charmed life, killing or wounding friend and foe alike, while he himself suffered neither danger nor hardship, nor any retribution. He must have been fairly confident not only that his sister's government was in no position to put him in jail, but also that the police would not dare to lay their hands upon him. He had also continued to adhere to his old belief that only through the use of force could one play an effective role in Pakistan's politics.[8] His acquittal in case after case had swollen his sense of self-assurance to the point that he once remarked: 'They cannot afford to kill another Bhutto.' By 'they', he too meant the Pakistan army and the Pakistan state apparatus. The paranoia he displayed abroad had given way to a conviction of immunity – for a man of extremes such as Murtaza, perhaps the only way to maintain his self-assurance. Of course this conviction was unfounded. Murtaza failed to understand that the bullet fired by an armed functionary of the state was just as blind and insensitive as the system in whose name it was fired. It did not discriminate between the just and the unjust, the peasant and the prince.

Besides Ashiq Jatoi, those who died with Murtaza on the night of 20 September 1996 were the following.

Sajjad Haider Ghakro: Born in a Punjabi family settled in Sind's Badin district, his uncle Ghulam Qadir was an enthusiastic worker of the PPP during Zulfikar Ali Bhutto's time. In the 1983 Movement for the Restoration of Democracy (MRD) launched against General Zia, the young Sajjad Haider spent twenty-two months in prison. In 1986, he recruited many young men for Al-Zulfikar and also became the senior vice-president of the PPP in Bedin. In 1995, Murtaza nominated him as the finance secretary of his party in Sind. He was about thirty-five when he died.

Yar Mohammad Baloch: Belonging to Hala in Sind, this thirty-seven-year-old Murtaza faithful was once a firebrand leader of the Sind People's Students' Federation (SPSF) and had also been jailed for a year during the 1983 MRD uprising. He was a card-carrying member of Al-Zulfikar, and also a member of the central committee of Murtaza's party since 1995.

Wajahat Hussain Jokhio: He came from Wahdat Colony in Hyderabad, Sind, and had always been a PPP activist. He joined Al-Zulfikar in 1986 and was jailed several times because of his loyalty to the Bhutto family.

Sattar Rajpar: He came from Nowshehro Feroz in Sind, having been born in the neighbouring village of Kandyaro. He was a member both of SPSF and Al-Zulfikar. He had been in jail several times over the years.

Mohammad Rahim Barohi: This twenty-two-year-old young man from Dadu in Sind was one of Murtaza's faithful security guards, and the youngest among those who were gunned down with their leader on 20 September.

All these men had one thing in common: their blind loyalty to the Bhutto family for whose sake they sacrificed their education, their careers and, ultimately, their lives. Is it not ironic that these devotees of the Bhuttos should have been slaughtered when there was a Bhutto in power? Had they been killed during martial law, they too would have been raised to the pantheon of PPP martyrs like Ayaz Sammu. Instead, the PPP declared them to be RAW agents and had them liquidated. Their dead bodies were not even returned to their families, but to the charitable Edhi Trust, which picks up unclaimed dead from the streets of Pakistani cities.

Even if no state agency was involved in a conspiracy to murder Murtaza, it will not do to file his death away as an unfortunate accident. It is significant that a few days after the incident, the station house officer of Clifton police, Haq Nawaz Sial, died mysteriously. He was said to have committed suicide while under police guard, but his widow insisted that she herself had seen two men running from the scene just after the event. A month after her brother's death, finding that public rumour had implicated herself and/or her husband in the killing, Prime Minister Benazir Bhutto invited a stream of former Scotland Yard detectives led by Roy Herridge to conduct their own independent investigation of the event. The interim report found evidence of a police conspiracy, and of an unidentified gunman at the scene. As soon as President Farooq Leghari had dismissed Benazir in November 1996, the Herridge team was quickly paid off and flown out.

Only time will tell who Murtaza's killers were. One cannot help observing though that his life dictated his death. He had started his political journey with a gun, and on 20 September 1996 it was a gun which brought it to an end. Nothing could save him, neither his guards, nor his bullet-proof jacket, nor his braggadocio. Like Al-Zulfikar, his death too would remain shrouded in mystery. Unlike Al-Zulfikar, the secret machinery of states rests upon an institutionalized ruthlessness that individual savagery can never match.

In the elections of February 1997, Benazir Bhutto suffered a decisive defeat that stemmed partly from the impact on Pakistan's politics of the return and violent death of Murtaza. Her brother's assassination and Benazir's eclipse may mark the end of an era in the country's history. So it seems apt at this point to take a general look at the chequered history and changing fortunes of the Pakistan People's Party. When it came into being in 1967, it appealed at once to the deprived masses that constitute the bulk of Pakistani society though they exercise no power. In the PPP they saw the promise of hope and change for the first time. Exactly four years later, in the wake of Pakistan's military defeat and the secession of its eastern wing, the PPP came into power. During the five and a half years that it stayed in office, it only brought severe disappointment to the people. Apart from cheap slogan-mongering, the party did little to bring about any change in the social, economic and political structure of Pakistan.

Massive street demonstrations mounted by the opposition against the PPP's misrule encouraged the army to take over. However, Bhutto's trial and execution in April 1979 became a grand act of expiation, and the people forgave him all his excesses. Once more, the masses set out on their journey of illusion, chasing the shadow called Bhutto and his promise of a just and equitable order. Bhutto was gone but there was Benazir, his daughter. A slogan that was current at the time would sum up the people's feelings and aspirations. 'Bhutto ki tasveer – Benazir, Benazir' (Benazir is Bhutto's true reincarnation) echoed on the streets of Pakistan. Benazir twice came to power, first from 1988 to 1990 and again from 1993 to 1996. On both occasions, her government failed to complete its term, dismissed on a host of charges by Presidents Ghulam Ishaq Khan and Sardar Farooq Leghari respectively. On both occasions, all she seemed to have achieved was to satiate her limitless hunger for power and privilege, doing very little for the people who had elected her. A party which had started out in 1967 with a platform promising the abolition of feudalism, turned into its last outpost. The people who for thirty years had followed first Bhutto and then his daughter were fated to be led around in circles while feudalism and gangster entrepreneurship ran rampant.

The PPP is presently the party of widows, divorcees and ex-wives, many of them foreigners. The leadership of one faction (the Shaheed Group) is in the hands of Murtaza's widow (Ghinawa Bhutto, a Syrian–Palestinian by origin), while the other faction is headed by Benazir, the daughter of Zulfikar Ali Bhutto. Begum Nusrat Bhutto, Benazir's mother and Ghinawa's mother-in-law, an Iranian by origin, is at the mercy of her daughters

Sanam (a divorcee) and Benazir. Shahnawaz's widow and Murtaza's divorced wife because of their daughters Sasi and Fatima are also taking part in family feuds over the control of the party and distribution of Bhutto's vast wealth. However, these Bhutto ladies have refused to relinquish the party leadership and free it from the family's clutches.

It is shameful for a party standing on the threshold of the twenty-first century to be run as a family concern and to have a chairperson-for-life elected by a bunch of non-elected pawns. According to one Pakistani intellectual,

> What is needed to make a new democracy is a new direction, new ideas, and of course a new leader. At this junction the substantive leaders, workers and supporters of PPP must reclaim their party, cleanse it of sycophants, rabble rousers, monarchists and monarchs, and make it worthy of a meaningful role in the next century. This task is by no means easy, but that is the only realistic choice there is.[9]

Those who refuse to march with history get run over by it. The history of the Liberal Party in Britain, the Peronists in Argentina, and the Communist Party in the Soviet Union amply illustrate the point.

It is a strange coincidence that on 27 October 1996, a month after Murtaza's murder, the Afghan mullahs the world has come to know as the Taliban executed former Afghan President Dr Najibullah in the most cruel manner. His death was like a final nail driven into the coffin of Al-Zulfikar because without Najibullah's personal support, there would have been no Al-Zulfikar in the first place. The hijack of the Pakistani aircraft – a joint Murtaza–Najibullah operation – would never have come about, nor any of the bloody Al-Zulfikar forays into Pakistan from Afghan soil. Najibullah was the iron man of Afghanistan for twelve years, the first civilian in Afghan history raised to the rank of major-general. Between 1980 and 1986, as head of KHAD commanding three brigades, he exercised the power of life and death over his country. Arrest and release, interrogations, imprisonments, and hangings were his to order at will. Even the Afghan jails were under his direct control. He was the last communist president of his country, having ruled it from 1987 to 1992. One of his initiatives was the transformation of the Afghan intelligence directorate into a fully-fledged ministry.

In 1992, when Najibullah arrived at Kabul airport hoping to escape to Delhi, his generals Azami and Babajan foiled the bid. He took refuge in the UN compound, where he remained for four years until he emerged on 27 October 1996 to be tortured and hanged in public along with his brother.

A few hours before the Taliban took Kabul, a minister in the fleeing

Burhanuddin Rabbani administration offered to take Najibullah to safety in the north. He rejected the offer. He had seen many rebel groups take control of Kabul during his long confinement safely in the UN compound, and he was sure that it was best for him to stay where he was. This decision proved to be his final error of judgement. The Taliban are said to have lured him out of the UN compound by saying that their leader wished to consult him on certain important matters; after the consultations, he would be returned to his sanctuary. The moment he left the building, Najibullah knew that the Taliban were going to kill him. He asked them to let him record his last statement but they set about beating him with the butts of their rifles and burning his hands with lighted cigarettes. These true believers then cut off his testicles. Even so, their feelings of revenge were not satisfied. They shot him several times, and dragged his mutilated body through the streets of Kabul, stuffing currency notes into his mouth. He swung from a pole in the city centre for three days.

While it is true that Najibullah was no angel, and that thousands lost their lives during his rule, what the holy warriors acting in the name of Islam did to him violated the teachings of every religion, broke every law and made nonsense of every moral value. Was it this 'Islamic system' for whose establishment thousands had died in the seventeen years preceding?

It is tragic but true that these mad and inhuman fundamentalists had the complete support of the Benazir government and according to some, much of the Taliban force was constituted by the border militia maintained by Pakistan. The tragic fate of Najibullah, seen that way, is directly linked to the Afghanistan policy of Benazir Bhutto. In a broader perspective, both his and Murtaza's death are monuments to the Cold War, and the billions of dollars and roubles worth of weaponry that it poured into Afghanistan and Pakistan. The West has yet to see the full repercussions of these weapons as they travel through the Middle East and farther, and by the approved regimes established at the cost of destabilizing the prospects of democracy. The career of Murtaza Bhutto was an exemplary episode in the history of an obsolescent feudal regime propped up beyond its time by outside forces. He never perceived how helpless he was in their grasp.

211

Appendix I

Al-Zulfikar's Operations

Operation	Names of Al-Zulfikar men involved
1. February 1981: Pope John Paul's public meeting, Karachi. One killed.	Lala Aslam died handling a time-bomb
2. March 1981: PIA plane takes off from Karachi, is hijacked to Kabul. Murder of Tariq Rahim.	Salamullah Tipu (executed by firing squad in Kabul 1984) Nasir Jamal (missing since 1992 in Libya) Arshad Khan (missing since 1992 in Libya) Nasir Baloch (hanged in Karachi 1984) Ayub Kabaria (jailed for 14 years 1984) Saifullah Khalid (jailed for 14 years 1984)
3. September 1981: Chaudhri Zahur Elahi and his driver Nasim murdered.	Razzaq Jharna (hanged in Lahore 1983) Lala Asad (killed in police encounter, Karachi 1981) Rehmatullah Anjum (died planting a bomb, Lahore 1983) Javed Malik (jailed in Austria, returned to Pakistan, jailed and freed 1995)
4. February 1982: Operation against Justice Anwar-ul-Haq, Rawalpindi. Two policemen killed.	Usman Ghani (hanged in Lahore 1984) Idris Toti (hanged in Lahore 1984) Idris Beg (hanged in Rawalpindi 1984)
5. September 1982: Zahoor-ul-Hassan Bhopali and four others murdered.	Ayaz Sammu (himself later hanged in Karachi 1985) Ilyas Siddiqui (shot on the spot in 1982 by Sammu) Javed Malik (see above) Rehmatullah Anjum (see above) Six members of the local PPP were arrested and given long prison sentences in 1983: Eizaz Khan, Ashraf A. Kolachi, Maula Bux, Ahmed Kahn, Zahid Hussain, N. Mohammad Brohi.

213

6. Canada Day reception, 1 July 1984, in Vienna, Austria, to be attacked and hostages taken. All nine assigned to the operation arrested before it began.

Javed Malik (jailed in Austria)
Akhtar Beg (jailed in Austria)
Ghulam Mustafa Memon (jailed in Austria)
Sher Bahadur (jailed in Austria)
Muhammad Karim (jailed in Austria)
Sheikh Iqbal (jailed in Austria)
Muhammad Zubair Minhas (jailed in Austria)
Umer Hayat (jailed in Austria)
Yaqub Cheena (jailed in Austria)

Appendix II

Al-Zulfikar men killed or jailed outside Pakistan

Note: This list does not include those who were jailed on account of Al-Zulfikar in Pakistan

1. Subedar Buneri (Tribal Areas) — Killed in Kabul on Murtaza Bhutto's orders (1981)

2. Mazdoor Yar Afridi (Peshawar) — Killed in Kabul on Murtaza's orders (1981)

3. Pervez Shinwari (Peshawar) — Killed in Kabul by Salamullah Tipu (1983)

4. Shahnawaz Bhutto (Larkana) — Died in mysterious circumstances in Cannes (1985)

5. Azam Chaudhri (Faisalabad) — Killed in Amsterdam by fascist group (1986)

6. Manzer Alam (Karachi) with 7 others — Lost/killed 1981

7. Tajbar Khan (Mardan) — Killed in 1984 or 1985

8. Baba Mohsin (Lahore) — Died in Kabul (1983)

9. Muhammad Ashraf (Faisalabad) — Died in Libya (1985)

10. Raja Anwar (author) — Jailed in Kabul (1980–83) at Murtaza's instance

11. Shaukat Ali Rana (Sheikhupura) — Jailed in Kabul (1980) at Murtaza's instance

12. Fazlur Rehman Kayani (Peshawar) — Jailed in Damascus (1981) at Murtaza's instance

13. Mueenullah Zahid (Peshawar) — Jailed in Damascus (1981) at Murtaza's instance

14. 'Vienna-9' (see Appendix I) — Jailed in Vienna (1984) for different terms ranging from 4 to 9 years.

215

Appendix III

PEOPLE'S LIBERATION ARMY

23ʳᵈ Dec 1980.

Since Shaukat Ali has decided to expose the plot hatched by counter-revolutionary criminal Raja Anwar against the P.L.A and its leadership, he will be provided the status of a witness in this case.

Also, with immediate effect I, in accordance with my powers conferred in the Constitution, request the Polit buro to pardon Shaukat Ali. His death sentence has been commuted and his release from detention will be arranged without any further delay.

Nabil.
Head of Central
Security Committee.

Murtaza Bhutto
Secretary General.
PLA

Murtaza Bhutto's hand-written orders on 'Pakistan Liberation Army' letter-head, dated 23 December 1980, commuting the death sentence of Shaukat Ali. The letter is co-signed by 'Nabil, Head of Central Security Committee'. 'Nabil' was Shahnawaz Bhutto's code name.

Patron:

   The LADY PALMER

President:

   Mrs. WILLIAM PALMER

County Branch Director:

~~Lieut~~Clozelzkzkz2Hbzn

Mrs. B. Aird.

British Red Cross Society

Royal County of Berkshire Branch

48, LONDON ROAD,
READING, RG1 5AR

Tel: Reading 81208-9
Welfare Dept: 82165

Mr. Hussein,
c/o 50 Bradley Road,
SLOUGH,
Berks.

                11 May 1982

Dear Mr. Hussein,

Re: Enquiry regarding Raja Mohammed ANWAR

Our Director of International Welfare in London has communicated with the International Committee of the Red Cross in Geneva to get further guidance on your problem. I hope we will soon hear further news of your brother.

Please let me know if you have any further communication from Mr. Anwar.

Sincerely,

Trips Bartlett.

Trips Bartlett
County Welfare Officer

A letter from the British Red Cross to Raja Anwar's brother Raja S. Hussein who lived in Britain.

HOUSE OF COMMONS
LONDON SWIA OAA

5 March 1984

TO WHOM IT MAY CONCERN

Raja Anwar

The above-named person is known to me. He was imprisoned
by the Afghan authorities from 23 October 1980 to
1 March 1983, being released thanks to representations
from Western socialists, including myself.

However, he makes the point that his jailing was a mistake
and that General Zia's regime were responsible for making
false allegations aginst him.

Raja Anwar wishes to remain in Europe and it is hoped that
you will be able to help him with this request.

Ron Brown
Member of Parliament

A letter from Ron Brown, MP, confirming Raja Anwar's wish to remain in
Europe.

Appendix IV

Facsimiles from *Jang*, London, 5 April 1981 and *Mashriq*, Lahore, 5 April 1981 saying that Raja Anwar had been shot dead in Kabul on Murtaza Bhutto's orders.

219

Appendix V

Position of political prisoners in the 1980s

Note: Most of the prisoners were arrested because of their suspected affiliations with Al-Zulfikar, though in many cases such affiliations did not exist. I have attempted to make the list as accurate and complete as possible, though in the absence of any available records this has proved difficult.

Kot Lakhpat Prison, Lahore (Punjab), mid-1985

Name	Date of arrest	City	Name	Date of arrest	City
1 Ch. M. Aslam	15/04/81	Lahore	2 A. Waheed Bokhari	20/04/82	Sialkot
3 Azhar Hussain	20/04/82	Sialkot	4 Hakim Ejaz Bhatti	26/12/81	Gujranwala
5 Khalid Pervez Mirza	16/03/81	Gujranwala	6 M. Sabir Hussain	04/12/81	Lahore
7 Riaz Sajid	28/01/82	Rawalpindi	8 Riaz Shahid	16/08/83	Lahore
9 Dr Islam	16/03/79	Lahore	10 Abbas	16/03/81	Gujranwala
11 Sufi Amin	1981	Faisalabad	12 Ch. Ghulam Qadir	25/12/82	Lahore
13 Iqbal Javed	04/12/81	Lahore	14 Hafiz-ur-Rehman	08/08/81	Lahore
15 Abdur Rauf	May 1981	Lahore	16 Agha Naveed	August 1981	Lahore
17 M. Rafique Babar	07/10/81	Lahore	18 Yousaf Khattak	02/10/81	Lahore
19 Akhlaq Shah	1981	Lahore	20 Abdul Khaliq	October 1981	Lahore
21 Naveed Iqbal	15/12/81	Lahore	22 Attaullah Moghal	08/08/81	Lahore
23 Mahboob Ali Shah	30/03/83	Lahore	24 Naseem Iqbal	02/05/83	Lahore
25 Sufi Iqbal	22/04/83	Lahore	26 Nadir Ali	29/04/83	Lahore
27 Agha Mobin	01/04/83	Lahore	28 Agha Naeem	01/10/83	Lahore
29 Ch. M. Ashraf	22/09/83	Lahore	30 M. Boota Khokar	06/06/83	Lahore
31 Baqar Ali Shah	18/04/83	Lahore	32 Abdul Haque	May 1983	Lahore
33 Javed Iqbal	18/04/83	Lahore	34 Mirza Khalid Beg	06/08/83	Lahore
35 M. Anwar Munshi	06/08/83	Lahore	36 Hakim Ali	16/08/83	Lahore
37 Kamal-ud-Din	17/10/83	Lahore	38 Abdul R. Bajwa	18/04/83	Lahore
39 Aftab Ahmed	08/09/81	R Y Khan	40 M. Hussain Manoo	02/08/82	Bahawalpur
41 Khan Mohammad	22/07/81	R Y Khan	42 Mohammad Younis	08/06/82	Sialkot
43 Fazal Elahi Shakil	20/04/83	Sialkot	44 Mohammad Arshad	12/05/83	Sialkot
45 Mohammad Abid	12/05/83	Sialkot	46 Dilbar Shah	23/04/83	Sialkot
47 Zahid Butt	23/04/83	Sialkot	48 M. Shafi Mufti	19/04/83	Sialkot
49 M. Pervez Changa	20/04/83	Sialkot	50 Baqir Hussain Kazmi	20/04/83	Sialkot
51 Dilshad Shah	20/04/83	Sialkot	52 Pervez Akhtan	20/4/83	Sialkot
53 Atiq-ur-Rehman	25/04/83	Sialkot	54 Salim Abbas	18/04/83	Sialkot
55 Fiaz Mohammad	02/10/82	Dera Ghazi Khan	56 Ghulam Shabbir	08/09/82	Bhakkar
57 M. Azim Butt	18/04/83	Faisalabad	58 Sh. Gul Mohammad	since 1981	Gujranwala
59 Zubair Shad	since 1981	Faisalabad	60 Pervez Azam Butt	01/10/81	Faisalabad

61 Shahid Gogi	January 1981	Faisalabad	62 M. Hussain Manj	08/05/81	Sheikhupura
63 Mohammad Ishaque	27/09/81	Narang	64 M. Shaheen Bhatti	08/10/81	Gujranwala
65 M. Akbar Butt	03/09/83	Gujranwala	66 Hamid Pervez	since 1983	Gujrat
67 Munawar Atif	April 1983	Gujrat	68 Anwar Baig	09/10/81	Rawalpindi
69 Amir Hussain Shah	January 1984	Faisalabad	70 Hamid Saeed Pia	22/01/82	Rawalpindi
71 Sh. Qayyum	16/11/81	Rawalpindi	72 Aurangzeb Zafar	16/01/82	Rawalpindi
73 Naeem Akbar	01/07/82	Rawalpindi	74 S. Masroor Ahsan	March 1983	Karachi
75 Mohammad Sharif	March 1983	Jacobabad	76 Mohammad Mumtaz	March 1983	Jacobabad
77 Shaukat Rizvi	December 1983	Gujranwala	78 Umar Farooq	since 1983	Taxila
79 Z. Maqsud Ahmed	12/08/81	Lahore	80 Qazi S Mahmood	since 1981	Rawalpindi
81 Talat Shakeel	02/12/82	Sialkot	82 Imtiaz Khan	25/01/82	Rawalpindi
83 Javed Akhtar	unknown	Lahore	84 A. Hamid Niazi	08/09/81	Mianwali
85 Ch. Yousaf	unknown	Sialkot	86 M. Atta Mohammad	15/09/81	Bhakkar
87 Ghulam Abbas	unknown	Sialkot	88 M. Maqbul Ahmed	14/09/81	unknown
89 M. Sadiq Tarar	1981	Sialkot	90 Abid Hussain	since 1981	Sialkot
91 Rana Laeeq	unknown	Sialkot	92 Iqbal Pervez Mashih	16/11/81	Faisalabad
93 Dr Khalid	unknown	unknown	94 Asif Butt	since 1981	Sialkot
95 Tariq Mahmood	unknown	Gujranwala	96 Mohammad Tahir	since 1981	Sialkot
97 Ayub Rana	unknown	unknown	98 Arshad Mahmood	since 1981	Sialkot
99 Islam Shah (QMA)	unknown	unknown	100 M. Atiq-u-Rahman	since 1981	Sialkot
101 Ch. Bashir Ahmed	11/12/82	Sialkot	102 M. Zubair Shad	since 1981	Gujaranwala
103 M. Qadeer Khokhar	11/11/81	Sialkot	104 Talat Jaffry	since 1983	Sialkot
105 Q. Sadiq Hussain	16/09/82	Sialkot	106 R. Farhat Ali	since 1981	Sialkot
107 M. Mohammed Rafi	26/01/82	Faisalabad	108 Ghulam Hussain	since 1981	Sialkot
109 Aslam Ludhianvi	11/05/81	R. Y. Khan	110 Mohammed Azam	since 1981	Sialkot
111 Hafiz Nusrat	08/06/81	R. Y. Khan	112 Laiq Ali	since 1981	Sialkot
113 Tahir Bhatti	11/05/81	Khanpur	114 Mohammed Saeed	since 1981	Sialkot
115 Amjad Hussain	since 1981	Sialkot	116 M. Anwar	since 1981	Sialkot
117 S. Iftikhar Shah	since 1981	Sheikhupura	118 Akram Khan	since 1981	Sheikhupura

Fifty-four of the above were imprisoned for life in March 1985 by a military court in Lahore. They were dubbed as Al-Zulfikar members.

Central Jail, Bahawalpur (Punjab), mid-1985

119 Farooq Kashif	3 years R.I.	Lahore	120 Tariq Nawaz.G.	3 years R.I.	Sialkot
121 Mohammed Akarm	3 years R.I.	Lahore	122 Mehdi Hasan	since 3 years	Gujranwala
123 Haji Afzal	since 3 years	Ghujranawala	124 Shekh Sajjad	since 3 years	Sialkot
125 Sharafat Hussain	since 3 years	Lahore	126 Sh. Hamid	17 years R.I.	Lahore
127 Shafique Ahmed	since 3 years	Lahore	128 Sarfaraz Ahmed.S.	since 3 years	Rawalpindi
129 Rana Farooq	14 years R.I.	Gojra			

District Jail, Gujranwala (Punjab), mid-1985

130 Rafiq Khan	7 years R.I.	Gujranwala

District Jail, Sialkot (Punjab), mid-1985

131 Mirza T. Hussain	since 1981	Gujranwala	132 N. Hussain Moghal	since 1981	Gujranwala

District Jail, Jhelum (Punjab), mid-1985

133 Ali Haider Shah	since 1981	Larkana	134 Jamil Abbasi	since 1981	Rawalpindi

Rawalpindi Jail (Punjab), mid-1985

135	Mahoob A. Khan	since 1982	Faisalabad	136 Zamir Gilani	since 1982	Lahore
137	Tanvir Zaman	since 1982	Lahore	138 Tariq Khurshid*	since 1981	Lahore
139	Zawar Hussain*	since 1981	Lahore	140 Jehangir A. Khan*	since 1981	Lahore
141	Rana Mansha*	since 1981	Lahore	142 Inayat A. Hashmi	since 1981	Lahore
143	Kamran Rizvi*	since 1981	Islamabad	144 Prof. Zahoor Ahmed*	since 1981	Mianwali
145	Saeed Akhtar	since 1981	D.I. Khan	146 Mubarik Shah	since 1981	D.I.Khan
147	Mohammad Ramazan	since 1981	D.I. Khan	148 Munawar H. Bokhari	since 1981	Sheikhupura
149	Ahmad N. Bokhari	since 1981	unknown	150 Samiullah Khan	since 1981	Bannu
151	Abdul Wahid	since 1981	Bannu	152 Mansoor Ahmed	since 1980	Bhakkar
153	Iqbal Mustafa	since 1983	Lahore			

* In March 1985, these prisoners were given life sentences.

Central Jail, Sahiwal (Punjab), mid-1985

154	Rozi Khan	since 1981	Lahore	155 Ghulam Rasool	since 1981	Lahore
156	Javed Iqbal	since 1982	Lahore	157 Zaman Butt	since 1982	Lahore
158	Mian Munir	since 1982	Lahore			

Central Jail, Hairpur N.W.F.P., mid-1985

159	Imtiaz Alam	unknown	Bahawalnagar	160 Sheri Ali Bacha	34 months	Mardan
161	Abdul Naeem	Advocate	Swabi	162 Babu Fazal Khaliq	23 months	Peshawar
163	Isa Khan	6 months	Peshawar	164 Zar Mohammad	23 months	Peshawar
165	Jahan Zeb	22 months	Peshawar	166 Kamran Haider Kiani	28 months	Khanpur
167	Banyad Hussain	2 months	Peshawar	168 Mohammad Ali	35 months	Kurrum Agency
169	Inam Khan	22 months	Kohat	170 Jehanger Khan	16 months	Kohat
171	Shams-ul-Haq	13 months	Charsada	172 Meer Ahmad	6 months	Charsada
173	Zafar	2 months	Charsada	174 Jehangeer Khan	2 months	Charsada
175	Shoaib Saqib	2 months	Charsada	176 Ghulam Ali	4 months	Parachinar
177	Iqbal Hussain	10 months	Parachinar	178 Sabir Hussain	10 months	Parachinar
179	Jafar Ali	10 months	Parachinar	180 Shah Baba	26 months	Peshawar
181	Lal Mohammad	6 months	Peshawar	182 Shah Rehman	49 months	Afghanistan
183	Gul Baz	21 months	Tribal Area	184 Ajar Khan	21 months	Tribal Area
185	Hilmat Shah	22 months	Tribal Area	186 Sikandar	22 months	Tribal Area
187	Ghazi	21 months	Tribal Area	188 Said M Umar	8 months	Tribal Area
189	Amir M. Wahiz	49 months	Afghanistan	190 Mohabat Khan	29 months	Charsada
191	Rahim Dad Khan	18 months	Charsada	192 Ismail Khan	22 months	Charsada
193	Gul Bacha	17 months	Charsada	194 Zabir Shah	16 months	Charsada
195	Ajab Gul	16 months	Charsada	196 Mohammad Zada	19 months	Charsada
197	Dr Masood	31 months	Charsada	198 Mohammad Jan	6 months	Charsada
199	Gul Jan	21 months	Mardan	200 Mohib Gul	34 months	Mardan
201	Iqbal Zahid	2 months	Marden	202 Asi Hashtnagri	20 months	Mardan
203	Tammas Mohammad	21 months	Mohmand Agency	204 Jan Said	4 months	Mohmand Agency
205	Mohammad Ikram	24 months	Lahore	206 Masood Iqbal	14 years R.I.	Lahore
207	Ihsan Nabi	25 months	Malakand	208 Noor Mohammad	27 months	Malakand
209	Akhwan Zada	21 months	Dir	210 Bakhat Zaman	25 months	Dir
211	Aijazulhaq	22 months	Karachi	212 Saleem Jan	4 months	Karachi
213	Khalil Qureshi	35 months	Parachinar	214 Gul Hussain	17 months	Parachinar
215	Qadam Ali	20 months	Parachinar	216 Said Mohammad	23 months	Chitral
217	Umer Zada	27 months	Swat	218 Mohammad Ghulam	22 months	Kurram Agency
219	Dr M. Salim	29 months	Ghazi	220 Masood Afridi	25 months	Kyber Agency
221	Master Mir Ali Shah	16 months	Bannu	222 Ghazi Gul	19 months	Kyber Agency
223	Bakht Jan	23 months	Waziristan	224 Majeed Khan	32 months	Kohat
225	Tariq Zeeshan	8 months	Abbottabad	226 Noor Rehman	56 months	Darbani
227	Nasir Butt	unknown	Sialkot	228 Tariq Gul	unknown	Sialkot

Appendices

Central Prison, Karachi, Jamia Cloth Market Bus-Burning Case, 1979

Name	Date of Arrest	Province	Name	Date of Arrest	Province
229 M. Rafique Memon	since 1979	Sind	230 A. Haq Sherapao	since 1979	Sind
231 M. Saleem Ansari	since 1979	Sind	232 Mohsin Raza	since 1979	Sind
233 Sahid Ali Raana	since 1979	Sind	234 Saleem Mughal	since 1979	Sind

Lala Asad Case, 1981

235 Rukhsar A. Qureshi	since 1981	Sind	236 M. Ashraf Sheikh	since 1981	Sind
237 M. Ramazan Mughal	since 1981	Sind	238 Mrs Rubina Qureshi	Since 1981	Sind

Bhopali Murder Case, 1982

239 Eizaz Khan	since 1982	Sind	240 Ahmed Khan	since 1982	Sind
241 Ashraf A. Kolachi	since 1982	Sind	242 Zahid Hussain	since 1982	Sind
243 Maula Bux	since 1982	Sind	244 N. Mohammad Brohi	since 1982	Sind
245 Ayaz Sammu	Death Sentence	Sind			

Conspiracy Case, mid-1985

246 Rafiq Safi Munshey	14 years R.I.	Sind	247 Maulana J. Naumani	since 1983	Sind
248 Ghulam M. Baloch	since 1983	Sind	249 Shareef Brohi	since 1983	Sind
250 Mumtaz Lashari	since 1983	Sind	251 Dr H. Zaffar Arif	since 1984	Sind
252 Hanif Ahmed Patel	since 1983	Sind	253 Sikander Baloch	since 1983	Sind
254 Mohammad Ali Patel	since 1984	Sind			

Jam Saqi Case, 1980

255 Jam Saqi	since 1980	Sind	256 Prof. Jamal Naqvi	since 1980	Sind
257 Dr Jabbar Khattak	since 1982	Sind	258 Amar Lal	since 1980	Sind
259 Shabbir Shah	since 1980	Sind	260 Ahmed Kamal Warsi	since 1980	Sind

D.S.F. Case, mid-1985

261 Ghansham Das	under trial	Sind	262 Imdad Chandio	7 years R.I.	Sind
263 M. Khan Solangi	7 years R.I.	Sind	264 S. Mohammad Mangrio	7 years R.I.	Sind

Miscellaneous Cases, mid-1985

265 Wali M. Saito	25 years R.I.	Sind	266 Syed Muheb Ali Shah	under trial	Sind
267 Ali Hyder Shah	25 years R.I.	Sind	268 M. Khaliqui-uz-Zaman	under trial	Sind
269 Zafar Chatta	1 year	Sind	270 Mairaj M. Khan	under trial	Sind

Landhi Jail, Karachi, mid-1985

271 Rasool B. Palijo	since 1979	Sind	272 Fazil Rahoo	since 1983	Sind
273 Pir Mazhar-u-Haq	since 1983	Sind	274 Mushtaq Ali Bhutto	since 1983	Sind
275 Manzoon Wasan	since 1983	Sind	276 Shah Nawaz Rapuar	since 1983	Sind
277 Noor Mohammad Dahri	since 1983	Sind			

Central Prison, Hyderabad (Sind), mid-1985

278	Ghulam M. Korai	detained	Sind	279	Aziz Phal	detained	Sind
280	Gulam H. Zardari	detained	Sind	281	Jewan Thebbo	detained	Sind
282	Sikander Abrejo	detained	Sind	283	Pir S. Jan Sarhindi	3 years R.I.	Sind
284	Mehrab Rajpar	detained	Sind	285	Anwar Shabani	detained	Sind
286	Barkat G. Jahtial	detained	Sind	287	Ali Ahmed Junejo	detained	Sind
288	Shah Jahan Shah	detained	Sind	289	Arif Leghari	detained	Sind
290	Yousuf Zardari	detained	Sind	291	Zaffar Rajper	detained	Sind
292	Sardar Leghari	detained	Sind	293	Mumtaz Sheikh	detained	Sind
294	Sher Khan Punnal	detained	Sind	295	Dr Sattar Rajpar	detained	Sind
296	Talib Jakhro	detained	Sind	297	Syed Anwar Ali Shah	25 years R.I.	Sind
298	Nizam Pakawad	detained	Sind	299	Ishaque Barhamani	detained	Sind
300	Qurban Soomro	detained	Sind	301	Haji Hassan Khusk	detained	Sind
302	Roshan Memon	detained	Sind	303	Dur M. Solangi	detained	Sind
304	Ishaque Punnal	detained	Sind	305	Faudi Khan Panwar	detained	Sind
306	Ali Nawaz Paind	detained	Sind	307	Roshan Mallal	detained	Sind
308	Ramzan Machi	detained	Sind	309	Maula Bux Bhrambro	detained	Sind

In addition, thirty-six students of Sind University, arrested during the Thori Incident Case, are still in detention.

District Jail, Nara (Hyderabad Sind), mid-1985

310	Yousaf Jakhrani	since 1983	Sind	311	Agha Saifullah	since 1983	Sind
312	Ghulam Mustafa	since 1983	Sind	313	Dulha Nahar Malakani	detained	Sind
314	Dost Ali Rind	detained	Sind	315	Anyat Rind	detained	Sind
316	Mohammad L. Hatir	detained	Sind	317	Younus Hamdam	detained	Sind
318	Pir S. Sirhandi	detained	Sind	319	Maharab Rachar	detained	Sind
320	Anayat Chital	detained	Sind	321	Ovais Mataihani	detained	Sind
322	Hasan Rachar	detained	Sind	323	Sikandar Abro	detained	Sind
324	Ismail Saho	detained	Sind	325	G. Qadir Solongi	detained	Sind
326	Bachal Daphar	detained	Sind	327	Dad Phand	detained	Sind
328	Layar Wahid	detained	Sind	329	Saban Dharejo	detained	Sind
330	Gulab Jatoi	detained	Sind	331	Manthar Jatoi	detained	Sind
332	Ghulam Jatoi	detained	Sind	333	Imam Bakhsh Jatoi	detained	Sind
334	Safar Jatoi	detained	Sind	335	Ghulam D. Pakhlai	detained	Sind
336	Ahmad Khan Kobar	detained	Sind	337	Shair Khan Lund	detained	Sind
338	Ayub Antar	detained	Sind	339	Mohuddin Kerano	detained	Sind
340	Ghansham Parkash	detained	Sind	341	Bashir Lashari	detained	Sind
342	Haji Shaffi M. Jatoi	3 years R.I.	Sind	343	Ali Nawaz Jatoi	3 years R.I.	Sind
344	Jeawan Jatoi	3 years R.I.	Sind	345	Muharram Jatoi	3 years R.I.	Sind
346	Mahboob Jatoi	3 years R.I.	Sind	347	Khudda Bux Jatoi	3 years R.I.	Sind
348	Khudda Bux Khan	detained	Sind	349	Ayub Jatoi	detained	Sind
350	Punhal Jatoi	detained	Sind	351	Allah Warrao Jatoi	detained	Sind
352	Soomar Jatoi	detained	Sind	353	Ali Murrad Jatoi	detained	Sind
354	Ghazi Jatoi	detained	Sind	355	M. Hashim Jatoi	detained	Sind
356	Ali Gul Chunno	detained	Sind	357	Mohammad Bux Jatoi	detained	Sind
358	Mithoo Ahmed	detained	Sind	359	Akhbar Sunabat	detained	Sind
360	Maan Piyaro	detained	Sind	361	Saffar Khamisoo	detained	Sind
362	Ali Hassan Pupat	detained	Sind	363	Gulzar Dilawar	detained	Sind
364	Ghulam R. Mithal	detained	Sind	365	Ghullab Ghaus Bux	detained	Sind
366	Allah Ditto	detained	Sind	367	Imam Bux	detained	Sind
368	Ali Hassan	detained	Sind	369	Ali Sher	detained	Sind
370	Ghullam Hussain	detained	Sind				

Central Prison, Khairpur, mid-1985

371	Pervaiz Ali Shah	since 1981	Sind	372	Ali Taqi Shah	since 1981	Sind
373	Nazir Hussain Dhoki	detained	Sind	374	Sabir Ali Shah	25 years R.I.	Sind
375	M. Suleman Sheikh	detained	Sind	376	M. Arif Jalbani	detained	Sind
377	Abdul Ghani Jatoi	detained	Sind	378	M. Qassim Pathar	detained	Sind
379	S. Wali M. Shah	detained	Sind	380	Mohammad Punhal	1 year R.I.	Sind
381	Abdur Rehman	1 year R.I.	Sind	382	Abdul K. Wassan	1 year R.I.	Sind
383	Shamsheer Wassan	detained	Sind	384	Irshad A. Lashari	detained	Sind
385	Ahmed Ali Khalhoro	detained	Sind	386	Haji Dhani Bux Watni	detained	Sind
387	Mureed Ali Rajpar	detained	Sind	388	Ghulam Nabi Soomro	detained	Sind
389	M. Hassan Lohar	detained	Sind	390	Abdul Qayyum	detained	Sind
391	A. Rauf	detained	Sind	392	Dil Murrad	detained	Sind
393	Azizullah	detained	Sind	394	Hazoor Bux	detained	Sind
395	A. Rasool Solangi	detained	Sind	396	Himmayat Ali Solangi	detained	Sind
397	Shaukat Ali	detained	Sind	398	Allah Dino	detained	Sind
399	Ghullam Q. Mangejo	detained	Sind	400	Habibullah Manejo	detained	Sind
401	Damman Ali Dahar	detained	Sind	402	Humzoo Majeedano	detained	Sind
403	Fido Hussain	detained	Sind	404	Nazuk Ram	detained	Sind
405	Gul Sher Jamroo	under trial	Sind	406	Mazhar Ali Abro	under trial	Sind
407	Anwar Ali Kanhar	under trial	Sind	408	Ali Murrad Kanhar	under trial	Sind
409	Nawab Ali Phalphatta	under trial	Sind	410	Rabbon Narejoo	under trial	Sind
411	Umar Niazi	under trial	Sind	412	Shah Murrad Rind	under trial	Sind
413	Hazoor Bux	under trial	Sind	414	M. Ali Chandio	under trial	Sind
415	Zaharral Shah	under trial	Sind	416	Dust Mohammad	under trial	Sind

Central Prison, Sukkur (Sind)

417	Rafique Ahmed Rind Baloch	under trial	Sind	418	Ali Hassan Khoso	under trial	Sind
419	Younus K. Baloch	under trial	Sind	420	Lal M. Bhutto	under trial	Sind
421	Dust Ali Rind Baloch	under trial	Sind	422	Enyet Ali Rind	under trial	Sind
423	Dhani Bux Malkani	under trial	Sind	424	Nooh Faqeer Sahato	under trial	Sind
425	Shah Nawaz Rajpar	detained	Sind	426	Jehangir Farhan	detained	Sind
427	Shabbir Sheikh	detained	Sind	428	Bashir Sheikh	detained	Sind
429	Hakim Ali Chandio	detained	Sind	430	Imdad Ali Chandio	detained	Sind
431	A. Razzak Khawar	detained	Sind	432	Saifal Mallah	detained	Sind
433	Niaz Bhatti	detained	Sind	434	Manzoor Chandio	detained	Sind
435	Yar M. Mahar	detained	Sind	436	Asad Ullah Bhutto	3 years R.I.	Sind
437	Qazi M. Bux Dhamra	3 years R.I.	Sind	438	Karim Bux Mallah	3 years R.I.	Sind
439	Abdul Latif Mallah	3 years R.I.	Sind	440	Baro Choo Hakro	3 years R.I.	Sind
441	Pirral Sheikh	3 years R.I.	Sind	442	Dil Sher Jatoi	1 year R.I.	Sind
443	Mohammad Hassan	1 year R.I.	Sind	444	Maharram Jatoi	1 year R.I.	Sind
445	Ali Nawaz Khan	1 year R.I.	Sind	446	Chotto Mohammad	1 year R.I.	Sind
447	Ali Gul Bux	1 year R.I.	Sind	448	Mano Nooral	1 year R.I.	Sind
449	Qadir Bux Hashim	1 year R.I.	Sind	450	Pathan Khan	1 year R.I.	Sind
451	Mattaro Khan	1 year R.I.	Sind	452	Saddro Masti	1 year R.I.	Sind
453	Ranno Mohammad	1 year R.I.	Sind	454	Ghullam Hyder Khan	1 year R.I.	Sind
455	Rano Khan Mithal	1 year R.I.	Sind	456	M. Bachal Bux	1 year R.I.	Sind
457	Allah Obhayo Sultan	1 year R.I.	Sind	458	Piyaro Mohammad	1 year R.I.	Sind
459	Hashim Mohammad	1 year R.I.	Sind	460	Allah W. Jumman	1 year R.I.	Sind
461	Darya Khan	1 year R.I.	Sind	462	Saffar Mohammad	1 year R.I.	Sind
463	Jarro Jeewan	1 year R.I.	Sind	464	Saleh Hashim	1 year R.I.	Sind
465	Malook Shah Baig	1 year R.I.	Sind	466	Suleman Nazzar	1 year R.I.	Sind
467	Umar Sawan	1 year R.I.	Sind	468	Muhrram Shikari	1 year R.I.	Sind
469	Hassan Piyaro	1 year R.I.	Sind	470	Faqir Mohammad	1 year R.I.	Sind
471	Mohammad Rano	1 year R.I.	Sind	472	Shah Jahan Panwar	1 year R.I.	Sind
473	Bashir Samejo	1 year R.I.	Sind				

Baluchistan Province

474	Ali Dost Umrani	since 26.09.83	Osta Muhammad	475	Liaqat Umrani	since 29.09.83	Nasirabad
476	Fabrid Umrani	since 15.08.83	Nasirabad	477	Javed Ahmed	under trial	Quetta
478	Haji M. Akbar Loni	1 year R.I.	Sibbi	479	Dr A. H. Pandarani	1 year R.I.	Temple Dera
480	Iqbal Shah	1 year R.I.	Quetta	481	Nasrullah Baluch	1 year R.I.	Jat Pat
482	Abdul Jabbar	since 18.03.83	Osta Muhammad	483	Ghulam R. Bambul	1 year R.I.	Jat Pat
484	Abdul Sattar	since 18.12.83	Osta Muhammad	485	Muhammad Faghan	since 18.12.83	Nasirabad
486	Ghulam Qadir Keri	since 18.12.83	Osta Muhammad	487	Ali Ahmed Kurd	since 12.08.83	Quetta
488	Shahban Maggi	since 14.03.83	Osta Muhammad				

Notes

1 The Fall of Zulfikar Ali Bhutto

1. Since 1969 Thulla has been settled in Denmark.
2. See Stanley Wolpert, *Zulfi Bhutto of Pakistan*, Oxford University Press, 1994, p. 263. According to Wolpert, when in his cups, Bhutto would call Zia his 'monkey General'. He also used to make fun of his false teeth. I did not see, hear or know of this. However, Bhutto's attitude was generally insulting to Zia and his own ministers. He had a fortnightly intelligence report and dossiers compiled on them. It is said that Zia later showed those dossiers with Bhutto's humiliating written remarks on them to some of Bhutto's important ex-ministers to win them over secretly to his side.
3. During this period, at various times, the governors and chief ministers of three provinces were all feudals. Punjab: Governor, Abbas Abbasi, Nawab of Bahawalpur, Chief Minister, Nawab Sadiq Hussain Qureshi. Sind: Governor, Dilawar Khanji, Nawab of Junagarh, Chief Minister, Rais Ghulam Mustafa Jatoi. Baluchistan: Governor, Mir Ahmed Yar Khan, Nawab of Kalat, Chief Minister, Nawab Ghaus Bakhsh Raisani.
4. I recall an incident which is relevant to the point I am making. In December 1976, on the occasion of the Muslim festival of Eid, I accompanied Bhutto to Larkana where I learnt during meetings with the *haris* (landless peasants) who had come to greet the Prime Minister that the landlords had hit upon a novel method of sabotaging the land reform programme. In league with local officials, they had made paper transfers of land above the maximum point of holding under the law to dead or non-existent *haris*. Most of those who had worked the land had been thrown out and labour on daily wages contracted from other areas to keep the locals away from the land which they had tilled for generations. Bhutto was very upset when he heard those stories and ordered an inquiry into the racket. However, seven months later, before it could produce any results, he had been overthrown by his army chief.
5. This was Malik Muhammad Hayat Khan Tamman, an old feudal-type Punjabi politician whose advice was said to be devoid of all redeeming political morality.
6. Bhutto was lucky enough that he did not survive to see the outcome of his dream. A corrupt, incapable and superstitious Benazir government would have given him a heart attack.
7. Bhutto recalled this exchange with Zia in a conversation during his 'protective custody' at Murree. He was allowed to meet members of his staff.
8. *The Pakistan Times*, Lahore, 15 July 1977, reporting Zia's press conference.
9. Ibid.
10. Ibid.
11. In accordance with an amendment to the constitution pushed through by Bhutto on 24 May 1974, which entitled the executive to outlaw any political party considered to be working 'in a manner prejudicial to the sovereignty or integrity of the country.'

227

12. Barrister Kamal Azfar, who was appointed Governor of Sind by Benazir Bhutto in 1995, was a member of the lawyers' panel defending Bhutto in 1977. He met the former Prime Minister in Kot Lakhpat jail, Lahore, and told him that Begum Bhutto, in order to avenge herself because of Bhutto's secret marriage to Husna Sheikh (this marriage was widely believed to have taken place in 1972), was determined to have him liquidated at the hands of the army. Next day when Bhutto repeated to Begum Bhutto what Azfar had told him, she became hysterical and left the jail. She was staying at Khagga House, Lahore, and narrated this incident to the author. Soon afterwards, she threw Azfar out of the party.

2   Al-Nusrat: The Campaign to Save Bhutto

1. Qazi Anwar, a famous student leader of 1968, had been Vice President of the Mazdoor Kisan Party, a pro-China left-wing peasantry-based grouping. Later on he joined the PPP. He is currently in Wali Khan's Awami National Party.
2. Dr Zafar Niazi, who started as Bhutto's dentist, was a lifelong loyalist of the Bhuttos. He and his daughter Yasmin became mainstays of the family after Bhutto's overthrow in 1977. However, inside the family it was often believed that he worked for various intelligence agencies, an unkind charge that it is hard to find a basis for.
3. After the 1970 elections in Pakistan, the Jamaat-i-Islami had started to organize in white-collar labour unions such as those that operated inside Pakistan International Airlines and the major nationalized banks.
4. A military court sentenced Bashir Bhutta to be lashed. He died of a heart attack in 1995. In 1994, Benazir Bhutto's government decorated Zia Iqbal Shahid with the Tamgha-i-Khidmat, an award for serving the country.

3   The Human Torches

1. *Qatil Kaun*, London, Azad Publishers Ltd, 1979, p. 206.
2. Sadiq Umerani was a very militant youth who suffered many years in prison. In 1988 he won elections and was a minister in Baluchistan. From 1990 to 1993 he was again imprisoned by Jam Sadiq's government in Karachi Sind.
3. I accompanied Benazir, and wrote her speeches.
4. *Musawaat*, Lahore, 28 September 1978.
5. *Musawaat*, Lahore, 29 September 1978.
6. *Musawaat*, Lahore, 15 October 1978.
7. Malik was a staunch PPP woman. In 1988 she was elected to the National Assembly. She died in 1995.
8. Benazir Bhutto, *Daughter of the East*, London, Mandarin, 1994, p. 148.
9. Ibid., pp. 3–4.
10. Col. Muhammad Rafi, *Bhutto ke Akhri 323 Din*, Lahore, Jang Publications, 1991.

4   Kabul Hosts People's Liberation Army

1. Murtaza's conversation with the author, Kabul, July 1979.
2. Begum Bhutto told me this story in September 1978, during the movement launched through the People's Action Committee.
3. Rafi, *Bhutto ke Akhri 323 Din*, p. 54.
4. It is an irony of history that in 1976, Zulfikar Ali Bhutto had the Supreme Court of

Pakistan declare the National Awami Party (NAP) a pack of traitors because of its links with Kabul. Yet here, three years later, was his son seeking Afghan assistance to set up a guerrilla base to operate against Pakistan. Nor far from Murtaza's residence lived Ajmal Khattak, the Pushtun intellectual and NAP leader, who had opened the first such base against Pakistan in Kabul. A Pushtunistan flag flew over his house, representing the dreamt-of Pushtun republic to be carved out of areas that constituted Pakistan's Frontier province, and every year he would go on Afghan radio and TV to celebrate Pushtunistan Day. After the rout of the Soviets from Afghanistan, this 'father of Pushtunistan' returned to Pakistan in 1988 and became such a super Pakistani patriot that it was as if he (like Murtaza) had spent all those years in Kabul to fight the battle for Pakistan's solidarity. Such somersaults are yet another symptom of the moral bankruptcy of our politicians. The fact is that Pakistan's political families, leaders and parties are often only interested in their personal agendas, on which they stick different labels to make them look respectable. Their commitment to Pakistan goes up or down according to whether they are in or out of power.

5. *Zindigi* weekly, Lahore, 24 September 1979.
6. Author's conversation with Asadullah Sarwari.
7. *Qatil Kaun*, p. 54.
8. Hazrat Usman died after a long illness in June 1995.
9. Among the prominent PPP workers and Bhutto partisans who came to Kabul as part of the first group were: 'Chacha' Safdar Hamdani, (Rawalpindi); Pervez Akhtar Malik (Bahawalpur); Rana Farooq (Faisalabad); Tariq Cheema (Bahawalpur); Arshad Awan (Faisalabad); Muhammad Boota (Lahore); Shahbaz (Faisalabad); Mehr Abdul Rashid (Faisalabad); Sheikh Gul (Gujranwala); Zubair Shad (Lahore); Hamidullah Zahid (Peshawar); Moeenullah (Peshawar); Mir Nazir Hussain (Peshawar); Fazlur Rehman Kayani (Peshawar); Rehman Haider Kayani (Peshawar); Noorul Amin (Peshawar); Misbahuddin (Dir); Niaz Adil (Peshawar); Muddasar Aziz (Peshawar); Fayyaz Ahmed (Peshawar); Tajbar Khan (Mardan); Jamal Shah (Nowshehra); Akmal Shah (Nowshehra).
10. This camp was in existence until 1990.

5 Murtaza's Ragtag Army

1. Shahnawaz had abandoned his schooling and flown to Afghanistan after a prank in London when he telephoned the police from his Knightsbridge flat threatening to bomb the Prime Minister's residence. He was taken in for questioning and while it is not clear if he was asked to leave, he felt that he belonged in Kabul with his brother.
2. Muzaffar Shah was a minister in the 1989 Benazir cabinet. However, in 1993 he left the PPP and joined the Pakistan National Party, which was Wali Khan's old National Awami Party in a new garb.
3. These tribesmen were named Painda Khan, Angoor Shah Afridi, Khyal Abad Afridi, Mastan Shah Afridi and Ali Man Shah Afridi.
4. Moeenullah visited me in Germany in 1989.
5. In July 1980 I saw Amir Muhammad Wa'aiz's mother wailing outside the office of Shah Wali.
6. Misbahuddin told me the story in Tripoli in 1986.
7. A Pakistani journalist who lived in London and brought out an Urdu weekly called *Musawaat*. He had migrated to England from Pakistan, and later became a stringer for *Nawai Waqt*, the Urdu daily from Lahore. In 1975, when the Bhutto government's case for treason against the National Awami Party (NAP) came up for a court hearing, he appeared as a prosecution witness against the NAP chief Khan Abdul Wali Khan. His

detractors have always maintained that he did so at the behest of Pakistani intelligence agencies. However, that is a charge quite commonly hurled at one another by Pakistani politicians.

8. Imtiaz Alam was a famous left-wing student leader of the Punjab University from 1970 to 1971. He later became the General Secretary of the MKP. In 1979, he formed his own group. He came to Kabul between 1981 and 1982 to get Soviet patronage, and on his return to Pakistan was arrested and thrown into prison. After the disintegration of the USSR, he joined the PPP.

9. See Daniel Sneider, 'The plot against Bhutto', *New Solidarity Weekly*, issue no. 6, London, 30 March 1981.

10. Tipu told me that it was at one point decided to kill Nashha through cyanide poisoning but he was lucky to have escaped this fate.

6   The Indian Link

1. *Kayhan International*, Tehran, 18 September 1977.
2. Benazir Bhutto, *Daughter of the East*, London, Mandarin, 1994.
3. *Kabul Times*, 15 March 1980.
4. This was not the end of the story. On 17 November 1992, Pakistan television showed a poorly made and heavily slanted documentary about Al-Zulfikar which began with the assertion that Raja Anwar had set up Al-Zulfikar in India. Once again our intelligence agencies had advertised a level of misinformation that only true incompetence achieves.

7   Pul-i-Charkhi

1. After General Zia's death in 1988, when the PPP asked for applications for party tickets, for every assembly seat there were scores of *jiyalas* who wanted to be considered. However, 1988 was not 1970 and they were mostly ignored.
2. Conversation with Qayyum Butt in London in 1987.
3. Conversation with Shaukat Ali and his wife Fakhra in Tripoli, September 1986.
4. Fakhra told me that she had obtained information about her husband and me from Sohail Sethi's wife, whom she had befriended.
5. For a copy of Murtaza's letter, see Appendix.

8   Drawing the Sword

1. I acted as interpreter when Murtaza presented the hijacking plan to Asadullah Sarwari. The Afghan official did not speak English and Murtaza spoke no Persian.
2. See 'Revenge of Baby Bhutto' by Anthony Mescrenhas, *Sunday Times*, 7 March 1981. This article refers to a statement of Murtaza's reported on 12 September 1980.
3. See Raja Anwar, *The Tragedy of Afghanistan: A First-hand Account*, London, Verso, 1988.
4. Following the fall of the Shah in Iran, students seized the US Embassy on 4 November 1979, and took about ninety hostages, most of whom were not set free until 20 January 1981.
5. Kausar Ali Shah, Muhammad Hussain Nashha and the two Agha brothers from Lahore were sent to Denmark through East Germany by Dr Najibullah, where they took political asylum. Kausar and Nashha, however, came back in 1988.
6. For an account of Tipu's career before and after the PIA hijack, see chapter 12.
7. Since 1992, Nasir Jamal and Arshad Ali Khan have been in jail in Libya.

9   The Hijack to Kabul

1. Nasir Baloch collected their boarding cards from the PIA counter.
2. Afghan TV news, 3 March 1981.
3. General Asmat was one of the authors of General Tanai's plot against Najibullah in 1988. He has lived in Germany since 1992, and told me this story during one of our meetings.
4. News conference by General Rahimuddin, *The Pakistan Times*, Lahore, 7 March 1981.
5. An interesting story starring Wolf happened on a balmy August evening in 1980. Murtaza and I were taking a walk, as was our custom, in a park that faced our house. Wolf was with us, jumping around in high spirits. Suddenly we saw a huge Alsatian leaping towards Wolf, with a young woman hot at his heels. The two dogs sized each other up and, after some cautionary exchanges, decided that they could be good friends. Next we knew they were running in every direction, chasing each other playfully and having a great time of it. The young woman looked at Murtaza and smiled. Then they looked at their dogs and they both smiled. From then on, this became a routine. Every evening, Murtaza would appear with his dog from one direction to find the young woman waiting with hers. Her father was a senior official at the Ministry of Foreign Affairs, and unlike the average Afghan, she spoke good English. One evening, after much introspection, Murtaza plucked a rose from our garden and told me that he was going to present it to her. When he offered her the flower, she got the message, and it was clear that she liked him too. We would often see her with her sister and sometimes friends, and they would come as far as our house. This very pretty but unfortunate girl later became Murtaza's first wife, and Murtaza cajoled his younger brother, Shahnawaz, into marrying her sister. So in a way, it was Wolf who was responsible for these ill-fated unions.
6. The name of this child, Hafizullah Amin's grandson, was Ghammay. He is now a young man in his teens and lives in Hamburg, Germany, with other members of the family.
7. Tipu told me that Murtaza ordered him not to disclose Tariq Rahim's identity to the Afghans, saying that he would handle the matter himself.
8. Mrs Hubble's interview in the *Guardian*, London, 24 March 1981.

10   Flight to Damascus

1. The list of pro-Moscow communists provided by Ajmal Khattak was as follows: Jam Saqi, son of Mohammad Sachhal, Tharparkar, Sind; Rasul Bux Paleejo, son of Ali Mohammad, Hyderabad, Sind; Amar Das, son of Thakur Das, Sukkur, Sind; Mohammad Sohail Sanghi, son of Mohammad Ramzan, Hyderabad, Sind; Prof. Jamal Naqvi, son of Nihal Din, Karachi; Ghulam Shabbir, son of Abdul Razzaq, Karachi; Mohammad Sharif, son of Fazal Mohammad, Lahore; Ahmed Kamal Warsi, son of Abdul Waheed, Karachi; and Hamid Baloch, Quetta.
2. *Guardian*, London, 24 March 1981.
3. *The Times*, London, 17 March 1981.
4. Until 1996, at least ten thousand Arab fundamentalist and extremist Muslims were playing hide-and-seek with the Pakistani authorities in the Peshawar area. The CIA no longer required them because the situation had changed. Their own governments had put a price on their heads. As for Afghanistan, to which they had come to take part in the jihad, the awful shambles to which the country has been reduced by the 'Islamic' forces is perhaps the saddest chapter in the eternally tragic history of that country. They are no longer welcome in the country they came to liberate from the communists.
5. *Jang*, London, 19 April 1996.

6. A typical indifference to facts is displayed by the newspaper report which claimed that those whom Al-Zulfikar assigned to terrorist missions had to swear: 'I will remain loyal to the PPP and Leninism. I will remain faithful to the Parcham Party of Afghanistan. I will conduct sabotage activities in Pakistan on receiving orders from Shahnawaz . . .' (*Pakistan Times*, Lahore, 1 April 1981). After their induction, the newspaper report said, these volunteers were made to undergo hard military training. This was mostly fabrication, and clumsily devised. First, there was no such party as Parcham in Afghanistan. Second, if a man like Murtaza had pretended that he was a communist, the people in Kabul would have burst out laughing. Third, Murtaza had no military training facilities. The only plain truth among the falsehoods was that the Bhutto brothers were indeed sending men across from Afghanistan to commit terrorist acts in Pakistan. However, this was not a secret since they themselves were the first to claim every sponsored or unsponsored operation as their work.
7. Hamid Mir in *Jang*, Lahore, 12 September 1992.
8. *Pakistan Times*, Lahore, 7 March 1981.
9. Murtaza pronounced the sentences of death on Mazdoor Yar Afridi and Subedar Buneri in Kabul.
10. Begum Nusrat Bhutto's interview, *Moon Digest*, issue 4, Lahore, April 1993.
11. Begum Nusrat Bhutto interviewed by Hamid Mir, *Jang*, London, 21 January 1993.
12. The Nishan-i-Haider is Pakistan's highest gallantry award.
13. See pp. 175–7.

11 Al-Zulfikar's Hit-List

1. See First Information Report (FIR) No. 211/84, filed with the Old Anarkali police station, Lahore, in which the government places the total number of Al-Zulfikar rebels at ninety-six. The case against Al-Zulfikar was registered in September 1981. One PPP advocate, Jehangir Khan, was arrested by the police and confessed that hijacker Tipu had stayed at his residence in January 1981, when returning from Kabul. He brought letters from his colleagues in Kabul and handed them over to Jehangir Khan to be posted to their respective addresses in Pakistan. Those un-posted letters were found by the police three months later. For this careless mistake he earned seven years in prison.
2. Murtaza Bhutto's letter to Rao Rashid, *The Nation*, Lahore, 14 September 1993.
3. Abdul Khaliq Khan has been living in political asylum in France since 1982.
4. *Amal*, London, September 1984.
5. Conversation with Benazir Bhutto in London, 6 January 1985.
6. I was present in the courtroom all through the trial, and base these remarks on personal observation.
7. Benazir Bhutto, *Daughter of the East*, p. 218.
8. *Nawai Waqt*, Lahore, 16 January 1983.
9. *Nawai Waqt*, Lahore, 21 November 1981.
10. Amnesty International report, 1984, pp. 5–7.

12 Zia Escapes Al-Zulfikar Attack

1. Murtaza's interview, *Jang*, London, 29 October 1992.
2. In the 1993 elections in Pakistan, Azam Chaudhri's elder brother was elected member of the National Assembly from Faisalabad on a PPP ticket. Was it an attempt on the part of Benazir to compensate the family?
3. Their real names were Agha Tasneem and Agha Walid. They remained close lieutenants

of Murtaza until 1993. In 1994, Benazir gave a job in Pakistan's Information and Broadcasting ministry to one of their brothers, Agha Naveed. That marked the end of their association with her brother.

4. These code-names were disclosed to me by an Al-Zulfikar man, but I have not been able to make an independent verification.

5. An officer from the Indian Punjab who was very friendly with the Punjabi operatives of Al-Zulfikar. The author was told by various Al-Zulfikar members that he would go to any lengths to help them. It is said that Chawala was in league with the young Pakistani military officers who planned to overthrow General Zia in 1983.

6. *Jang*, Karachi, 16 September 1982.

7. *Dawn*, Karachi, 19 September 1982.

8. Benazir's BBC interview, *Jang*, Karachi, 27 June 1985.

9. ibid.

10. *Pakistan Times*, Lahore, 15 and 16 September 1983.

11. This triggered a sequence of events that would make a vivid story had it not endangered a totally innocent person. The tailor told the interrogators that he had stitched the clothes on an order placed by the wife of a former member of the Punjab Provincial Assembly, Muzaffar Cheema. For the next three years, the police kept carrying out raids here and there in an effort to arrest Mrs Cheema, finally placing her on its most wanted list. The story was that Muzaffar Cheema, her husband, had some local rivalries, and there had been a running feud between his family and another. Even a number of murders had taken place as a result. In order to escape arrest, Cheema had managed to get to Delhi, where he met Azam Chaudhri (the Al-Zulfikar member later to be killed by an unknown hand in Holland). When Chaudhri came to Pakistan in 1982, he called on Mrs Cheema to bring her news of her husband. On his return to Delhi some months later, he brought Cheema a couple of suits that his wife had had stitched for him in Faisalabad. Cheema gave one of these suits, a blue one, to Azam as a present. When Rehmatullah Anjum was leaving for Pakistan in 1983, he borrowed that suit from Azam and was wearing it when the bomb exploded in his hands. The sticker that tailors sew on the inside pocket with their name and address survived the blast, which is how the police got to know about the link with the Cheemas.

12. Interview with one of them in 1990 in Vienna.

13. Murtaza had set up an Al-Zulfikar passport cell under Sohail Sethi.

14. The names on the passports were Lias Khan, Andrew John Limon, Kevin Francis Taylor, Barry John Caan, Kenneth James Mascakel, Mazizurehman, M. Rashid, M. Aslam Khan and Reginald Hopi Smith.

13 A Killer for Murtaza

1. I was later told a similar version of the story by some Karachi youths, that Tipu had fired at Jamiat-i-Tuleba. Though no one was killed, a case of attempted murder was brought against him. In order to avoid arrest and a possible fourteen years in prison he approached Mrs Bhutto, who sent him to Kabul with Qayyum Butt. Three months later he returned to Karachi to hijack a PIA airplane. On 26 February 1981 a military jeep was burnt by pro-PPP students in front of Karachi University where one of them, Akram Qaim Khani, was putting up slogans against the military regime. A group of Jamiat-i-Tuleba students then started to beat him up. On hearing that, Tipu apparently rushed to the spot and fired at them, killing Hafiz Aslam.

2. Conversation with Nasir Jamal in August 1983, after he grew tired of Tipu's misconduct.

3. Conversation with Tipu in May 1983.

4. Tara Masih was the man assigned to the task of hanging Zulfikar Ali Bhutto in Rawalpindi Central Jail in April 1979.
5. Conversation with Najibullah in May 1983.
6. ibid.
7. Conversation with Faruq Yaqubi, a close aide to Dr Najibullah, August 1983.

14   Forgotten Victims

1. Begum Bhutto used to send messages to Murtaza through her London-based sister Bejat Harreri, who would phone them to him in Kabul.
2. 'Open Reply to Rao Rashid', Murtaza Bhutto, *The Nation*, Lahore, 14 September 1993.
3. *Jang*, London, 11 April 1994.
4. It may amuse readers to know that in 1970, while out shooting sparrows with a cousin of his, armed with a .22 airgun, Murtaza accidentally received a slug in his back and had to be taken to hospital to have it removed. His father told this story at a public function at Lahore's Ambassador Hotel on 6 September 1970, while talking about the deplorable condition of hospitals in Pakistan. (See *Musawaat*, Lahore, 7 September 1970. The function had been held to mark the entry of the eminent lawyer and leftist liberal, Mian Mahmud Ali Kasuri, into the PPP.) Perhaps it was the mark from that stray airgun slug that Murtaza sometimes presented as evidence of an attempt made on his life by General Zia.
5. Benazir Bhutto, *Daughter of the East*, p. 299.
6. *Sunday Times*, London, 23 March 1981. Also *Inqilab*, London, 10 April 1981; *Pakistan Times*, Lahore, 20 April 1981; *Jang*, London, 10 April 1981.
7. I saw this grave with my own eyes after my release in 1983
8. Author's press statement, *Nawai Waqt*, Lahore, 22 December 1992
9. Begum Bhutto's interview, *Jang*, Lahore, 22 January 1993. Also see *Jang*, London, 29 January 1993.
10. *Khabrain*, Lahore, 24 April 1994. According to a news story, I was the devil behind all plots against her sons.
11. Conversation with Tipu in Kabul in July 1983.
12. This was what Tipu later told me in 1983.
13. He was elected as a Member of the Provincial Assembly in March 1977. As Bhutto's close aide, I know that he was denied a ministership only because of his outspoken manner.
14. Conversation with Tipu in Kabul in July 1983
15. Conversation with Moeenullah Zahid in 1988.
16. Tipu told me this part of the story in Kabul in 1983.
17. Information from a letter written to me by Nagi and Tanvir Begum from Canada on 15 October 1985.
18. Nashha, Nasir Jamal and the Agha brothers made arrangements for his burial. Unfortunately I could not attend the funeral.
19. Benazir Bhutto, *Daughter of the East*, p. 287
20. Ibid., p. 293.
21. Ibid., p. 299.

15   Sindhi Ambitions and Laundered Reputations

1. The three veterans were Sardar Salim, Sohail Sethi and Ehsan Bhatti. Sardar Salim rose to head the PPP in Rawalpindi, while Ehsan Bhatti became a member of the central committee of the Murtaza group, and Sohail Sethi its general secretary for the NWFP.

2. *Takbeer* weekly, Karachi, 10 October 1996.
3. For blowing up the oil storage tanks of the National Refinery, police cases were registered against the following: Abdul Ghani, son of Haji Nathar Din, Badin; Yunus Bhan, son of Haji Bhan, Thatta; Dudu Jatoi, son of Chotoo Khan Jatoi; and Rafiq Memon, son of Abdullah, Kharadar, Karachi.
4. This conversation took place in London over a meal. I had travelled from Germany to inquire after Jam Sadiq Ali's health. He was suffering from cancer and died in 1992.

16   One More Assassination

1. BBC broadcast of 5 January 1994. Also *Nawai Waqt*, Lahore, 6 January 1994.
2. Though there were many cases of terrorist acts brought to court against Murtaza, including one of hijacking, Benazir's government had allowed him to take armed guards onto planes while travelling to other cities.
3. *The News*, the English version of *Jang*, London, 23 October 1996.
4. *Khabrain*, Lahore, 5 October 1996.
5. Other allegations have emerged about the role played by Ali Mohammad Sonara. Benazir Bhutto claims to believe that he was an agent provocateur working for Zia's former chief of intelligence, Brigadier Imtiaz Ahmed. She alleges that the events of 16 September were staged with Sonara's help: 'My brother was sucked in by Sonara's plan – it was all a set-up.' See Seumas Milne, 'The crumbling house of Bhutto', *Guardian Weekend*, 25 January 1997.
6. Statement in court by Shoaib Suddle, Deputy Inspector-General of Police, Karachi, *Jang*, London, 10 October 1996.
7. *The News*, London, 20 October 1996.
8. *The News*, London, 2 October 1996, report by Kamran Khan.
9. 'PPP Reform or Perish', Dr M.L. Ali, *The News*, London, 23 April 1997.

The Furies of Indian Communalism
Religion, Modernity and Secularization
ACHIN VANAIK

The Furies of Indian Communalism is a powerful and rigorous analysis of the growing phenomenon of Hindu communalism which currently threatens to tear India apart. Placing the politics of Hindu nationalism and anti-Muslim hatred in a global context, Vanaik explains the specific nature and modernity of communalism, distinguishing it both from fascism and from mere religious extremism. In defending both the reality and the desirability of the secularization of the Indian state and society, Vanaik engages in a rich and subtle examination of the relationship between religion and culture, critically appraising the contributions of figures such as Émile Durkheim, Charles Taylor and Anthony Giddens to questions of identity and modernity.

Whilst rejecting simplistic readings of religion as nothing but ideology, Vanaik is scathing about the postmodernists and cultural essentialists who assert the inescapable centrality of religion to Indian culture and society. Moving beyond purely theoretical considerations, he assesses India's political future, the possible obstacles to the development of communalism, and the forces that exist on the Left which might be brought into an alliance to halt the march of chauvinism.

(1997) Hardback ISBN 1 85984 921 0

Paperback ISBN 1 85984 016 7

The Painful Transition
Bourgeois Democracy in India
ACHIN VANAIK

India is in a state of transition in domestic politics and in external relations. Its emergence as a dominant regional power raises questions about India's commitment to a policy of non-alignment, the platform which has supported important and distinct relationships with both the West and the former Soviet Union. As a developing capitalist economy, India continues to maintain a strained rapport with the external influence of the multinational corporations, whilst upholding an internal economic structure based on inequality and domination.

At the centre of this system of contradictions is the endemic crisis of ruling-class leadership, within a durable and decentralized democratic framework which itself bears the marks of the residual caste system. Achin Vanaik roots his analysis of modern India in the specific character of Indian social relations and on either side of India's transition to new political forms: both the traditional bourgeois forms from which it has not fully emerged, and the struggles over dramatic objectives, authoritarianism and Hindu nationalism which are dictating its progress. *The Painful Transition* is an original and accessible dissection of the forces at work in shaping the world's largest democratic state.

(1990) ISBN 0 86091 504 2

Lineages of the Present
Political Essays
AIJAZ AHMAD

Despite the attention of the world's media to the 50th anniversary of India's independence, the complex diversity of the subcontinent's societies and cultures is likely to remain largely enigmatic to outsiders. In his first book since the landmark *In Theory*, Aijaz Ahmad untangles the intricacies of history and politics in South Asia, providing invaluable insight.

Opening with two general pieces on the theory of imperialism and the post-colonial state, *Lineages of the Present* analysis Pakistani politics in the Bhutto period, the construction of ideas of nation and community and the rise of Hindu fundamentalism. Closing with a fascinating account of India's 1996 parliamentary elections, this book confirms Aijaz Ahmad as one of India's most lucid and authoritative contemporary analysts.

(1998) Hardback ISBN 1 85984 877 X

Paperback ISBN 1 85984 114 7

In Theory
Classes, Nations, Literatures
AIJAZ AHMAD

Erudite and brilliant . . . one of the few books in recent years which deserve to be taken completely seriously.'

Guardian

'A brilliant polemic which remorselessly undoes some Western illusions about post-colonial societies.'

Times Literary Supplement

'Ahmad's voice is one of the most important in the current critical debate on the literatures and cultures of Africa and Asia.'

Financial Times

(1994) ISBN 0 86091 677 4

Class, Caste and Colony
India from the Mughal Period to the British Raj
IRFAN HABIB

In this major new work by the doyen of Indian historians, Irfan Habib ranges across the political and economic landscape of pre-colonial and British India.

Class, Caste and Colony opens with an examination of Marxist historiography and Marx's own perception of India. Habib goes on to examine the place of the peasantry and caste in Indian history, the potential for indigenous capitalist development, the various forms of class struggle, the nature of capital accumulation under the Mughals, and the impact of colonialism on the Indian economy. He provides an authoritative account of Indian history which is also a refreshing riposte to current fashions in the study of colonialism.

(1998) Hardback 1 85984 812 5

Paperback 1 85984 143 0

Viramma
A Pariah's Life

VIRAMMA, JOSIANE RACINE
and JEAN-LUC RACINE
Translated by Will Hobson

Viramma is an agricultural worker and midwife in Karani, a village near Pondicherry in south-east India. This extraordinary book is the story of her life, which she told, over ten years, to Josiane and Jean-Luc Racine. Her story is both fascinating and moving. She describes her brief, happy childhood; the ordeal of leaving her village to live with her husband when she had just reached puberty and their subsequent loving marriage; her experiences as the mother of twelve children, nine of whom have died; the oral culture of her community and the interplay between the different castes; the divine forces which influence her and the effects of modernization, which are becoming increasingly apparent. Threaded through the personal stories she tells is her sence of profound change, a constant dialogue between the old certainties of the caste system and institutional and political initiatives to improve the lives of her people.

Officially Viramma is a Jarijan, a member of the 'scheduled castes'. To emancipationists, she is one of the 'dalits', the oppressed. But in her village, she is still what she has always been: an 'Untouchable', a 'Pariah'.

Taking its place alongside the immensely successful *I, Rigoberta Menchu*, *Viramma: A Pariah's Life* is a rare and important publication: the vivid portrayal of a proud and expressive woman living at the margins of society.

(1997) Hardback 1 85984 817 6

Paperback 1 85984 148 1

Divide and Fall?
Bosnia in the Annals of Partition

RADHA KUMAR

Divide and Fall? analysis the post-Cold War revival of what is essentially a British colonial theory of ethnic division. In a timely and elegant intervention, Radha Kumar looks at the Bosnian partition process in relation to earlier partitions of Ireland, India-Pakistan, Israel-Palestine and Cyprus.

She traces the way ethnic mobilization developed in parallel with changing colonial policies of administration, contending that the shift from divide and rule to divide and quit, which was made between the two world wars, stimulated rather than diminished conflict.

Kumar points to the irony of reviving a British colonial practice to deal with a country that was not a colony, in a period which is not only post-colonial but in which a post-Cold War vision of reintegration is being implemented through NATO expansion and the ending of Cold War partitions. She raises the possibility that the Western powers' acceptance of the Bosnian partition indicates that the reversal of Cold War partitions will be accompanied by the revival of ethnic partitions. Kumar concludes that such an eventuality is unlikely because the revival of a colonial theory of partition in the present period would damage both NATO expansion and European integration, to the point of divide and fall.

(1997) ISBN 1 85984 852 4

The History of Doing
An Illustrated Account of Movements for Women's Rights and Feminism in India, 1800–1990

RADHA KUMAR

A thematic history of the women's movement in India both before and after independence, this book covers the period from the nineteenth century to the present day. It looks at how women's issues were raised, initially by men and as part of the movements for social reform, and then with the involvement of women in the nationalist movement, by women themselves. Using photographs, old and new documents, excerpts from letters, books and informal writings, the author documents the growing involvement of women and the formation of the early women's organis-ations; she examines the foregrounding of the 'women's issue' during the reform and nationalist movements and its subsequent disappearance from the agenda of public debate until the post-independence period of the Sixties and Seventies when it surfaces again. Key questions are raised regarding the nature of the contemporary movement, the kinds of issues (such as rape, dowry, environment, work, health) it has taken up, its directions and perspectives, its differences from western movements, the role of autonomous women's organisations and their relationship with political parties, especially those of the Left. Visually rich, this book provides a wealth of information in an accessible style and should appeal to a wide cross-section of readers.

(1993) ISBN 0 86091 665 0